Museo Storico Alfa Romeo

Giorgio Nada Editore Srl

Editorial manager
Leonardo Acerbi

Editorial
Giorgio Nada Editore

Layout
Sansai Zappini

Cover
Sansai Zappini

Translation
Neil Davenport

Text
Lorenzo Ardizio

Giorgio Nada Editore
Via Claudio Treves, 15/17
I – 20090 VIMODRONE MI
Tel. +39 02 27301126
Fax +39 02 27301454
E-mail: info@giorgionadaeditore.it
http://www.giorgionadaeditore.it

Allo stesso indirizzo
può essere richiesto
il catalogo di tutte
le opere pubblicate
dalla Casa Editrice.

*The catalogue of
Giorgio Nada Editore
publications is
available on request
at the above address.*

Distribuzione:
Giunti Editore Spa
via Bolognese 165
I – 50139 FIRENZE
www.giunti.it

Acknowledgements
We would like to thank all those who in various ways made the publication of this catalogue possible. Particular thanks for their contributions to Architetto Benedetto Camerana, Nick Czap, Lorenzo Ramaciotti and Nino Vaccarella.

Photos
Centro Documentazione Alfa Romeo, Archivio Giorgio Nada Editore, Giunti Archive, © Marco Lanza, Giovanni Petronio

Museo Storico Alfa Romeo. The catalogue
ISBN: 978-88-7911-649-7

Museo Storico Alfa Romeo

The catalogue

GIORGIO NADA EDITORE

Contents

Preface

Whatever it exhibits, the function of a museum is above all to make connections. It is required to bring together two apparently distant worlds: that of the experts, the scientists and the academics and that equally heterogeneous world of the general public. The true essence of a museum therefore exists in the way that is chosen to achieve this result. And it is in this limbo that the infinite exhibition criteria, the languages, the layout, the colours and a whole variety of macroscopic and detail elements are discussed. An approach is selected, which may be didactic, playful, sober or ostentatious. The visitors themselves may range from school parties to enthusiasts, from adolescents to pensioners, the idea always being to attract a broad a spectrum as possible. Before all this, the exhibits themselves have to be chosen. A museum, in fact, should not become an immense encyclopaedia in which everything available is listed and explained. Quite the contrary, it should be a story in which characters and situations play determinant roles. It could become an academic essay — as museum were for many years — or a story that entices and entrances through to the last page.

The Alfa Romeo museum is an extraordinary story, one that is over a century long, one in which the characters and many of the episodes have become legendary. The cars have been involved in, interpreted and frequently even created unrepeatable situations: iconic cars, protagonists of their eras, mirrors of a society, dreams of a generation.

Like Alfa Romeo itself, there are infinite facets to the museum and it may be observed, discovered and experienced from diverse points of view. Some of which are fundamental: the cars, those which the TIMELINE section describes through the sequence of eras; the BELLEZZA of the coachwork, of the mechanical organs, of the designs. And finally the VELOCITA' that is a crucial element in the Alfa Romeo DNA, in the racing that has nourished the Alfa legend and in the driving experience that has always transformed every client into an enthusiast.

It is a world apart, waiting to be discovered, model by model, victory by victory in a story that builds and swells as the pages race by, through to the final line. Where we find not the end, but the future.

Alfa Romeo

THE PROJECT

The project

ARCHITETTO BENEDETTO CAMERANA

THE PROGRAMME

In 2013 I was asked by Sergio Marchionne to take charge of the redevelopment of the Alfa Romeo Museum in Arese. Several proposals had been put forward over a number of years (including a project of mine in 2002 for a new site for the museum in the Bicocca area) and the museum had been closed since 2011.

The aim of the project was to turn the office complex and the extraordinary historical collection in Arese into the focal point of the imminent project regarding the radical and global relaunch of the glorious Milanese marque. The strong propulsive thrust given to the programme by the Alfa Romeo brand, led by the CEO Harald Wester, had to fit in with the limitations imposed by the cultural heritage status of the collection and part of the complex.

The project had to work on two distinct but well-integrated fronts: the redevelopment of the complex's architecture according to its new functions and the redesigning of the installation according to contemporary criteria. Drawing on my experience in historic and exhibition contexts as a starting point, I initiated the project by aiming to enhance the value of the collection and the office complex while maintaining close contact with the people in charge of the Cultural Heritage in the regional administration, coordinated by Caterina Bon Valsassina. These aims were incorporated in the investment plan produced by Fiat Partecipazioni under the direction of Mario Lombardi and in constant dialogue with the technical staff led by Gian Pietro Surano.

THE ARCHITECTURAL DESIGN PROJECT

In the early phases of the work I concentrated on the construction of the exhibition space and tried to create an environment that would be appropriate for a contemporary museum. I had to rethink the nature of the exhibition areas and the paths through them and take into consideration the fact that the new museum would have very different requirements compared to those of the original museum designed by the Latis brothers and opened in 1976 as an addition to the administrative centre. The new plan grew out of a

The Museo Storico Alfa Romeo inaugurated in 1976 in a cross section revealing the chronological arrangement of the cars, distributed over the six floors of the building. Left, Cavalier Luigi Fusi, a designer in the Jano period and later artificer and curator of the museum. On the facing page, the new entrance to the museum, a contemporary addition to the renovated historical context. Top, an engineering drawing of the tubular frame. Bottom, a preparatory rendering of the structure.

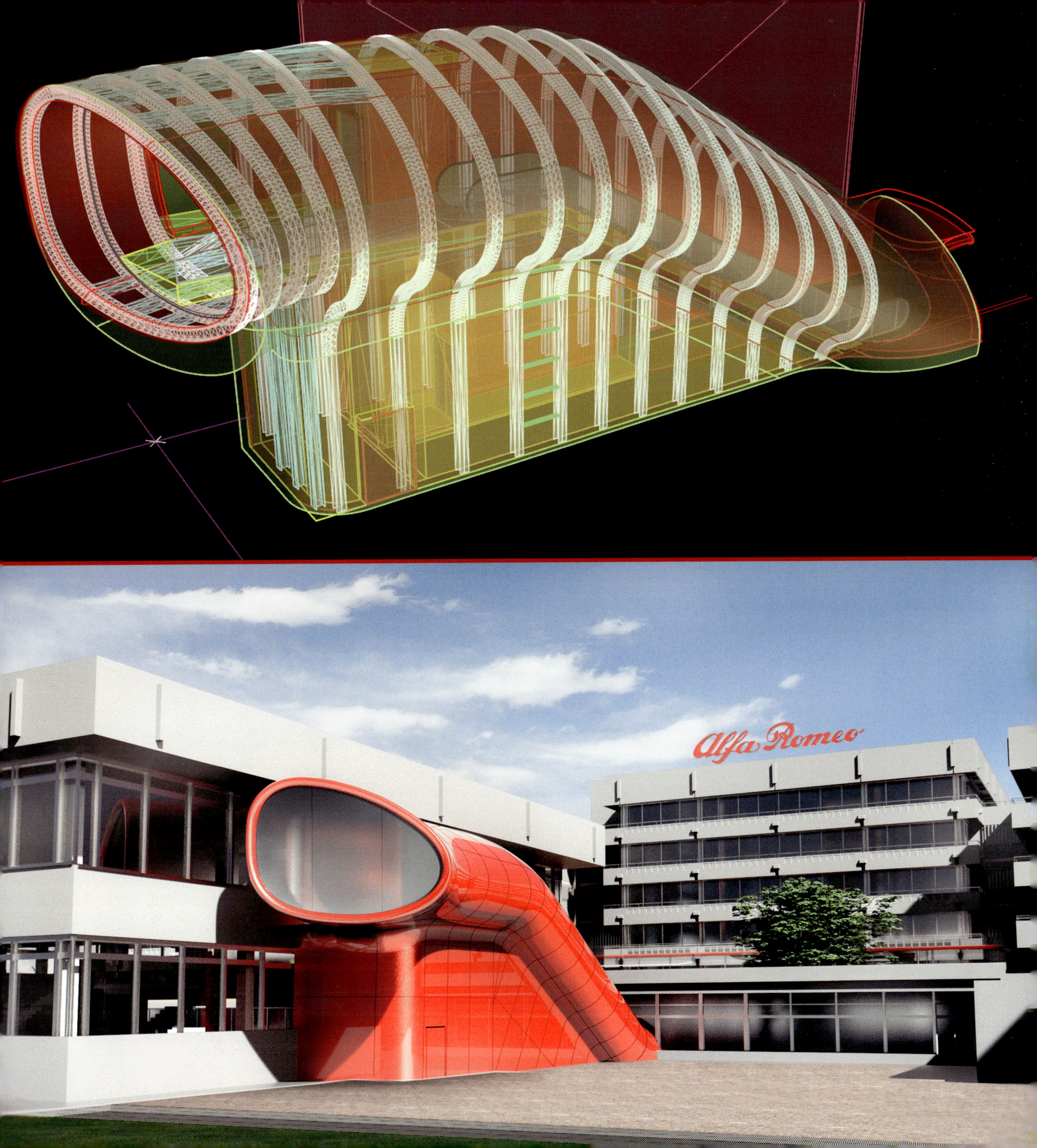

very different functional principle: not just a museum, albeit one enhanced by all the now standard secondary activities (shop, cafe, archives), but rather a brand centre complete with showroom, delivery area, space for events, test track, classics centre and workshop. A set of proposals aimed at a wide section of the public and rather than just specialists.

Out of this context arose the most striking architectural decisions: moving the entrance to the north side of the complex; upgrading the basement as an entrance and pre-museum area; the red ribbon used to guide the public from the car park to the exhibition; the new exterior construction allowing people access to the higher main museum; the continuity of the exhibition layout; the inclusion of new compulsory through-ways between floors; the opening of a level in the empty space in the centre of the museum; downgrading the mezzanine area in the entrance to a scenographic space; the enlargement of the areas in the basement of the museum; the dropped ceiling of the museum seen as a "technological machine"; the "colonisation" of the spaces in the administrative centre with new functions.

Regarding the architecture I still had to resolve the relationship between the historical and the contemporary. With the complete agreement of the Cultural Heritage authorities I worked on the "implant" principle: the new forms/functions generated by the new elements became signs of all that was contemporary, embedded in the Sixties architecture. So I made no use of camouflage in the language of the work. I used the "new" Alfa Romeo red and an architectural design that underlines the continuity of the brand. As a result, there are innovative features which serve to show the timelessness of the new Alfa Romeo (neither retro nor futuristic). In contrast, the architecture of the administrative centre, jointly designed by Cassi Ramelli, Ceretti and Latis, has been restored to its former state, in full respect of the original plan. The result is a balance between context and modernity, which could be seen as a statement about the relationship between protection and redevelopment in modern-day Italy, going beyond the principles of mere conservation or mimesis.

The red band generated by the new flows through the museum complex and entrance: the first sketches by the architect Benedetto Camerana and its development within the area if the former Alfa Romeo Administration Centre, on the following page.

THE EXHIBITION DESIGN

In a subsequent phase I worked on the exhibition design, again working alongside the Cultural Heritage authorities and with the crucial contribution of a working group, guarantors of the history and future of the Alfa Romeo brand, led by Stefano d'Amico, president of the RIAR, and more especially, Lorenzo Ramaciotti, the then head of design for FCA. As a benchmark we chose the most recent and successful projects such as the Museo Nazionale dell'Automobile and some of the brand museums of other European car manufacturers. Added to this, I wanted to create a more Italian identity for the project, more closely linked to the Alfa brand. I worked at trying to arouse excitement and the idea of a show with interactive systems, immersive spaces and above all, I tried to create continuity with the architecture of the external implants, by means of a coherent matrix of the brand, composed of dynamism, lightness, technology and appropriacy to every single thematic area. The exhibition concept reduces the synthesis of the essence of the Alfa Romeo brand to three principles and a floor of the museum is allocated to each of these: the Timeline which represents industrial continuity, Beauty, which covers style and design, and Speed, the synthesis of

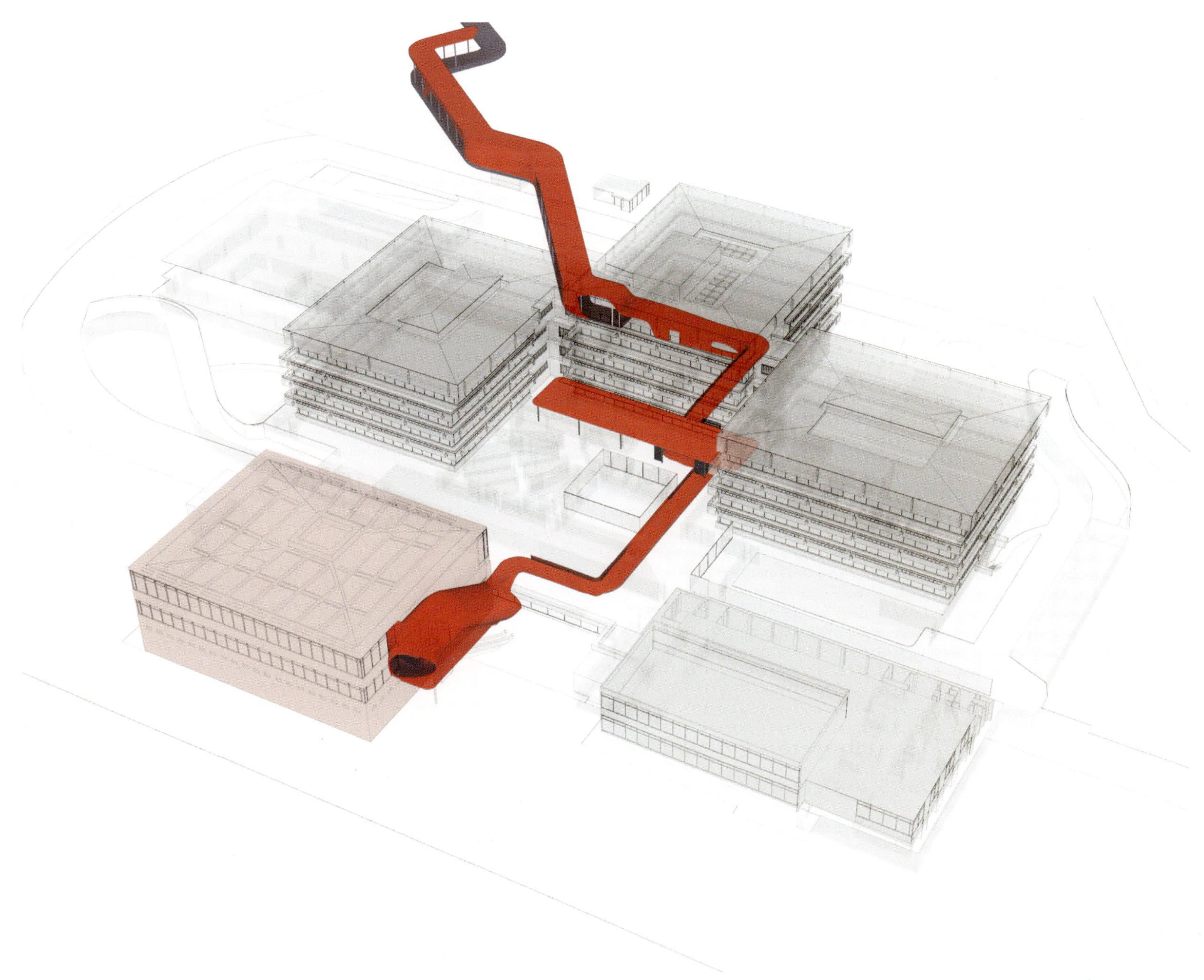

technology and lightness. Now that I have presented the underlying principles of the project, I will continue by describing the exhibition layout, which I have imagined as the storyboard of an experience, almost a film, which in which the visitor is immersed from his or her arrival in the car park to the end of the itinerary, in a crescendo of emotions that succeed each other in a tightly-structured and varied sequence.

THE MUSEUM ITINERARY: A STORYBOARD

On arriving at the museum the visitor is struck by the red canopy, an eye-catching new sign that shows how the administrative complex has been transformed and that guides the visitor from the car park to the museum. The design is dynamic and brings to mind "Alfa Romeo genetics". The canopy then penetrates the building and continues as a red band running along the whole itinerary through the "basement": like a Virgil guiding visitors to the real museum. After traversing the

building the red band emerges to create the new volume of the entrance to the Museum. This tubular volume, with a very automotive design, is highly visible from the motorway and is integrated in the museum building like an architectural implant. The interior space contains the escalator that carries visitors up to the exhibition, enveloping them in the projection of films showing cars in motion. At the end of the ascent the large space of the museum opens out. The vision begins.

The first area on the itinerary is the Timeline, which takes up the whole of the first floor. Here there is a visual summary of the evolution of the marque, with a selection of the 19 most characteristic cars, arranged like the spokes of a wheel in a great chronological circle. Each car has its own multimedia information panel, with historical and technical information, pictures and video clips outlining the value of the model on display. The exhibition concludes with a smart-tech "interactive memory" workstation allowing visitors to access a database giving in-depth information about the history of Alfa Romeo cars.

In the centre of the circle is the Alfa Romeo DNA installation, consisting

Renderings offering a preview of the interior of the red tubular structure in which the escalator leading to the museum is situated and the red canopy, on the following page, that welcomes visitors and accompanies them towards the entrance.

of lights, words and styling motifs. The installation is suspended in the large central void that links the various levels of the Museum and reminds one of the double helix of DNA, a symbol of Alfa Romeo's stylistic continuity . The luminous signs are activated in a descending corkscrew movement linking the three floors to one another.

This floor also features the "The Alfa Romeo People" installation that narrates how, over a period of more than a hundred years, a legend has been created thanks to the work of thousands of men and women who have dedicated their lives to the growth of the company. Factory workers, mechanics, testers, draughtsmen and office workers who have believed in the legend: the anonymous and silent majority who have made Alfa Romeo great.

Beauty is the second part of the itinerary and occupies the whole of the ground floor with various thematic areas. The installation here consists of a series of dynamic and fluid lines that bring to mind those drawn by the great Italian designers who have worked with Alfa Romeo. From the "Masters of Style" bringing together nine extraordinary examples of design from every era, to "The Italian School", where the extraordinary cars bearing the Superleggera name created by the Touring coachbuilding firm are on display.

At the centre of the itinerary we find "Alfa Romeo in film", an ellipsoidal volume dedicated to the presence of the great marque in the cinema

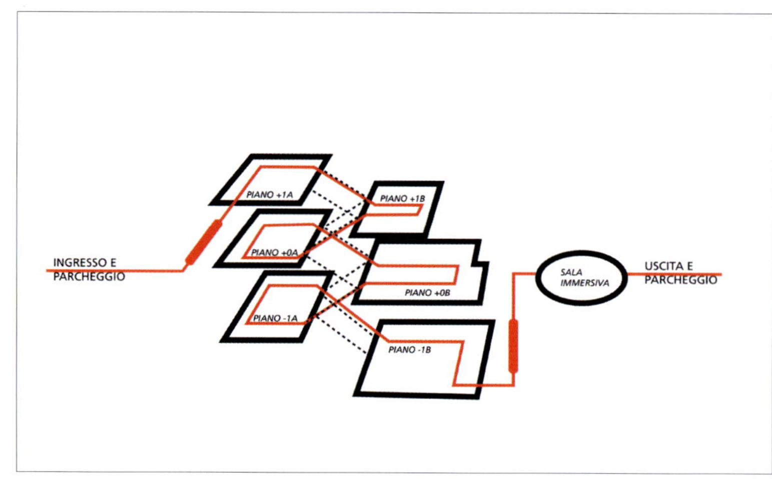

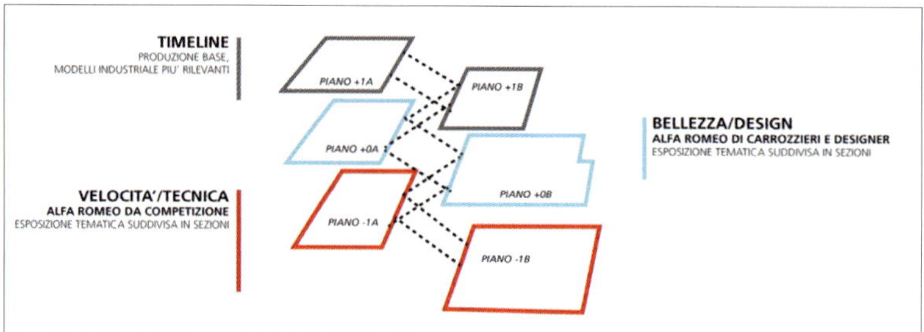

Top, a three-dimensional representation of the exhibition concept with the division into three sections: Timeline, Beauty, Speed. Bottom, a photograph of the collection of historic Alfa Romeos still displayed in a department of the plant, before the creation of the museum in the Administration Centre. On the following page, renderings of the "Timeline", top, and the "World Champions" sections, and bottom, one of the five "Speed" sections.

JUAN MANUEL
FANGIO

NINO
FARINA

and featuring clips from Italian and international art or popular films. There follows a combined installation, "The Giulietta Phenomenon" and "Giulia: Designed by the wind" with the models that were popular during the period of economic growth in Italy in the Fifties and Sixties.

The third part of the itinerary is Speed, with a tauter and more angular design that takes up the whole of the lower ground or -1 floor that has been considerably extended during the redevelopment work. This is the most exciting area, where the enthusiast will find the legendary protagonists of the great Alfa Romeo victories: from "The birth of the Legend", a spectacular multimedia space bringing together the protagonists of the epic inter-war races, to the debut of F1, "Project 33" and "A Racing DNA". At the centre of this floor, visitors enter the "Temple of Victories", another space where a display of images, sound and video presents the ten greatest victories in Alfa history.

The exhibition itinerary concludes with a spectacular grand finale. "Emotional bubbles" are dedicated to the experience of the Alfa Romeo world, with 360° virtual reality film clips and competitive videogames. From here visitors enter the "Immersive Room", where there are interactive armchairs from which they can watch an exciting computer graphics film devoted to the legendary successes of Alfa Romeo in competition, from the Twenties to the Eighties.

In summing up I cannot fail to draw attention to the almost impossibly tight schedule given the realisation of this project: less than twelve months have gone by from the approval of the concept to the opening of the museum. Three years would have been an appropriate length of time. However, speed of action, which is one of the hallmarks of today's FCA, has helped us to complete this project to this timescale, a project that will be a point of reference in relations between the Cultural Heritage authorities and private enterprise and a model of how to organise an exhibition of a marque (not necessarily cars). Therefore I would like to thank everyone and in particular my colleagues led by Marco Caretto for the architectural part and Giulia Mondino for the exhibition part.

A view of the compluvium of the Museo Storico Alfa Romeo, opened on the 18th of December 1976 and the poster for the inaugural event. On the facing page, renderings previewing "Giulietta. Italy's Sweetheart", "Giulia. Designed by the wind" and "The Masters of Style", three of the five "Beauty" sections.

BELLEZZA
I MAESTRI DELLO STILE
THE MASTERS OF STYLE
Carabo 1968
Bertone
Iguana 1969
Bertone
Zagato
De Silva
Carabo 1968

Disco Volante

ALFA ROMEO

From the origins to the future

The Alfa Romeo story is long, tormented and passionate. The firm was officially registered in Milan on the 24TH of June 1910 as just A.L.F.A. (Anonima Lombarda Fabbrica di Automobili), but its roots stretched as far as Naples, London and Bordeaux and in particular its origins were intimately bound up with the destiny of Darracq & Co. Founded in 1897 as a bicycle manufacturer, Alexandre Darracq's company was soon to devote itself to the production of motor cars, with a success and rapidly led to the birth of an English branch and an Italian one established in Campania to take advantage of the law favouring the "economic rebirth of Naples" promulgated in 1904. This was in 1906, and by the month of December problems had forced the investors to move the company to the Portello area in Milan, in what was then a peripheral area district the city, with the objective of producing 600 cars a year. This phase too was to be short-lived and by early 1909 the company was in liquidation: it was to be Cavaliere Ugo Stella, the managing director of the company, who redressed the situation, promoting the constitution of a new firm, A.L.F.A., capable of taking over the factory and employing the 200 workers of the Società Italiana Automobili Darracq.

While this was occurred on the 24TH of June 1910, work had begun behind the scenes much earlier: at a meeting in September 1909 at the Automobile Club in Milan, Ugo Stella and the Piacenza-born designer Giuseppe Merosi had in fact come to an agreement for two cars that were to fall within the 12 and 24 hp taxation bands. From his Milan

Darracq 8/10 HP, 1908

Portello, 1910

A.L.F.A. 24 HP, 1911

Poster A.L.F.A. 24 HP, 1910

Nicola Romeo, A.L.F.A. 24 HP, 1911

A.L.F.A. 24 HP, 1910

home in Via Cappuccio 17, the new technical director prepared drawings consigned on the 1ST of January 1910 that were to be developed by the Technical Office.

The company badge was created in the same way: as the story goes, Romano Cattaneo (a young draftsman, brother of the better known Giustino Cattaneo, a designer at Isotta Fraschini) told Merosi about being struck by the Visconti serpent he had seen on the Filarete tower in Piazza Castello while waiting for the No. 14 tram one morning. Immediately sketched by Merosi, who added a red cross on a white ground, the symbol of the city of Milan, and enclosed everything in a blue disc with the scripts A.L.F.A. and Milan in gold, separated by two Sabaudian knots, the design was approved by Ugo Stella and Cattaneo himself was ordered to prepare the definitive drawing for the badge to be put into production.

The 24 HP was a prestige car, fast, elegant and successful. As was its 12 HP counterpart, which helped make the company profitable as early as 1913. However, the firm's more sporting clients had soon begun to request a more powerful car suitable for competition and eagerly purchased the 40-60 HP that was soon collecting the marque's first racing honours.

This success immediately demonstrated the marketing potential of competition and encourged Giuseppe Merosi to aim for even more ambitious goals: in the October of 1913 he presented the A.L.F.A. board with a proposal for a new Grand Prix car. The project was approved by Ugo Stella and the GP 1914 adventure began: 4.5 litres, four in-line cylinders, a double camshaft valvetrain, four valves per cylinder and dual ignition made it a remarkably modern vehicle. Modern but unsuccessful: in 1914 it was still raw and development was then brusquely interrupted by the First World War. At the end of the conflict, the project was reprised and improved, but by then the time was ripe for a new generation of cars. The coup de grâce came at the start of the 1922 season when the sole example produced was to be found to be missing its crankcase and sump. Having been cast in Elektron, the components had disintegrated over the winter due to the humidity in the air.

When, on the 28TH of June 1914, Archduke Franz Ferdinand was assassinated in Sarajevo and the war broke out, A.L.F.A. saw the

40/60 HP Aerodinamica, 1913

24 HP, Targa Florio, 1911

Campari-Fugazza, Targa Florio, 40/60 HP, 1919

A.L.F.A. 15 HP Corsa, 1911

Giulio Ramponi, Parma-Poggio di Berceto, 40/60 HP, 1919

automotive market collapse and the beginning of its financial problems. Missing out on a commission for the construction of military vehicles led to the company being wound up by the Banca Italiana di Sconto (BIS). In the meantime, the young Neapolitan businessman, Nicola Romeo, thanks in part to BIS capital, had founded Società Ing. Nicola Romeo & C. which was soon to become the representative of the American firm Ingersoll-Rand and shortly afterwards won a major state munitions commission for the production of shells. The Romeo workshop was not of a sufficient size, but a short distance away were the well-equipped facilities of A.L.F.A. which was by then in liquidation. The BIS acquired the shares and control was entrusted to Nicola Romeo & C.

Growth was prodigious and war profits were sumptuous: the workforce expanded exponentially and the Portello factory was extended with new sheds. In February 1918, the investors decided to take the company public and it thus became Società Anonima Italiana Nicola Romeo & C., aka Alfa Romeo. In the same period investments were increased and numerous mechanical and railway engineering firms were acquired. With the end of the First World War, the birth of Alfa Romeo and the slow return to normality, car manufacturing recommenced at the Portello: by 1919 the assembly of parts in stock was already under way and the 20-30 ES was to be presented in 1921, the first car carrying the Alfa Romeo name. The model was actually an evolution of the pre-war 20-30 HP (series E), but the improvements in comfort and performance meant that it was still an up-to-date car.

In the meantime, numerous projects competed for space on Merosi's desk: the failure of the G1 and its successor the G2 – large, heavy and sophisticated but very slow flagships – was countered by the launch of the successful RL, the Italian designer's undisputed masterpiece. Its excellent engineering and sparkling performance made it one of the most prestigious cars on the market, while sales both home and abroad were boosted by the ringing endorsement of numerous victories. First and foremost the 1923 Targa Florio, with Ugo Sivocci's car carrying the Quadrifoglio or Cloverleaf symbol for the first time.

The firm's growth appeared to be unstoppable, but the disappointment of the GPR – otherwise known as the P1 – was to oblige it to change tack: designed for Grands Prix around the new two-litre formula, producing

Poster, 20/30 ES, 1920

RL Super Sport, 1925

RL Super Sport Zagato, 1925

Principe di Piemonte, RL Normale, 1928

95 hp and good for a top speed of 180 kph, the P1 was never to turn a wheel in anger and the fatal accident involving Ugo Sivocci during practice for the Monza GP in 1925 put an end to the project. This was to be Merosi's swansong at Alfa Romeo and the beginning of a new era. Shortly afterwards the young Vittorio Jano was to arrive from the Fiat racing department.

The Turin-born designer's first project was the Tipo P2 Grand Prix car that, following its victorious debut in the 1924 GP of Europe at Lyons, was to conquer the first World Championship for Grand Prix cars organized by the AIACR (International Association of Recognised Automobile Clubs). The title resulted in the laurel wreath being added to the badge.

The technical, sporting and commercial relaunch of Alfa Romeo appeared to promise a rosy future, but the new decade opened with the devaluation of the Lira and increasing debt with the Banca Italiana di Sconto. Then, on the 30TH of December 1921, the BIS – suffocated by the Ansaldo debts – was obliged to close, liquidated by the Banca Nazionale di Credito (BNC), founded by the government in April 1922 to cope with the crisis. This represented the collapse of the Italian industrial and banking system and the beginning of state control of Alfa Romeo. Initially the influence was discrete, with no interference, but the "old guard's" refusal of conditioning encouraged the BNC to act more decisively: the railway stock was sold off, while Nicola Romeo himself was demoted in operational terms from managing director to chairman. The BNC, which then became the Istituto Liquidazioni, would have liked to let Romeo go, but the Neapolitan's significant shareholding made such an agreement difficult. In the end, on the 28TH of May 1928, an understanding was reached and Romeo ceded his Alfa shares in exchange for an amnesty regarding the debts he had contracted. He had effectively been sidelined since 1925.

That same year the Paris Motor Show had seen the launch of the NR, named after Nicola Romeo, which was to be produced from 1927 as the 6C 1500. The following year it was the turn of the Sport and Super Sport versions, with and without supercharging, which soon began to enjoy sporting success. The pinnacle came in the 1928 Coppa delle Mille Miglia, dominated by Campari and Ramponi. The first of Alfa Romeo's 11 legendary victories in the "Freccia Rossa".

RL Targa Florio, 1923

RL Targa Florio, 1923

Antonio Ascari, Spa-Francorchamps, GP Tipo P2, 1925

Tipo P2, Gp Italia, 1925

6C 1500, Colle della Maddalena, 1928

6C 1500 Super Sport, 1928

The 6C 1500 then evolved into the 6C 1750, one of the symbols of the 1930s: from a sporting perspective, with an enviable palmarès, and in commercial terms, with an overall production total of 2,579 examples. The 6C 1750 was also a status symbol, the icon of an era, desired and "clothed" by the best-known and most prestigious coachbuilders. In racing the names were those of Campari, Nuvolari, Varzi, Caracciola and Sommer, in coachbuilding those of Zagato, Castagna, Touring, Brianza and Young.

As Alfa Romeo's fame spread throughout the world in the wake of the numerous victories and the prestige of its production cars, at the Portello attention was already turning to what were intended to be the cars of the years to come. The in-line six-cylinder and double overhead camshaft configuration of the 1750 was inherited by the 6C 1900 GT and the successive 6C 2300 models that were designed more for road and touring use than racing. With regard to competition, the baton was passed to the new 8C 2300. Its race debut came in the 1931 Mille Miglia, but the 8C 2300's of Nuvolari and Arcangeli were unable – a rare exception for the Biscione marque, accustomed to its sporting models enjoying victorious debuts – to impose themselves on the race due to poor fine-tuning of the cars which had just left factory with no time for testing. This failure in the Mille Miglia was made up for in the Targa Florio on the 10TH of May and the 8C 2300 went on to become a true star, with victories in the 1932 and 1933 Mille Miglias and the success of the Monza and Le Mans versions, this last dominating the legendary French 24 Hours races for four years in a row.

These were also the years in which the aviation division took on increasing importance, driven by the pragmatic general manager Prospero Gianferrari. Following the early experience of the testers Santoni and Franchini with their "biplane" from 1910 and the production under license of Isotta Fraschini engines in 1917, in 1925 the newly formed Regia Aeronautica entrusted Alfa with a commission to produce and maintain Bristol Jupiter radial engines under license, while Jano began work on a radial project of his own, the "D". Dedicated workshops and testing departments were built at the Portello as design work proceeded. An experiment was conducted with a 6C 1750 engine equipped with reduction gearing and fitted in a Caproni 100, which with Colonel

Campari-Ramponi, Mille Miglia, 6C 1750 SS, 1929

8C 2300 MM, Milano, 1932

6C 1750 GS, 1930

Nuvolari-Compagnoni, Mille Miglia 1930, 6C 1750 GS

Velardi at the controls completed the second Aerial Tour of Italy in 1931. However, the time was not yet ripe for aircraft produced in large numbers and the project was shelved.

These were controversial years in motor racing too: while awaiting a new and competitive single-seater, budgetary constraints led Jano to design the extravagant Tipo A Grand Prix, with two 6C 1750 engines mounted side by side. A very powerful but difficult car that, after just a few races and one victory in the Coppa Acerbo, was to give way to the Tipo B Grand Prix, soon nicknamed the P3 by the press in an attempt to connect it to the legendary World Championship-winning P2.

The car debuted in the 1932 Italian GP and in the best Alfa traditions won with Nuvolari at the wheel. Further wins followed in the French GP, the German GP (with three Tipo B's in the first three places), the Coppa Ciano, the Coppa Acerbo, the Circuito Principe di Piemonte and Monza. Unfortunately, the success enjoyed by these cars did not reflect the company's true situation: production levels were in constant decline, despite the contribution of the aviation division and the heavy goods vehicles built under license from Deutz & Bussing, the workforce was cut and the losses that almost exceeded the company capital seemed to presage the end for Alfa Romeo. The conditions of the factory also have to be considered: structurally inadequate and drifting in organizational and managerial terms. However, Alfa Romeo was also a social phenomenon as well as a calling card for industrial Milan and the "imperial" Italy: "the constructor of the finest Italian cars". As had been the case in 1923, state pressure once again opposed the equally insistent forces calling for closure. In the December of 1933, Alfa Romeo was acquired by the newly formed Istituto per la Ricostruzione Industriale (IRI) and Ugo Gobbato was appointed as general manager, a charismatic and talented figure, an expert in business organization with international experience and plenty of influence among the "powers that be". The first passage in the salvaging of Alfa Romeo was to be an in-depth reorganization of production, combined with an intuition regarding the potential of the military market: trucks, vans and aero engines. All waste was to be eliminated and even racing and "publicity" were to be considered distractions: at the end of the 1932 season the decision was taken to withdraw the Tipo from Grands Prix as it had

8C 2300 Monza, 1931

Poster Scuderia Ferrari, 1930-1933

Cortese-Guidotti, 8C 2300 Le Mans, 1932

GP Tipo B, 1932

Tazio Nuvolari, Benito Mussolini, Roma, GP Tipo B, 1932

Varzi, Chiron, Trossi, Montlhéry, GP Tipo B, 1934

already "demonstrated its invincibility", as the official line had it.

In the meantime, in 1929 Enzo Ferrari, an Alfa Romeo driver and concessionaire for the marque in Emilia Romagna and the Marche, founded with his own capital and that of private investors, the Società Anonima Scuderia Ferrari with the aim of managing races and cars for privateer drivers. The turning point came, however, in 1933: with the closure of the works racing department, Ferrari was appointed as a consultant for sporting and commercial activities. At Modena, the Scuderia enjoyed considerable independence and what originally was to have been a provision of services soon became a research and development programme for the cars in view of the new 1934 formula. An outline agreement between Alfa Romeo and Scuderia Ferrari was drawn up in 1934: the company committed to the construction of a certain number of cars which the Scuderia would run in all the races decided upon. The agreement was renewed for 1936 too, with further independence for what was now considered to be a true Alfa Romeo racing department.

Encouraged by the growing military market — the company was militarized in 1935 — Alfa Romeo became a large and efficient mechanical engineering company, the workforce expanded from 1,000 to 9,500 in less than ten years and, in order to satisfy the ever greater demand, work began on the construction of a new aviation factory "San Martino" at Pomigliano d'Arco near Naples in 1938.

The 6C 2300 and then the 6C 2500 were launched, continuing the marques success in the Sport category and in 1937 the 8C 2900 B also saw the light of day: "the fastest car in the world" read the titles in the specialist press. The other side of the coin was represented by the Grands Prix: making their debuts were the Tipo C GP and the 12C 1937, the last design by Vittorio Jano before he left the Portello, but racing was one of the issues that Gobbato was unable to resolve: the superiority of the German marques and the inefficiency of Alfa-Scuderia Ferrari led to years of disappointment, illuminated only by heroic individual enterprises, first and foremost Tazio Nuvolari's extraordinary victory at the Nürburgring in 1935. The decisive move came in 1937: Alfa Romeo acquired an 80% shareholding in the Scuderia, liquidated the company and transferred the machinery to a new building at the Portello under the name "Alfa Corse"

6C 2300 B Mille Miglia, 1938

Boratto-Guidotti, Mille Miglia, 6C 2300 B MM, 1937

GP Tipo A, 1931

GP Bimotore, 1935

of which Enzo Ferrari was appointed as director, although restrictions on his independence and severe internal competition meant that he left the Portello at the end of 1939 to set up his own company.

In the meantime, Wifredo Ricart, a Spanish engineer, had arrived at Alfa Romeo in 1936 and was soon appointed as head of the Special Research Service: his revolutionary but still immature Tipo 512 came up against the more conservative Tipo 158 assembled at Modena that benefited from the great experience in the field of its creators. This was merely the most obvious aspect of a fierce rivalry between Ferrari and Ricart that concerned technical, professional, hierarchical and personal matters. Then came the years of war, decentralization and destruction. But also the years in which thoughts turned to planning for the Alfa Romeo of the post-war period.

Ugo Gobbato led Alfa Romeo with skill and foresight during the war and the period of Nazi occupation: he was to attempt to protect the factory and the workforce, thanks in part to his relations with the upper echelons of the Italian and German political world. Unfortunately, he was never to see his masterpiece come to fruition as he was assassinated on the 28TH of April 1945, despite being cleared the previous day of accusation of collaborating by an infamous popular court: as he made his made his way to work, he was flanked by a Lancia Augusta. Gobbato greeted the occupants, shortly before being riddled with bullets.

Under the leadership of Pasquale Gallo, automotive production slowly revived in a Portello factory badly damaged by the allied bombing of 1943 and 1944, initially with assembly of mechanical components for the 6C 2500 already in stock, which were to give rise to the "Freccia d'Oro" bodied in-house by Alfa Romeo and the Super Sports bodied by Touring (including the "Villa d'Este", queen of the celebrated 1949 concours d'elegance) and the Pinin Farina Cabriolets.

However, the automotive world was changing. The costly craft-based production of the pre-war era was about to be replaced with mass production for the mass market and with the end of munitions contracts, the productive capacity of the factory had to be converted. Alongside alternative lines – cookers, roller blinds and railway equipment were manufactured at the Portello – the team led by Orazio Satta Puliga, Ricart's replacement as head of the technical department, developed

GP Tipo C 12C, 1936

GP Tipo 12C 1937

GP Tipo 316, Nino Farina, Monza, 1938

Sommer-Biondetti, 8C 2900 B Speciale Le Mans, 1938

Sommer-Biondetti, 8C 2900 B Speciale Le Mans, 1938

6C 2500 Sport, 1939

8C 2900 B Speciale Le Mans, 1938

GP Tipo 512, 1940

a project for a modern, more economical and rational car that would be reliable and easy to build in series: the 1900.

The over 17,000 examples produced in the various versions – prior to the war the average annual production was less than 300 cars – were to make the "race-winning family car" a great success in terms of sales and image.

Racing once again played a major role in promoting the marque throughout this period: German superiority in the Grands Prix was but a memory and the Alfetta 158's, hidden to escape requisitioning and bombing, were recovered, tested and raced successfully even before a true championship had been organized.

In 1949 – in part due to the deaths of Wimille, Varzi and Trossi – Alfa Romeo decided to withdraw from competition and prepare for the following season in which the first Formula 1 World Championship was to be run. The continuously improved Alfetta was to win all 11 of the races in which it was entered: the World Championship title went to Nino Farina, followed by the other two elements of the "Fa-Fa-Fa" team, Fangio and Fagioli.

In the 1951 season the competition, especially from Ferrari, was much stiffer and the Alfetta was so thoroughly revised that it was rebaptised as the Tipo 159 GP: now producing 450 hp, the engine permitted top speeds of over 300 kph. Of the four Grand Prix wins, three went to Fangio who, with victory in the Spanish GP, was crowned World Champion.

When direct control of Alfa Romeo passed to Finmeccanica and Giuseppe Luraghi joined the company directors, the main problem to be resolved was still that of the saturation of the factory. The great success of the 1900 was still insufficient to keep the assembly lines running at full capacity and the idea was mooted of a more modern car with a much smaller displacement. This marked the beginning of the period of gestation for the Giulietta, the project for which being the focus of all available human and economic resources, even at the cost of sacrificing other activities. The company abandoned Formula 1, which thus never saw the debut of the futuristic four-wheel drive Tipo 160, while the axe also fell on the three-litre six then under development at the Portello, the 2000 Sportiva, the "Disco Volante", the development of the 6C 3000 CM and a series of other nascent projects.

At Luraghi's behest, Rudolf Hruska arrived at the Portello to reorganize

6C 2500 S "Freccia d'Oro", 1946

6C 2500 SS "Villa d'Este", 1949

1900, 1950

Portello, 1950

Nino Farina, 1950

1900 Super Sprint, 1954

production of the Giulietta, which thanks to its performance and styling enjoyed immediate and overwhelming success. Production of the various versions was to continue for 11 years and a total of 177,513 examples, ten times that of the 1900, which had itself exceeded the total number of other Alfas produced: for Alfa Romeo this represented its definitive transformation into a major car manufacturer.

Success that was not just commercial but also sporting and which enhanced the reputation of the marque but also posed the question of a replacement: the Giulietta was a point of reference for the market, a dream for the public and creating a worthy heir was by no means easy. Orazio Satta Puliga's team took up the challenge enthusiastically, thoroughly revising the Giulietta mechanicals and designing for the Giulia new and revolutionary coachwork. It featured the first progressively deformable unitary body, focussing on safety years before its rivals, and the fruit of in-depth aerodynamic research — it was sold with the slogan "Giulia. Designed by the wind" — and boasted unexpected styling that initially provoked contentious reactions from the critics. These impressions were immediately belied by the public which was much more open than the press to the car's great innovative spirit. Class-leading performance and driving pleasure contributed to a success that is not fully represented by the over 570,000 examples produced in the diverse versions.

The Giulia era was also marked by an upheaval in the life of the company as the "old" Portello factory was by now too small and impossible to expand, surround as it was by the city of Milan. The decision was therefore taken, on the strength of the healthy balance sheets of recent years, to construct a new facility according to the most up-to-date criteria. A vast plot was acquired at Arese, around 15 km from the Portello, strategically located to the north-west of the city. Over two and a half million square metres were to be covered by the plant and the administrative centre, where a building was devoted to housing the collection of historic cars: the future Alfa Romeo Museum that opened its doors on the 18TH of December 1976. From 1963, production of the Giulia was gradually transferred to the new plant, through to the point where all departments were fully operational.

At the same time, a modern, safe proving ground equipped for the

1900 C52 Disco Volante, Monza, 1952

Sanesi-Zanardi, 6C 3000 CM, Monza, 1953

Giulietta Sprint, 1954

Portello, 1955

2000 Sportiva, 1954

Giulietta, 1955

Giulietta Spider, 1955

Giulietta TI, 1957

development of production and racing cars was constructed at Balocco, a village in the midst of the rice fields of the Vercelli countryside. At Alfa Romeo, road testing had historically played a major role in the definition of the cars: not so much the verification of design and engineer quality, but as an integral part of the design process. A true school in which the testers handed down from generation to generation the "recipe" that makes every Alfa Romeo immediately recognisable.

For Alfa Romeo, the Sixties brought a renewed desire for works participation in racing afters years — following the retirement of the "Alfettas" — in which sporting activities had been handled by privateers. Development began on the Giulia TZ, with assembly being entrusted to Delta of Udine, a company founded for the purpose by Carlo Chiti and Ludovico Chizzola. This firm soon became Autodelta and transferred to Settimo Milanese where it was acquired by Alfa Romeo and transformed into the official racing department. Autodelta was initially responsible for managing Alfa's racing activities, then the preparation of the cars — this was the era of the legendary GTA's — and finally for complete construction of the cars, from the Tipo 33 through to the Formula 1 single-seaters.

The TZ and TZ2 were very successful but the true turning point came with the Giulia Sprint GTA, in which the "A" for Allegerita or lightened summarised the main modification: a bodyshell that was 200 kg lighter thanks to the use of aluminium panelling. Sporting success was not slow to arrive: "A victory a day with a car for every day" and fame that was second only to that of the Duetto, the convertible from the Giulia family that debuted in 1966 and was immediately accorded iconic status, as had been the case a generation earlier with the Giulietta Spider.

The victories of the GTA — along with those of the GTA 1300 Junior and the GTAm — failed to satisfy the powers that be at Alfa Romeo who instead looked to ever more ambitious goals. This led to the project for a new sports prototype in an era in which the Sports Car Championship was perhaps even more popular than Formula 1. The 33 made a winning debut in the Fléron hillclimb in 1967 and took the title in the category the following year. In a sequence of highs and lows it had to wait until 1975. Not all the results in this adventure were concerned with racing. 1967 saw one of the marque's greatest ever icons emerge into the spotlight: the 33 Stradale. Sophisticated and exceedingly expensive, it represented

Giulietta Sprint Speciale, 1957

Giulietta TI, 1957

Giulietta SZ "Coda Tronca", 1961

Giuseppe Luraghi, Ugo Zagato, Elio Zagato, Nuccio Bertone, Giovan Battista Pinin Farina, Monza, 1962

Giulia TI Super, 1963

Giulia TZ, 1963

the point of contact between the world of racing and that of the road, but it was also a masterpiece of car design, penned by Franco Scaglione and immediately interpreted by many other coachbuilders who used the chassis for their own dream cars.

The Alfasud project was quite a different kettle of fish: a new car in a segment and with a configuration that Alfa Romeo had never previously explored. It was to be built in a new plant erected at Pomigliano d'Arco, not far from the aircraft factory founded in 1938. The newborn SICA (Studi Impianti Consulenza Automobilistica), directed by Rudolf Hruska, proposed a compact, four-wheel drive car with class-leading interior space and performance worthy of an Alfa Romeo: a brief that took shape in the form of a modern saloon designed by Giorgetto Giugiaro's Sirp and powered by a new four-cylinder boxer engine.

The dawn of the 1970s were instead marked by the decision to pension off the glorious 1900-Giulietta-Giulia-1750-2000 configuration and start thinking about an avant-garde new layout: the transaxle configuration, with a front engine and a gearbox in unit with the rear axle, to the benefit of handling. The Alfetta's gestation was long and difficult but when it saw the light of day in 1972 it inaugurated a new generation of Alfa Romeos.

Not everything in the garden was rosy however. While the Tipo 33 held great promise, there was a return to Formula 1 on the horizon, the GTA and the GTA, continued to monopolize the scene and the production range had few rivals, the same cannot be said for the business itself, which every day was increasingly afflicted by inefficiency, union struggles and difficulties that while having little to do with the cars undermined the firm's financial health. The situation was also worsened by the oil crisis, which hit the sporting marques hardest and began to focus their attention on issues that had previously been marginal: efficiency, comfort, fuel consumption, emissions and safety. The automotive world was changing rapidly.

On the track, however, Alfa continued to record major victories: in 1975, the 33 TT12 finally capitalized on years of work and development, dominating the World Championship for Marques by winning seven races out of eight. Two years later the 33 SC12 went one better by winning every round of what was to be the last championship for the sports

2600 Sprint, 1963

Giulia TZ2, 1964

Giulia Sprint GTA, Giulia TZ2, Balocco, 1965

GTA 1300 Junior, 1970

1960s   1970s

Giulia Sprint GT, 1963   Giulia Sprint GTA, 1965   1750 GTAm, 1970

prototypes. In the meantime, at the end of 1975, Alfa Romeo had signed a contract with Bernie Ecclestone's Brabham Martini Racing Team for the supply of 12-cylinder boxer engine from the 33 to be installed in the future BT45 Formula 1 car. In 1978, the same engine was also to power the Tipo 177, the car that marked Alfa Romeo's return to the blue ribbon F1 series as a constructor rather than an engine supplier. Its debut was to come in the 1979 Belgian GP.

The Alfetta and Alfasud ranges were expanded with new versions, from the Alfetta L to the Alfasud Sprint. Another debutante was the "new" Giulietta replacing the Giulia, the Alfa 6 flagship, the Alfa 33, introduced in the wake of the Alfasud and the Alfa 90 in 1984. A chapter apart might be devoted to the Arna, a utilitarian car slotting in below the Alfasud and created as a joint venture with the Japanese firm Nissan: the mechanical assemblies — with the exception of the rear suspension — were those of the Alfasud, while the bodyshell was derived from the new Nissan Cherry. Assembly took place in a new purpose-built factory at Pratola Serra in the province of Avellino. Unfortunately it never enjoyed the success the quality of the car deserved: it was the object of a smear campaign in the media — fomented by the competition — against what was seen as a Japanese "invasion". The styling was not particularly inspired and an unsuccessful advertising campaign did the rest. The industrial experiment was instead severely affected by the variations in the Lira-Yen exchange rate: with the agreements having been drawn up when the Yen was weak, following a sudden and significant strengthening of its value the supply costs became unsustainable and the joint venture with Nissan was no longer profitable. The experiment was terminated in 1987.

The Formula 1 adventure also failed to live up to expectations: following the debut of the 177, the rise of ground effects cars had made conventional single-seater obsolete, encouraging Alfa Romeo to develop a new car with a V12 engine: the 179. It was to make its debut in the 1979 Italian GP, with Bruno Giacomelli at the wheel. That season closed and for 1980 Alfa Romeo decided to flank the Brescian driver with Patrick Depailler, who tragically was killed during testing at Hockenheim early in August. The final races of the season were completed by Vittorio Brambilla and the young Andrea De Cesaris. In the meantime, Giacomelli — in an increasingly rapid 179 — secured pole

33 Stradale, 1967

33/2 Coupé Speciale, 1969

Carabo, 1968

Iguana, 1969

1600 Junior Z, 1972

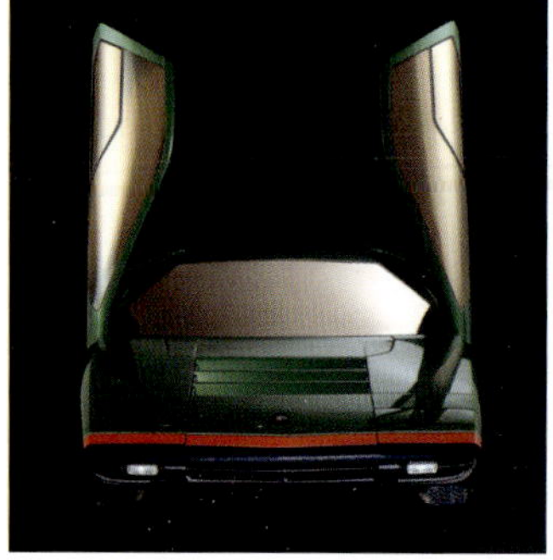

position and just missed out on victory in the United States East GP, betrayed by a simple casting.

1981 promised to be a turning point: the 179 was finally competitive and the American champion Mario Andretti had been signed. However, modifications were made to the regulations and the 179 was rendered obsolete overnight. Its best result was Giacomelli's third place in Las Vegas. The carbonfibre Tipo 182 designed by Gerard Ducarouge could do no better, with Andrea De Cesaris taking a single pole position and a third place finish. The 1982 season also saw the birth of the experimental 182 T powered by a 1497 cc V8 turbo: various features were tested ahead of the debut of the 183 T, this time entered by the Euroracing team rather than Autodelta. At the wheel were De Cesaris and Mauro Baldi. In 1984 it was the turn of Riccardo Patrese and Eddie Cheever, teammates again in 1985, when Alfa Romeo retired definitively from Formula 1.

The withdrawal from racing is just the most evident symptom of the profound crisis into which the Alfa Romeo company was sinking. Inefficiency, surplus productive capacity and an inability to achieve an international dimension: the IRI was pressing for a sale and the directors were beginning to investigate the possibility, but finding a partner able to take on the huge debts accumulated over the years was by no means easy. In 1985, Ford advanced a proposal for the gradual acquisition of Alfa Romeo. The news got out immediately and Fiat's response arrived promptly: total and immediate acquisition. IRI's choice soon fell on the Italian alternative and on the 6TH of November 1986, Alfa Romeo became part of the Fiat Group.

A year earlier the Alfa 75 had been presented, a compact saloon destined to replace the Giulietta, with which it shared much of the structural and mechanical parts while boasting more power and a more sporting configuration. Numerous technical innovations were introduced during the car's career, including Twin Spark ignition and the first turbocharged engine fitted to mass produced Alfa Romeo.

The 164 was instead launched during the period of the sale, a brand-new front-wheel drive flagship created on the Type 4 platform shared with Fiat, Lancia and Saab. However, the differences were substantial with technical features designed in the previous era, in agreement with

1600 Spider "Duetto", 1966

Tipo 33/3 Le Mans, 1970

Giuseppe Luraghi, Aldo Moro,
Alfasud (Pomigliano d'Arco), 1968   Alfetta, Balocco, 1972

Tipo 33/2 Daytona, 1968   Mugello, 1968   Montreal, Ginevra, 1970   Alfasud, 1971

Fiat, and sophisticated styling by Pininfarina. Performance was class-leading, as were comfort and the equipment levels: the public responded enthusiastically and by the time the 164 handed over the baton to the 166, no less than 270,000 examples had been produced.

1986 saw the creation of the "new" Alfa Corse which took up the heritage of Autodelta in order to bring together the marque's sporting activities in a single sector. The programmes included the supply of Formula 1 engines to the French Ligier team (work began on the development of a four-cylinder turbo and a new naturally aspirated V10, subsequently adapted for the new Group C and ProCar categories), a debut in Formula Indy, the intensification of the marque's participation in Formula 3 and the Touring Car Championships and the organization of single-marque series such as Alfa Boxer and Barchette.

Alfa Romeo presented the SZ at the 1989 Geneva Motor Show, an aggressive coupé with taut, angular lines born out of a collaboration with Zagato. A limited edition of 1,000 coupés (the RZ spider was to follow) with bodywork in Modar, an innovative thermo-hardening resin. The 155 was presented in 1992, the first car to come out of the Fiat acquisition. Derived from the shared Tipo 2 platform, it was intended to replace the 75, from which it differed significantly in mechanical terms thanks to front-wheel drive and independent suspension. Two years later it was the turn of the 33 to bow out, replaced at the Turin Motor Show by the 145, which was to be followed in 1995 by the 146. In the meantime, Alfa Corse's sporting activities had intensified. The 155 GTA's conquered the Italian Superturismo Championship, while from the following year the 155 2.0 Twin Spark won diverse titles in the D2 class, including the BTCC and the Spanish and Italian Touring Car Championships. 1993 also saw the marque triumph in the DTM with the 155 V6 TI driven by Nicola Larini.

It was a period of in-depth technical and stylistic renewal for Alfa Romeo. 1995 saw the presentation of the GTV and Spider with high level mechanical specifications and elegant coachwork by Pininfarina. However, real progress was represented by the presentation in 1997 at Lisbon of the 156, just a few months after the stunning Nuvola prototype. The new car was a sports saloon to replace the 155: the styling was all new and unusual, the work of the Alfa Romeo Styling

33 TT12, 1975

33 SC12, 1977

Niky Lauda, Brabham-Alfa Romeo BT46, 1978

Patrick Depailler, 179 F1, Montecarlo 1980

Arese, 1980

Centre directed by Walter De' Silva. Sleek and compact, interpreting in a modern key many of the marques traditional styling motifs, starting with the "trilobite" front end that had risked disappearing in the 1980s. The mechanical specification also proved to be of a very high level: a high wishbone front suspension layout was introduced and was to dictate fashions for years, while the JTD turbodiesel made its debut as the first common-rail system fitted to a production car. Elected as Car of the Year in 1998, the 156's greatest tribute was the response of the public: 90,000 orders in the first four months after going on sale. When the assembly lines were shut down in 2005, over 680,000 examples had been produced. In the meantime, the Sportwagon, GTA and Crosswagon versions had been introduced. The car also enjoyed sporting success with 13 Italian and European drivers', constructors' and team Touring Car championship titles. This car marked Alfa Romeo relaunch in terms of both sales and image following the excessive cost-cutting on the product range in the 1990s that had threatened to tarnish the marque's reputation.

The air of positivity extended to other segments: the flagship 166 debuted in 1998 followed in 2000 by the 147 and the 146 in the competitive C segment. Three years later it was the turn of the Alfa GT, a spacious coupé designed by Bertone.

Following an across the board facelift, in the March of 2005 at the Geneva Motor Show Alfa Romeo presented the 159, the new mid-range saloon with the unenviable task of replacing the best-selling 156, albeit in a higher market segment thanks to its dimensions, power and equipment. Giugiaro's styling of the front end and flanks was inspired by the much admired Brera concept car presented in 2002, while the mechanical specification was based on a platform developed with General Motors, a Fiat Group partner in those years. The saloon was soon flanked by the Brera coupé and the 159 Sportwagon, while Pininfarina, in collaboration with the Styling Centre was to introduce the new Spider.

A decisive and unexpected change of tack instead came with the presentation at the Frankfurt Motor Show in 2003 of the 8C Competizione, a seductive concept car that was to be produced in a limited edition of 500 examples from 2007, in part thanks to the immediate and unanimous approval of critics and public for the Alfa Romeo Styling

Alfa 75 2.5i QV, 1985

Alfa 164 3.0i V6, 1987

Nicola Larini, 155 V6 TI, 1993

Nuvola, 1996

Alfa 156, 1997

Alfa 156, 1997

Centre's sculpted forms. Similar success was soon met by the 8C Spider, which was also produced in 500 examples.

An iconic model whose influence was to wash down to the other segments: first up was the MiTo, presented in 2008 as the entry-level model with its styling inspired by the 8C and a mechanical specification designed to appeal to young people.

The Centenary of the marque came on the 24TH of June 2010. The car of the moment was the Giulietta, designed to replace the ageing, but still popular, 147 in Segment C, that of the compact saloons. An ambitious car that proved capable of fulfilling that original role and conquering new markets as well as constituting the backbone of the Alfa line-up thanks to a broad and varied range, culminating with the sporting Quadrifoglio Verde versions.

A true turning point came in 2011 with the presentation of the 4C Concept, a compact and extremely light supercar with a carbonfibre chassis and design by the Styling Centre led by Lorenzo Ramaciotti. It was but a short step from the prototype to the production car, which went on sale in 2013, and the result was a sports car that made performance, lightness, agility and driving pleasure its strong suits, while the styling kept faith with the forms previewed two years earlier. 2014 saw the presentation of the Spider version, due to go on sale in 2015.

The 4C marks Alfa Romeo's return to the North American market, a step in FCA's ambitious strategy, and anticipates a major relaunch of the marque involving new products, new projects and great energy.

June 24TH 2015. The future restarts from Milan.

156 GTA, 147 GTA, 156 Sportwagon GTA, 2002

Spider, 2003

Brera, 2005

Giulietta, 2010

4C, 2014

TIMELINE

TIMELINE

NICK CZAP

When I see an Alfa Romeo, I lift my hat

Henry Ford

According to the American automotive historian Griffith Borgeson, the oft quoted phrase sprang from a conversation between Henry Ford and Alfa Romeo's president, Ugo Gobbato, during a visit Gobbato paid to Ford in Dearborn, Michigan in 1939. Given the scarcity of Alfa Romeos in the States at the time, one wonders how many the magnate might have encountered. Gobbato's son Pierugo seemed to recall that in 1938, Ford had examined an Alfa Romeo 8C 2900 belonging to a member of the Rockefeller family. One can only imagine what the American engineer – who boasted to Gobbato that his factories built six cars a minute – made of the artisanal roadster's exotic double overhead cam engine and bullet-like coachwork.

Alfa Romeos started entering the US in significant numbers in mid-1950s, under the wing of Max Hoffman, an Austrian expatriate with a keen sense for the predilections of American drivers. Thanks to the modernization of the manufacturing process at Portello in the years following WWII, Hoffman's first import, the Giulietta, was magnitudes more affordable than the cars that Ford had so admired. When it first arrived on US shores, a 1956 Giulietta Spider sold for a mere $2500. Price, though, was not the primary attraction. A period advertisement from Hoffman Motors Corporation, featuring the image of a Giulietta Sprint, told Americans everything they needed to know about Alfa Romeo: "Italians Build Such Exciting Cars."

When journalists from the American magazine *Road & Track* took their turn behind the wheel of a Giulietta Spider in 1956, they were smitten, calling its engine "dreamy," a term more commonly associated, in the vernacular of the period, with teenage girls singing peans to their heavily pomaded idols. "Without a doubt," *Road & Track* continued, "the 1300-S Spyder is the most fascinating small sports car we have ever driven."

Fascination, generally speaking, leads two ways, to passion, or enduring love. In the case of Alfa Romeo in America, it was both. From the moment the Giulietta arrived, enthusiast clubs began to spring up, first in Detroit, in 1956, then Chicago in 1958. In the years that followed, America's Alfa Romeo clubs grew exponentially in number and size, reaching a peak of nearly 6,000 members in the late-1980s. Today the figure is smaller, about 3,500 but still impressive considering the advancing age of the clubs' founders, and the loss of cars due to corrosion, wrecks, and other forms of entropy.

TIMELINE

Each year in the US, more than 30 vintage racing associations organize nearly 200 vintage races. On any given weekend, from Watkins Glen to Indianapolis Motor Speedway to Laguna Seca, America's more adventurous Alfisti drive their cars to the limit, axle-to-axle with their historic nemeses, rekindling rivalries born in the earliest days of motorsports. While few of these events are broadcast in the 20TH-century sense of the word, thanks to the proliferation of miniature 21ST-century video cameras and the human penchant for self-documentation, one can now experience entire races vicariously from the points of view of the drivers — an attractive compromise for an Alfista lacking the skills, nerve, or funds necessary for such an undertaking.

Cultural and linguistic differences aside, the primary distinction between American Alfisti and their counterparts in Italy is that with the exception of a handful of 8C coupes and spiders, the Americans have been pining for their beloved for two decades. Judging by their enthusiastic response, over the years, to persistent rumors of Alfa Romeo's impending return, they have remained steadfastly optimistic. Their patience and optimism, it seems, have paid off.

With the 4C, Alfa Romeo marks both its return to the United States, and an unequivocal embrace of its historic DNA. Alfa Romeo's designers might well have begun with something innocuous. An inoffensive aerodynamic blob. A car that coddles its occupants in a cocoon. Instead, they turned for inspiration to the 1960s, to the ferociously beautiful and utterly uncompromising 33 Stradale. Despite its carbon fiber construction, the 4C, accordingly, conjures nothing so much as a mid-century racer, a car whose vocabulary consists of a single word: Drive.

While obeying this command over the course of several days in Northern California, I was struck just as much by the 4C's performance as by the public reaction. Hats are no longer the fashion they were in Henry Ford's time, and the tipping thereof long since replaced by a no less archaic yet remarkably durable symbol of approval, the thumbs-up. The gesture came at the 4C from every direction, and all walks of life. From a woman in a station wagon full of kids. From a fellow pushing a shopping cart loaded with his worldly possessions. From a manically grinning man who looked as if he would have abandoned his hybrid on the side of the road for a chance to ride shotgun. And from a black-leather-clad rider in a phalanx of Harley-Davidsons, who, at seventy miles per hour, extended a weathered fist and an upraised thumb before roaring away with the pack.

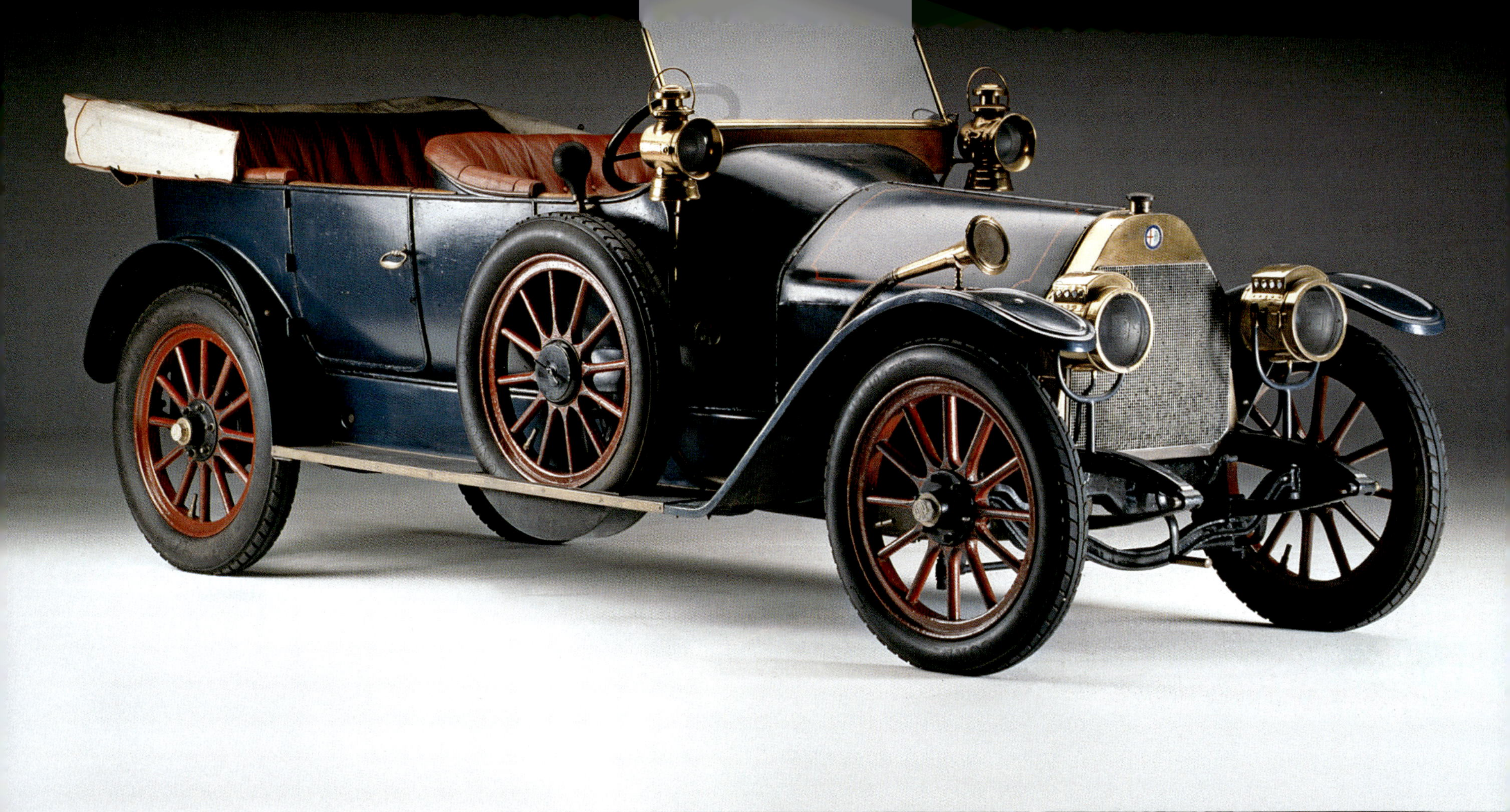

Pag. 8   MOTORI CICLI & SPORTS   25-26 Agosto 1910
CHASSIS 24 HP
ALFA
Cataloghi e preventivi per chassis nudi e carrozzati a richiesta
PRONTE CONSEGNE
ANONIMA LOMBARDA   ALFA   FABBRICA AUTOMOBILI
MILANO - Strada al Portello, 95   Telefono 71-99

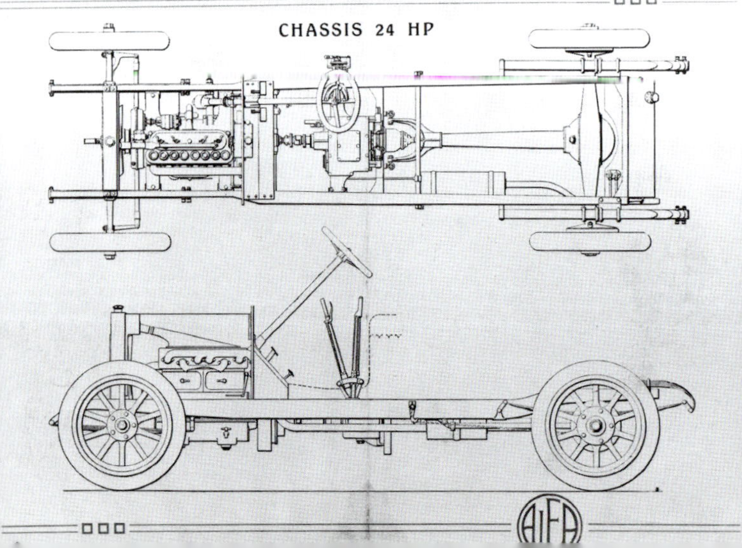

CHASSIS 24 HP
ALFA

7915

A.L.F.A. 24 HP

THE FIRST CAR. THE BIRTH OF THE LEGEND

Engine

Front-mounted, vertical longitudinal, straight-four, block and fixed head in cast iron, two side valves per cylinder, gear-driven lateral camshaft. Single carburettor, magneto ignition, wet-sump lubrication

Displacement

4084 cc (100x130 mm)

Power and torque

42 hp at 2200 rpm

Transmission

Rear-wheel drive, front-mounted multiple dry-plate clutch, 4 speeds + reverse

Chassis

Longerons and cross members in pressed steel

Coachwork

Torpedo (Castagna)

Suspension

Front: rigid axle, semi-elliptic leaf springs

Rear: live axle, semi-elliptic leaf springs

Brakes

Rear: mechanically actuated drums

Front: absent

Dimensions

Wheelbase: 3200 mm - Width: 4360 mm

Weight

1000 kg

Maximum speed

100 kph

Number of cars made

Over 200

A.L.F.A. (Società Anonima Lombarda Fabbrica Automobili) was registered as a company on the 24th of June 1910, when the design for the first car the 24 HP had already been completed. A few months earlier, in September 1909 at the Automobile Club di Milano, Ugo Stella — the faunder of A.L.F.A., who head taken over the factory and investments of the short — lived Italian company Darracq came to an agreement with the Piacenza-born designer Giuseppe Merosi to design two cars that would fit into the 12 and 24 HP tax bands. The new technical director started work at his home in Via Cappuccio 17, Milan and handed over the drawings to the Portello on the 1ST of January 1910.

The 24 HP was positioned at the medium to high end of the automotive market of the day. It had a traditional configuration but was not without certain innovative features: the chassis was fabricated from C-section sheet-steel longerons and cross-members, the front axle was an H-section pressing and the suspension featured semi-elliptical leaf-springs. Drum brakes that could be applied by a hand control or foot pedal were fitted to the rear wheels. The engine was an in-line four-cylinder design with a cast-iron cylinder block and a fixed head. The side-valves were operated by tappets driven by a camshaft situated in the crankcase. The engine had a capacity of 4084 cc and a power output of 42 hp at 2200 rpm (later increased to 45 hp at 2400 rpm).

The transmission was particularly sophisticated: the four-speed gearbox with reverse gear was connected to the wheels by means of a one-piece drive shaft running in a torque tube. The spoked wheels were made by Sankey. The car weighed 1,000 kg in running order.

The car's superior performance — with a top speed of 100 kph — and excellent workmanship made it an immediate success: around 200 chassis in four series were to be produced by 1913. Most of them were fitted with torpedo bodywork.

The "Corsa" version with two-seater open bodywork and a reduced weight of 870 kg successfully took part in a number of races, including a stunning performance by Nino Franchini in the 1911 Targa Florio. For a long time he led the race, which was held in terrible weather conditions, and he had a lead of more than six seconds over Ceirano in the Scat, but was forced to retire after being blinded by mud which caused him to lose control of the car and damage a wheel.

At the outbreak of the First World War, the firm began producing the 24 HP chassis for the Italian Army. Later, Nicola Romeo suspended this production and the facilities were used to produce other items. The chassis were improved and completed after the war, giving rise to the 20-30 ES.

The example on display, in perfect working order, features a torpedo body by Ercole Castagna that started a long and profitable working relationship between the two Milanese companies. In 1953, Alfa Romeo bought the car from one of its dealers in Switzerland, long before beginning to set up its own museum.

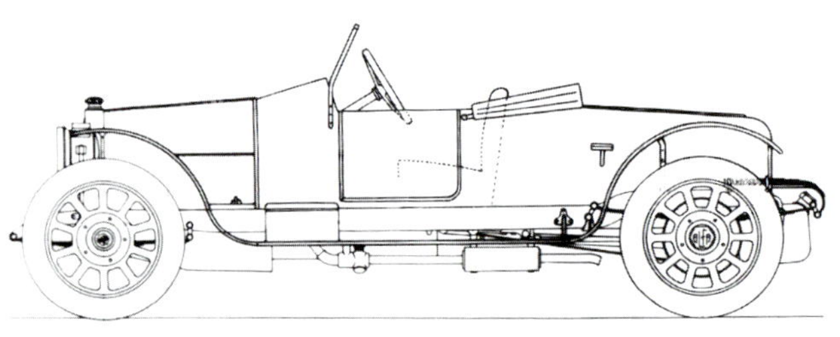

CHASSIS 15 HP

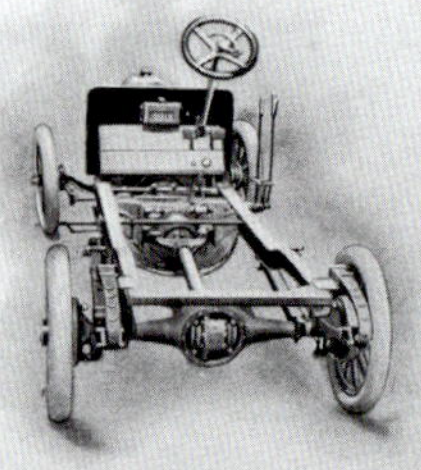

nibile per questa di metri 2,40 × 0,80. Interasse di metri 2,80, carreggiata di m. 1,30.

Pneumatici, uguali alle quattro ruote, di 760 × 100 o, a richiesta, di 810 × 90.

MOTORE a quattro cilindri, monoblocco. Alesaggio millimetri 80, corsa 120.
Le valvole sono comandate da un unico albero a cames, e sono rinchiuse in modo da essere difese efficacemente dalla polvere e da rendere più facile la pulizia esterna del motore.

TELAIO In lamiera d'acciaio stampata, può portare qualsiasi tipo di carrozzeria avendo uno spazio dispo-

A.L.F.A. 15 HP Corsa

THE "LITTLE SISTER" BEGINS
A LONG SPORTING TRADITION

Engine

Front-mounted, vertical longitudinal, straight-four, block and fixed head in cast iron, two side valves per cylinder, gear-driven lateral camshaft. Single carburettor, magneto ignition, wet-sump lubrication

Displacement

2413 cc (80x120 mm)

Power and torque

25 hp at 2400 rpm

Transmission

Rear-wheel drive, front-mounted clutch
3 speeds + reverse

Chassis

Longerons and cross members in pressed steel

Coachwork

"Quattro Baquets"

Suspension

Front: rigid axle, longitudinal semi-elliptic leaf springs

Rear: live axle, longitudinal quarter- and semi-elliptic leaf springs

Brakes

Rear: mechanically actuated drums

Front: absent

Dimensions

Wheelbase: 2920 mm – Width: 3783 mm

Weight

920 kg

Maximum speed

95 kph

Number of cars made

100

As soon as they met in September 1909, it became clear that Ugo Stella and Giuseppe Merosi intended to build A.L.F.A. on solid foundations and they immediately started designing a range based on two models. A more compact car was introduced alongside the 24 HP a few months later. This was the 12 HP, which was in a lower tax band and more affordable.

The engine bore a close resemblance to the one in its sister model, with a cast-iron cylinder block, and a crankcase and sump in light alloy. However, the displacement was reduced to 2114 cc; likewise the power dropped to 22 CV, for a top speed of 90 kph. The chassis, again fabricated with sheet steel longerons and cross members, was lighter and more compact, while the transmission featured a conical rather than multi-plate clutch and there was no fourth gear.

Shortly after the presentation of the car in January 1911, A.L.F.A., reluctantly at first, decided to enter a 12 HP in the first Modena reliability trial, scheduled from the 23RD to the 29TH of April. The competition was staged over a distance of 1500 km to be covered in a week. It turned out to be an even harder task to observe the rules of the race: no mechanical work, not even minor adjustments, was allowed on the cars and not even in the evenings – the cars were kept in a parc fermé and were closely guarded.

The engine of the "quattro baquets" was given an extra 3 hp and two of the company's testers took turns at the wheel: Nino Franchini, the very first head of testing, and Giuseppe Campari, still a young apprentice but destined for a brilliant career at the Portello, tragically cut short by a fatal accident at Monza in 1933. At the end of the gruelling marathon, the 12 HP had accumulated just 1/10 penalty points and finished first "ex aequo" among seven of the 19 that started.

A year later, Merosi drew on his racing experience to introduce the same modifications to the B series, giving rise to the 15 HP, now with four gears, a brake on the transmission and a multi-plate clutch.

1914 saw the debut of the third series, baptised as the 15-20 HP, now with a power output of 28 hp, wider tracks, single-plate clutch and a maximum speed of 100 kph.

330 of these cars were made in various versions (about ten of the engines were used during the First World War to power a portable generator).

The chassis of the car on display, a 15 HP, came to Alfa Romeo in 1962 when Luigi Fusi managed to obtain this car and a GP Tipo P2 from the Museo delle Scienza e Tecnica in Milan, in exchange for a GP Tipo 512 chassis. The "quattro baquets" bodywork was rebuilt in 1971 according to instructions given by an ex-employee of the Bollani firm, which had made bodywork for several of these chassis. In October the car was ready for display in the museum.

RL Super Sport

MEROSI'S MASTERPIECE AND THE BIRTH
OF THE QUADRIFOGLIO

Engine

Front-mounted, vertical longitudinal, straight-six, block and head in cast iron, two valves per cylinder, gear-driven lateral camshaft. Twin carburettors, high tension magneto ignition

Displacement

2994 cc (76x110 mm)

Power and torque

83 hp at 3600 rpm

Transmission

Rear-wheel drive, front-mounted multiple dry-plate clutch, 4 speeds + reverse

Chassis

Longerons and cross members in pressed steel

Coachwork

Torpedo (Castagna)

Suspension

Front: rigid axle, longitudinal semi-elliptic leaf springs, friction dampers

Rear: live axle, double longitudinal semi-elliptic leaf springs, friction dampers

Brakes

Mechanically actuated drums

Dimensions

Wheelbase: 3143 mm – Width: 4248 mm – Height 1760

Weight

1600 kg

Maximum speed

130 kph

Number of cars made

2631 (RL, 1922-1927)

Nicola Romeo intended to make the RL, Giuseppe Merosi's masterpiece, competitive with its leading international rivals. With this in mind, the engineer from Piacenza even went to the 1920 Detroit Motor Show to buy up avant-garde machine tooling as well as a Pierce-Arrow for "evaluation".
The RL was shown to the public on the 13TH of October 1921 in the Alfa Romeo Showroom at No. 18 Via Dante in Milan and was put on sale the following year, although only six cars were made. Initially it was available in two versions: Normale and Sport.
It had a traditional ladder frame chassis with pressed steel C-section longerons and cross-members, semi-elliptic leaf-springs and friction dampers. The engine was a newly designed straight-six with a block and fixed, flat cylinder-head in cast iron, its engineering being particularly elegant thanks to the innovatory induction and exhaust ducts cast as part of the block. The Normale version, with a displacement of 2916 cc, developed 56 hp, while the Sport, which differed by having a pointed rather than flat radiator and a larger displacement of 2994 cc had a corresponding increase in power to 71 hp thanks also to the adoption of twin vertical single-choke carburettors. The intake and exhaust sides were inverted and it now had dry-sump lubrication. The wheelbase was shortened too and the weight reduced. The maximum speed increased from 110 to 130 kph. From the third series dating from September 1923, the rear band brakes were replaced with an integral braking system with drum brakes on all four wheels.
Benefitting from the experience gained with the Corsa version, known as the Targa Florio after Ugo Sivocci's win in the 1923 edition of the exhausting Sicilian race, in 1925 the sixth series was launched with an increased power output of 83 hp and improved braking thanks to bigger drums. After these modifications the name was also changed to RL Super Sport.
A total of 393 RL Super Sport cars were made before 1927, added to which there were 1315 Normal versions of the chassis, 537 Sport versions and 387 Turismo versions. Although it was the Targa Florio versions which dominated the sporting scene, the road-going versions also had their fair share of victories, such as Enzo Ferrari's first place in the 1923 Coppa delle Alpi and the 1925 Coppa Acerbo, the 1925 Circuit de Eiffel, and the Baden Baden hill climb in 1926. Mention also has to be made of Willy Cleer's overall third place in the German GP in 1926 on the very fast Avus circuit.
The coachbuilders' creations, from Castagna to Sala and through to the newcomer Zagato, were also of note. The car on display was acquired in Pakistan in 1965. The flamboyant bodywork in handcrafted aluminium, apparently originally made by Castagna for an Indian maharaja, was partially rebuilt before it was included in the collection.

6C 1750 Gran Sport

NIMBLE, FAST, STYLISH. THE ICON OF AN ERA

Engine

Front, longitudinal, vertical straight-six, block and head in cast iron, two valves per cylinder, double overhead camshafts driven by layshaft and bevel gear pair. One twin-choke carburettor and supercharger, distributor ignition, wet sump lubrication

Displacement

1752 cc (65x88 mm)

Power and torque

85 hp at 4500 rpm

Transmission

Rear-wheel drive, front multiple dry-plate clutch, four speeds + reverse

Chassis

Longerons and cross members in pressed steel

Bodywork

Open racing two-seater (Zagato)

Suspension

Front: rigid axle, semi-elliptical leaf springs, friction dampers

Rear: live axle, semi-elliptical leaf springs, friction dampers

Brakes

Mechanically actuated drums

Dimensions

Wheelbase: 2745 mm, length: 3652 mm, width: 1615 mm

Weight

920 Kg

Maximum speed

145 kph

Cars produced

213 (6C Gran Sport, 1930-1932)

The 6C 1750, designed by Vittorio Jano, was the natural heir to the 6C 1500. Following on from the racing success of the earlier car, the intention was not just to develop a project from the ground up but also to offer a product that was perfect for the market and that in no time at all was to become one of the symbols of the early Thirties. On the sporting front, the car was to dominate Sport car races while it was also very successful in commercial terms too, with as many as 2,579 cars sold between 1929 and 1933, at a time when it was the norm to make only a few hundred cars a year. The 1750 was also one of the cars most cherished by racing drivers, by the so-called gentlemen drivers and by high society, who had stunning bodywork built by the most famous coachbuilders of the time — Castagna, Farina, Young, Touring or Zagato. These were cars that had as much success in concours d'elegance as they did in races.

The 1750 was presented at the 1929 Salone Internazionale dell'Automobile in Rome in three versions, Turismo, Sport and Super Sport. It reached the height of its success in 1930 with the addition to the range of the Gran Turismo version, which used the same mechanical components as the Sport, and above all with the Gran Sport, which took over from the Super Sport as the flagship model. The main difference was in the fuel supply, where a Roots-type supercharger made by Alfa Romeo was fitted coaxially to the crankshaft and twin-choke carburettors were fitted on the left side. Power output was still 85 hp and in this case too six examples, soon to be used for racing, were built using a fixed-head engine, with a power output of 102 hp giving a top speed of 170 kph.

The car on display was partially rebuilt before it was put on show. The open two-seater bodywork was made by Zagato and was presented at the 1931 Paris motor show. For this reason Luigi Fusi decided to draw attention to a detail relating to a small series of cars built between 1931 and 1934: in order to avoid paying export duty the components were exported as spare parts and later assembled in a small workshop in Paris. The French importer at that time was Luigi Chinetti, a well-known racing driver who had taken part in two Le Mans 24 Hour races at the wheel of an 8C 2300. He later emigrated to the United States where he became a Ferrari importer and in 1958 founded the North American Racing Team. Alfa Romeo had opened a sophisticated garage in 36 Rue Marbeuf several years previously. They went so far as to have it designed in such a masterful way by a famous modernist architect, Robert Mallet-Stevens in 1925, that in February 1927 the magazine *L'art Vivant* described it as "one of the most pure expressions of design". The characteristic feature of these cars was the badge on the radiator that, while retaining the same design, replaced Milan with Paris.

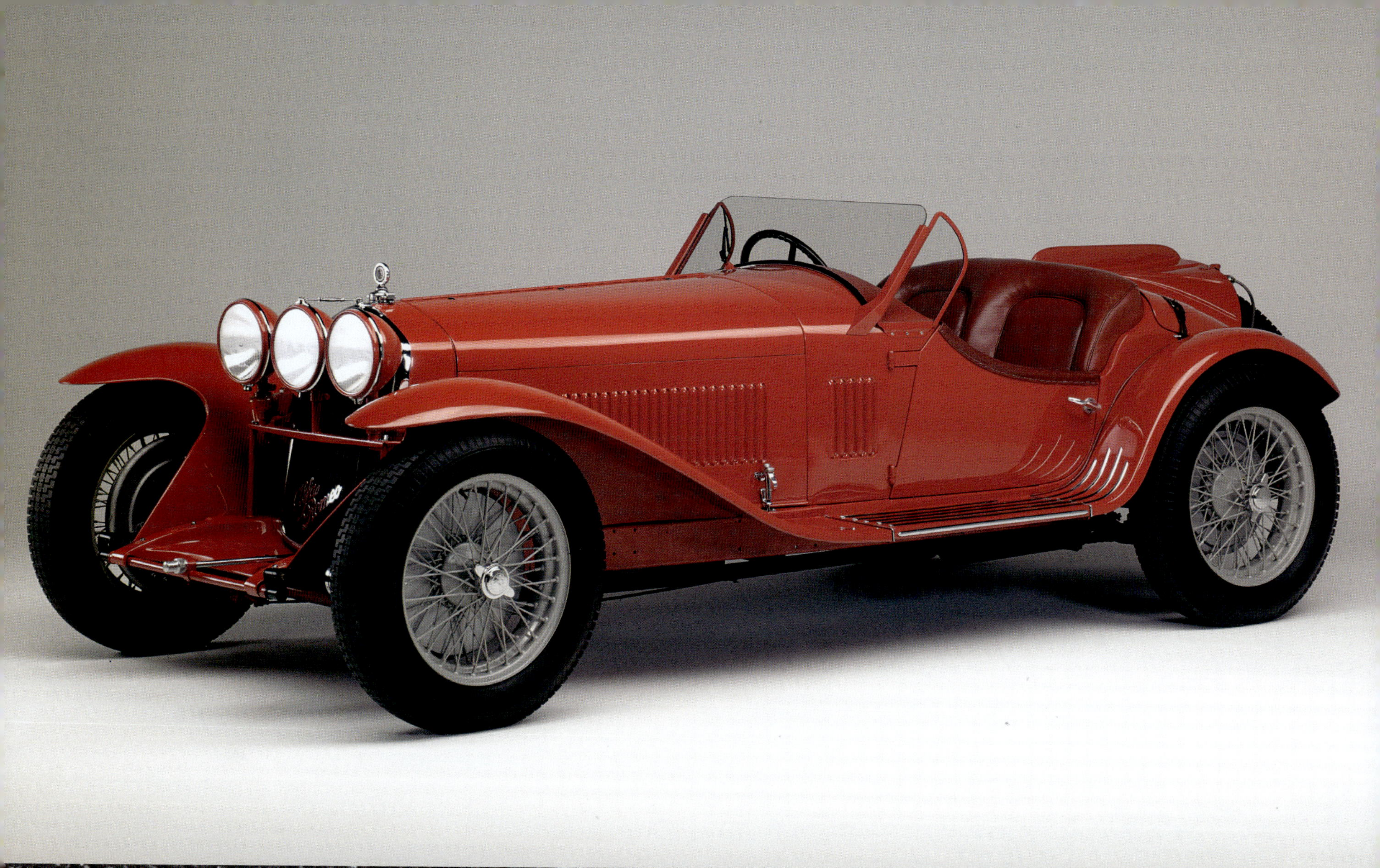

8C 2300 Corto "Mille Miglia"
AN UNSUCCESSFUL START TO A REMARKABLE CAREER

Engine

Front, longitudinal vertical, straight-eight, twin blocks and head in light alloy, two valves per cylinder, gear driven double overhead camshafts, single carburettor, supercharger, distributor ignition

Displacement

2336 cc (65x88 mm)

Power and torque

155 hp at 5200 rpm

Transmission

Rear-wheel drive, front multiple dry-plate clutch, four speeds + reverse

Chassis

Longerons and cross members in pressed steel

Bodywork

Open racing two-seater

Suspension

Front: rigid axle, semi-elliptical leaf springs, friction dampers

Rear: live axle, semi-elliptical leaf springs, friction dampers

Brakes

Mechanically actuated drums

Dimensions

Length: 4400 mm - Wheelbase: 3100 mm

Weight (dry)

1000 Kg

Maximum speed

185 kph

Cars produced

308 (8C 2300, 1931-1934)

The straight-eight engine had born fruit, and what fruit, in the P2, a Grand Prix car that proved capable of a remarkable degree of success at an international level, initially between 1924 and 1925 (for example, conquering the single-race World Championship at Monza in '25 with Gastone Brilli Peri) and then again in 1930 when Achille Varzi drove an updated version of the car to victory in the Targa Florio.

Vittorio Jano continued down this path in 1931 with the 8C 2300, equipped with a brand-new straight-eight displacing 2236 cc, with the two blocks of four cylinders cast in light alloy like the cylinder heads. The steel liners were dry and hot pressed. The gear train driving the valvegear and the auxiliary components, including the Roots-type supercharger, was again set between the two blocks. The camshafts were fabricated in two sections to avoid any torsional deformation, dry sump lubrication was adopted and the unit produced a maximum power output of 142 hp at 5000 rpm. However, the hand of the brilliant designer can also be seen in the chassis, closely derived from that of the 6C 1750 and offered in the new car in two versions: one with a wheelbase of 3100 mm (8C 2300 "Lungo") and 2750 mm (8C 2300 "Corto"). From the outset a Spider Corsa version was offered, with an engine producing 155 hp at 5200 rpm (165 hp at 5400 rpm in 1932), for a top speed of 185 kph (195/215 kph in 1932).

The leading coachbuilders of the era, from Touring to Zagato and others, were to find the 8C 2300 rolling chassis to be the ideal foundation for their creativity, producing superb examples in open and closed form. Among the latter, mention has to be made of the sleek "Victoria" berlinetta, built by Pinin Farina in 1933, while among the open cars, as well as a number of Touring variations on the Flying Star theme, the models prepared by Zagato were unforgettable, undisputed protagonists on the national and international sporting scene of those years.

The 1931 Mille Miglia (11-12 April) was the setting for the debut of the new 8C 2300 MM's, three Alfa Romeo works car entered for Nuvolari, Borzacchini and Campari and another four raced by the Scuderia Ferrari. Hurried fine tuning of the cars that had been introduced just a few months earlier and had yet to be road tested, along with excessive tyre troubles during the race (Nuvolari alone had to change 18…) were factors that compromised the outcome of the race, although in the successive Targa Florio the Flying Mantuan was to obtain the first in a long series of the victories for the 8C 2300.

"Revenge" in the Mille Miglia was to come over the following two years, with wins for Borzacchini-Bignami in 1932 and Nuvolari-Compagnoni in 1933.

6C 2300 B
CARATTERISTICHE TECNICHE
L'Auto Italiana
ANNO XVIII - N. 18 - 30 GIUGNO 1937 XV - SPEDIZ. IN ABBON. POSTALE - LIRE

ALFA ROMEO

2300 B
ALFA-ROMEO MILANO

6C 2300 B Corto

RACING, BUT ALSO COMFORT AND SOPHISTICATION.
THE GRAN TURISMO

Engine

Front, longitudinal vertical straight-six, block in cast iron and head in light alloy, two valves per cylinder, chain and gear driven double overhead camshafts. One twin-choke carburettor, distributor ignition, wet-sump lubrication

Displacement

2309 cc (70x100 mm)

Power and torque

76 hp at 4400 rpm

Transmission

Rear-wheel drive, front single dry-plate clutch, four speeds + reverse

Chassis

Welded box-section longerons and cross members

Bodywork

Saloon

Suspension

Front: independent, wishbones, coil springs hydraulic dampers

Rear: independent, trailing arms, longitudinal torsion bars, hydraulic dampers

Brakes

Hydraulically actuated drums all round

Dimensions

Wheelbase: 3000 mm

Weight (dry)

1440 Kg

Maximum speed

130 kph

Cars produced

86

In the innumerable books dedicated to the history of Alfa Romeo, few pages are devoted to a car that remained in production for just one year, 1933, and which was powered by the glorious straight-six from the 6C 1750 bored out to 1917 cc (68x88 mm). The car was known as the 6C 1900 Gran Turismo and its technical specification was not without interest, starting from the aluminium cylinder head in place of the cast iron version, the adoption of a twin-choke carburettor and the use of a box-section chassis to increase overall stiffness. And yet this car, whose name contained a figure, 1900, that was to become synonymous with Alfa Romeo in years to come, was a transitional model, replaced from 1934 by the new 6C 2300 Turismo which appeared at the Milan Motor Show that year, equipped with a new generation straight-six engine. A cast iron block, a total displacement of 2309 cc (70x100 mm), light alloy cylinder head and chain driven (for the first time) double overhead camshafts were just a few of the main features of the new engine that developed a maximum power output of 68 hp at 4400 rpm (good for a top speed of 120 kph).

As with the previous 1900, the chassis with box section steel longerons was retained, perforated for lightness (with a wheelbase of 3210 mm), while the rigid axle suspension featured semi-elliptical leaf springs outside the longerons and friction dampers, those at the rear adjustable from the cockpit. Mechanically actuated drum brakes were fitted.

The chassis of the 6C 2300 was to be one of the most sought-after of the era: mention has to be made of the wonderfully evocative "Soffio di Satana" or "Satan's Breath" by Carrozzeria Touring, and the no less admirable "Pescara" models (the name chosen as a tribute to the team's feat in finishing first, second and third in the 1934 Pescara 24 Hours with three 6C 2300 berlinettas), forerunners of the GT's with a "sporting heart" that were capable of performing as prestige road cars as well as winning important races.

Pinin Farina and Castagna also used the same chassis, testimony to the success and versatility of the model, with a series of more sober closed cars, with two-light bodywork, similar to the one featuring in the museum today, an example acquired in Switzerland in 1965 and added to the collection two years later.

6C 2500 Sport "Freccia d'Oro"

ALL THE ELEGANCE OF THE MARQUE AND OF ITALY. BUT THE WORLD WAS CHANGING

Engine

Front, longitudinal vertical straight-six, block in cast iron and head in light alloy, two valves per cylinder, chain and gear driven double overhead camshafts. One twin-choke carburettor, distributor ignition, wet-sump lubrication

Displacement

2443 cc (72x100 mm)

Power and torque

90 hp at 4600 rpm

Transmission

Rear-wheel drive, front-mounted multiple dry-plate clutch, four speeds + reverse

Chassis

Welded box-section longerons and cross members

Bodywork

Saloon (Alfa Romeo)

Suspension

Front: independent, wishbones, coil springs, hydraulic dampers

Rear: independent, trailing arms, torsion bars, dual hydraulic dampers

Brakes

Hydraulically actuated drums all round

Dimensions

Wheelbase: 3000 mm, Length: 4950 mm, Width: 1850 mm, Height 1530 mm

Weight (dry)

1550 Kg

Maximum speed

155 kph

Cars produced

680

When the Second World War was still raging in Europe, Alfa Romeo was already beginning to think about what would come "after", and what it would be able to do in industrial terms once peace had been re-established. With this in mind, in the early Forties Wifredo Ricart, the Spanish engineer then leading the Special Studies department, had been given the task of designing a new mid-high range saloon that would be innovative and avant-garde but also relatively simple and economical to construct. A car that, in substance, took up the heritage of the glorious 6C 2500 family, but which could arouse the interest and expectations of a less elitist public. The 6C 2000 "Gazella" was born out of this brief and was not without elements of interest but remained at the prototype stage after being rejected out of hand by the firm's great test driver, Consalvo Sanesi, who slated the car as "… not suitable for production".

At the end of the war, in a Portello factory semi-demolished by allied bombing, the powers-that-be at Alfa preferred to focus once again on the "old" 6C 2500 from 1939, laboriously restarting automotive production on that basis.

It was out of this difficult situation that the 6C 2500 Sport "Freccia d'Oro" was born, exploiting the ladder chassis of the 6C 2500 Sport with a wheelbase of three metres grafted onto which was a brand-new Alfa-designed body. The car was an elegant two-door, two-box, all-metal saloon that, in aesthetic terms, was distinguished by voluminous and prominent wings that, at the front at least, blended progressively into the body, a long, narrow Alfa shield at the front that, with the two horizontal lateral grilles, formed the usual "trilobite" front end, and the close-coupled rear that balanced the imposing nose. The two-light upper body was particularly airy and was characterised by ample glazing.

In mechanical terms, the "Freccia d'Oro" was equipped with the front-mounted longitudinal straight-six with a block in cast iron and a light alloy cylinder head and a displacement of 2443 cc. Fitted with a single carburettor, the unit produced 90 hp at 4600 rpm (a figure which rose over the course of the years to 93 hp) for a declared maximum speed of 155 kph. The transmission had four speeds + reverse and featured a steering-column gear change.

Despite being something of a fall-back model in view of an all-new design in the future, the "Freccia d'Oro" nonetheless marked an important chapter in the history of the marque during what was a very delicate phase of rebirth. A few examples were actually used in racing: Consalvo Sanesi and Franco Venturi started the 1949 Mille Miglia aboard a 6C 2500 carrying race number 346 which they drove to an honourable 12TH place overall.

The example on display in the museum was added to the collection in 1965 after having been purchased in running order two years earlier from Alfa's Bassano Concessionaire.

Alfa Romeo
1900
1900   BERLINA ALFA ROMEO
1900 C   COUPÉ TOURING
          CABRIOLET PININ FARINA
1900 L   CABRIOLET VICTORIA
          STABILIMENTI FARINA
ALFA ROMEO
-MILANO-

1900

THE RACE-WINNING FAMILY SALOON

Engine

Front, vertical, longitudinal straight-four, cast iron block, removable alloy cylinder head, two valves per cylinder, chain actuated double overhead camshafts. One single-choke carburettor, distributor ignition, wet sump lubrication.

Displacement

1884 cc (82.55x88 mm)

Power and torque

80 hp at 4800 rpm

Transmission

Rear-wheel drive, front single dry-plate clutch, four speeds + reverse

Chassis

Pressed steel unitary construction

Bodywork

Saloon

Suspension

Front: independent, wishbones, coil springs, hydraulic dampers

Rear: live axle, trailing arms, triangular central element, coil springs, hydraulic dampers

Brakes

Hydraulically actuated drums all round

Dimensions

Wheelbase: 2630 mm, length: 4400 mm, width: 1600 mm, height: 1490 mm

Weight

1100 kg

Maximum speed

150 kph

Cars produced

17,390 (1900, 1950-1958)

At the end of the Second World War the 6C 2500, and its derivatives, still represented the core of the Portello's output but market trends and the new society's tastes were changing fast. The few people who, in that extremely difficult period of history, could afford to buy a car, certainly no longer aspired to own sophisticated and expensive cars and were more likely to be looking for a stylish but reliable car for everyday use.

At the Portello, where fortunately work on projects had never stopped, these new demands certainly did not go unnoticed and the idea of a new mid-range car with a displacement of around 1800 cc soon gained ground. A car of modern design that could be produced and therefore sold in very large numbers. A car that could guide Alfa Romeo to a truly industrial scale of production, but without losing sight of those qualities of excellence and vitality that were the building blocks of the company's DNA.

The 2ND of October 1950 thus became a key date in the history of Alfa and Italian motoring: the 1900 saloon was unveiled at the Hotel Principe di Savoia in Milan.

Work had actually begun on this revolutionary car two years earlier, in November 1948, when the chief engineers at the Portello decided to go down the road of a 4-cylinder twin-cam engine in a load-bearing body. At an early stage, front-wheel drive was taken into consideration but then a more conventional design was chosen with the engine was mounted longitudinally at the front and rear-wheel drive. With regard to the suspension, the technical specification of the 1900 lists a live rear-axle, with a single lower trailing arm and a triangulated central link, while at the front there was independent suspension with wishbones, coil springs and an anti-roll bar.

The 1900's four-cylinder engine, which initially at least looked like heresy to "purists" of the marque, had a displacement of 1884 cc (82.55 x 88 mm), two chain-driven overhead camshafts and a single-choke Solex carburettor. It delivered a maximum power output of 80 hp at 4800 rpm, while, in terms of performance, the early cars were capable of around 150 kph.

The bodywork, for which several prototypes were made, took the form of a simple but sleek four-door sedan with a typical "trilobate" or "three-lobed" Alfa Romeo front end.

The 1900 earned the well-known slogan "The family car that wins races" because in 1952 the "Casa del Biscione" had already brought out a new version with the initials TI (Turismo Internazionale) with 110 hp and a top speed of 170 kph.

From the car's debut in the Giro di Sicilia that year, the new TI revealed first-class competitive qualities and won the 2-litre class with Carini-Artesani. This marked the beginning of a long run of successes.

alfa
romeo

1900ᶜ

super
sprint

1900 Super Sport

TOURING WITH ALFA ROMEO AGAIN FOR A TRUE "SPECIAL"

Engine

Front, vertical, longitudinal straight-four, cast iron block, removable alloy cylinder head, two valves per cylinder, chain actuated double overhead camshafts. One single-choke vertical carburettor, distributor ignition

Displacement

1975 cc (84.50x88 mm)

Power and torque

115 hp at 5500 rpm

Transmission

Rear-wheel drive, front-mounted single dry-plate clutch four speeds + reverse

Chassis

Pressed steel unitary construction

Bodywork

Touring Superleggera coupé

Suspension

Front: independent, wishbones, coil springs, anti-roll bar

Rear: live axle, trailing arms, triangular central element, coil springs

Brakes

Hydraulically actuated drums all round

Dimensions

Wheelbase: 2500 mm – Length: 4475 mm - width: 1630 mm, height: 1325 mm

Weight (dry)

1000 kg

Maximum speed

190 kph

Cars produced

599 (1900 Super Sprint 1955-1958)

As well as whetting the appetites of the well-established sports car customers who found the TI to be the ideal car to "show off" in on road and track, the immediate success of the 1900 encouraged Alfa Romeo as early as 1951 to complement the saloon with new coupé and cabriolet versions, the styling and construction of which were entrusted to external coachbuilders, Touring and Pinin Farina above all, as the Portello did not have the resources to undertake such a task in-house.

The famous Milanese body coachbuilder created the first 1900 C Sprint using a shortened 2500 mm wheelbase (compared to the 2630 mm of the 1900). The car had elegant lines distinguished by the inevitable trilobate front and strongly accentuated rear wings framing a restrained tail. The 4-cylinder twin-cam was still the 1884 cc from the TI but, thanks to a slightly revised compression ratio, the power output rose to 110 hp.

The launch of the 1900 Super in 1954 (1975 cc) represented the ideal opportunity to prepare a new series of coupés under the Super Sprint name. Thanks to the two twin-choke carburettors the engines now boasted a maximum power output of 115 hp at 5500 rpm and a new 5-speed + reverse gearbox was also adopted. In terms of styling, while the Super Sprint retained Touring's classic configuration, some of the detail work was more slender and modern: a progressive lightening of the rear pillars can be seen and thin chromed rods are to be found inside the two horizontal lobes of the radiator grille in place of the classic mesh.

However, in 1955 the need to update the coupé version of the 1900 became pressing and after submitting a number of prototypes (Tipo 55) that failed to meet with Alfa Romeo's approval, Touring finally got it right in 1956, giving rise to a new model that had a simpler and more clearly-defined lines that also had something of the design features used on the new Giulietta Sprint introduced in 1954. There was the same innate Pinin Farina stylishness in the way the sides were barely "sullied" by the tiny door handles and on some models, by a thin chrome strip running beneath the doors. It is worth drawing attention to an upper body distinguished by its extensive glazing and by the extremely elegant rear pillars barely highlighted with slim pieces of chrome trim. In some of Touring's drawings it appears that a two-tone upper body had been considered, although this option was never seen in the small batch of cars that was produced.

Using the same chassis as the Super Sprint, but without the upper body, Carrozzeria Touring unveiled an extremely elegant cabriolet 2+2 at the 1957 Geneva Motor Show, but the proposal was never followed up. Just as the 1956 Super Sprint coupé inevitably suffered from internal competition with the Giulietta Sprint, this cabriolet, which came out two years after the debut of the iconic Giulietta spider (1955), was destined to make very slow progress right from birth.

alfa romeo Giuli
1300 cmc.
berlina 4 posti

Giulietta

ALFA ROMEO ENTERS THE WORLD OF MASS PRODUCTION WITH "ITALY'S SWEETHEARTH"

Engine

Front, longitudinal vertical straight-four, block and head in light alloy, two valves per cylinder, chain driven double overhead camshafts One single-choke vertical carburettor, distributor ignition, wet-sump lubrication

Displacement

1290 cc (74x75 mm)

Power and torque

53 hp at 5500 rpm – 8.5 kgm at 3000 rpm

Transmission

Rear-wheel drive, front single dry-plate clutch, four speeds + reverse

Chassis

Pressed steel unitary construction

Bodywork

Saloon

Suspension

Front: wishbones, coil springs, hydraulic dampers, anti-roll bar

Rear: live axle, upper triangular element, trailing arms, coil springs, hydraulic dampers

Brakes

Hydraulically actuated drums all round

Dimensions

Wheelbase: 2380 mm, Length: 3990 mm, Width: 1550 mm, Height: 1400 mm

Weight (dry)

870 Kg

Maximum speed

136 kph

Cars produced

131,775 (Giulietta, 1955-1964)

The events in 1954 that led up to the launch of the Giulietta Sprint before the saloon version were part and parcel of the company, of its state overship. Despite the car's immediate and overwhelming success Alfa Romeo's management had ambitions that went well beyond production of the coupé. They were in fact aiming at transforming the company into a major automotive manufacturer, something that could only happen if they presented a less sporting car that would lend itself to mass production on the assembly line that Rodolf Hruska was setting up at the Portello, putting to good use the experience he had gained while working on projects for Volkswagen and Simca.

After a lengthy period of gestation, during which Alfa Romeo had to make the sacrifice of withdrawing from racing and devoting all its energy and resources to the project, the Giulietta saloon was presented in 1955. Its first official appearance was at the Turin Motor Show. For this version of the car too a show was put on with actors naturally playing the parts of the Shakespearian characters Romeo and Juliet. The mechanical configuration of the car was similar to that of the Sprint: a 1290cc twin-cam engine made of light alloy at the front, with rear-wheel drive and a live axle, a unitary construction bodyshell and independent front suspension. The engine, using just one single-choke carburettor, still managed to produce 53 hp, good for a top speed of 136 kph. In the mid-Fifties the Giulietta didn't have to freaking confront: top speed, acceleration, pick-up, road-holding and braking decreed an immediate and overwhelming success. In the years to follow changes were made to the bodywork, with less rounded and more protruding light units being recessed in the tail section, newly designed instruments installed and modifications to the engine, with a power output that in 1961 was increased to 62 hp for a top speed of 145 kph. The car was a true icon of its time and soon made a name for itself as "Italy's sweetheart" symbolising a position in society which was aspired to by many, but which for many more – in a country that was picking itself up again after the gloom of the war – was only a dream. Production ended in 1963 after 39,057 cars had been made, excluding the TI versions and the coupé and spider version.

The car on display was acquired in 1973 from an Alfa Romeo employee who had bought it from new and used it for nearly twenty years. It was restored in January the following year and then introduced to the museum.

2600 Sprint

SIX CYLINDERS AND A COUPÉ BODY FOR A TRUE GT

Engine

Front, vertical, longitudinal straight-six, light alloy block and cylinder head, two valves per cylinder, chain driven double overhead camshafts. Three twin-choke carburettors, distributor ignition, wet sump lubrication.

Displacement

2584 cc (83x79.60 mm)

Power and torque

145 hp at 5900 rpm - 18.8 kgm at 2000 rpm

Transmission

Rear wheel drive, front single dry-plate clutch, five speeds + reverse

Chassis

Pressed steel unitary construction

Bodywork

Coupé

Suspension

Front: wishbones, coil springs, hydraulic dampers, anti-roll bar

Rear: live axle, upper triangular element and trailing arms, coil springs, hydraulic dampers

Brakes

Hydraulically actuated discs

Dimensions

Wheelbase: 2580 mm, length: 4580 mm, width: 1706 mm, height: 1380 mm

Weight (dry)

1370 kg

Maximum speed

197 kph

Cars produced

6,999 (2600 Super Sprint 1962-1966)

Two years after the presentation of the 2000 saloon, which was designed but failed to replace the 1900, the launch of the Spider with Touring bodywork and the exit of the last 1900 Super Sprint cars, the Alfa Romeo range was missing a mid- to high-range GT. For this reason, following the success of the Giulietta Sprint, Bertone was asked to design a modern body for the 2000 chassis, which was itself an evolution of the 1900. Giorgio Giugiaro, at the time barely twenty years old and working at Bertone, designed a sleek coupé with clean flanks, an expansive glazed area and a spacious and bright interior. Another minor revolution was to be found in the high and imposing front end of the car, where the lighting clusters were no longer recessed in the bodywork but embedded in a single radiator grille bearing the Alfa Romeo badge, styling that anticipated that of the Giulia GT. Limited by an undersized engine, the 2000 Sprint reached full maturity in 1962 when a new straight-six engine with a displacement of more than two and half litres saw the light of day. It was made of light alloy, had a very respectable power output and shared many of the components of the "twin-cam" engine from the Giulietta. There were only small differences between the new 2600 Sprint and the 2000, the most obvious being the air intake on the bonnet, which gave the front of the car a more aggressive appearance. With its three carburettors, the power output was increased to 145 hp with a top speed of nearly 200 kph. It had a five-speed gearbox and disk brakes, at first only at the front, but later fitted to all four wheels. However, apart from a few appearances in races in the hands of privateers, the track was hardly its favourite environment. The 2600 Sprint was an elegant and refined Grand Touring car, as *Quattroruote* magazine stated in its test report at the time of its presentation during the Geneva Motor Show. "The six-cylinder engine, which is smooth and vibration-free, gives this car a level of comfort which the '2000' certainly does not offer. The larger displacement and therefore the increased power provide an outstandingly supple driving experience. Braking is gentle, powerful and at the same time easily dosed; the suspension is soft and comfortable and we have no comments to make about the road-holding — racing experience and the fact that the Alfa Romeo test drivers are almost all former racing drivers means that this company's cars in this category are all extremely well set up."

Some specially equipped cars were used by the police forces and in particular those allocated to the Italian Polizia di Stato became known as "Panthers".

The car on display had been stored in the Research Department. It was restored and repainted at the beginning of the Seventies.

Giulia

FAST, MODERN, SAFE, ICONIC: "DISEGNATA DAL VENTO"

Engine

Front, vertical, longitudinal straight-four, light alloy block and cylinder head, two valves per cylinder, duplex chain driven double overhead camshafts. Single twin-choke carburettor, distributor ignition, wet sump lubrication

Displacement

1570 cc (78x82 mm)

Power and torque

90 hp at 4400 rpm - 12.1 kgm at 4400 rpm

Transmission

Rear wheel drive, single dry-plate clutch, five speeds + reverse

Chassis

Pressed steel unitary construction

Bodywork

Saloon

Suspension

Front: Independent, wishbones, coil springs, hydraulic dampers, anti-roll bar

Rear: live axle, upper triangular element and trailing arms, coil springs, hydraulic dampers

Brakes

Hydraulically actuated discs with servo (first 22,000 examples fitted with drums)

Dimensions

Wheelbase: 2510 mm — Length: 4130 mm
Width: 1560 mm, height: 1430 mm

Weight (dry)

1000 kg

Maximum speed

169 kph

Cars produced

572,646 (Giulia, 1962-1978)

At the end of the Fifties, Alfa Romeo, boosted by the enormous success of the Giulietta, had to start thinking about a car that could take its place. There were various opinions on the subject — for many the best answer was to develop and improve the existing car which so many people liked, but Orazio Satta Puliga strongly supported by Giuseppe Luraghi, decided to aime at a completely new project, which would put them ahead of their time and win back the marque's position as leader in technology and performance.

The Giulia TI (Turismo Internazionale) was presented at Monza on the 27TH of June 1962. It provoked mixed and conflicting opinions, mainly because of its unusual and distinctive styling, which found a place in the general public rader than in critical evaluation.

The mechanical design of the car was developed from the Giulietta using the twin-cam engine with new castings to increase the displacement to 1570 cc and uprated suspension, now without lubrication points, while the bodywork was instead completely new and in many ways revolutionary: larger, more spacious, more square-cut, safer and more aerodynamic.

This last point was perhaps the most important: the aerodynamic design was carried out on the drawing tables, in the wind tunnel of the Milan Polytechnic and on the road, resulting in a slim, sleek car with a reduced frontal area, a tapering nose and a high, truncated rear end. This last feature needed a massive advertising campaign to help a still sceptical public by no means reassured by the Cx figures to understand the new concept and the excellence of the project.

Not only was the active safety of the car of the highest level, thanks to its performance and reliability but the Giulia was also a class leader in terms of passive safety — the body shell had a deformable end section. The chassis was designed to buckle progressively and gradually absorb the kinetic energy of an impact. The passenger area was also free of sharp edges and a collapsible steering column was fitted. At a time when legislation enforcing minimum standards in the case of frontal impacts had yet to be introduced in the USA, with the same laws being introduced in Europe a few years later, the Giulia that had been presented long before then, would have easily passed any crash-test.

As much an icon of its age as the Giulietta had been, the Giulia was produced from 1962 to 1978 in several different guises and eventually 572,646 cars were made, to which have to be added the coupé and spider models. This was a time of great innovation for Alfa Romeo with the opening of its new factory in Arese and the Balocco track at around the same time.

Montreal

THE "HEART" OF THE 33 FOR "MAN'S UTMOST AUTOMOTIVE ASPIRATION"

Engine

Front, longitudinal, 90° V8, block and cylinder heads in light alloy, chain driven double overhead camshafts per bank. Spica indirect fuel injection, capacitance discharge electronic ignition, dry sump lubrication

Displacement

2593 cc (80x64.5 mm)

Power and torque

200 hp at 6500 rpm - 24.8 hp at 5100 rpm

Transmission

Rear-wheel drive, hydraulically actuated single dry-plate clutch, five speeds + reverse

Chassis

Sheet steel unitary construction

Bodywork

Coupé

Suspension

Front: Independent, double wishbones, coil springs, hydraulic dampers, anti-roll bar

Rear: live axle, central triangular element, trailing arms, hydraulic dampers, anti-roll bar

Brakes

Dual circuit with servo, self-ventilating discs all round

Dimensions

Wheelbase: 2350 mm – Length: 4220 mm
Width: 1672 mm, height: 1205 mm

Weight (dry)

1270 kg

Maximum speed

220 kph

Cars produced

3925 (Montreal, 1970-1977)

Expo 1967 in Montreal celebrated the centenary of the Canadian Confederation and opened with a futuristic pavilion called "Man the Producer". No exhibition of man's achievements over the last century would have been complete without a car and it had to be a prototype which represented, in the organisers' opinion "man's utmost automotive aspiration." So not a dream car but one that could be adapted for road use. The choice fell on Alfa Romeo, but the Portello only found out about the assignment nine months before the official opening. There was no time to build a new engine and chassis so Bertone was given a Giulia Sprint GT chassis fitted with the softly-tuned engine from the Giulia 1600 TI. Marcello Gandini, who had just taken over from Giorgetto Giugiaro, designed a low, sleek coupé defined by a series of vents in the rear roof pillar and headlights concealed behind slatted eyelids.

The two prototypes were painted in a unique pearl-white finish and flown to Montreal. The cars were positioned between two mirrors (a Norton motorcycle was suspended above them) so that their image was reflected into infinity. The car's appealing lines and unusual proportions were so popular that the Alfa management were forced to consider putting it into production.

The four-cylinder twin-cam engine was completely inappropriate considering the ambitions of the car, and with the six-cylinder 2600 having just gone out of production, Giuseppe Busso's choice fell on the new V8 from the Tipo 33.

The capacity was increased to 2593 cc, while its power delivery was "softened" for road use, with a reduction in power output to 200 hp at 6500 rpm (compared to the 270 hp of the two-litre engine in the 33). After various experiments to decide on the choice of transmission - tests that were also carried out on the engine, leading to the "sacrifice" of one of the two concept cars - it was decided to use a five-speed ZF gearbox. The chassis retained the same configuration as the Giulia, with "adjustments" to the suspension set-up and the fitting of self-ventilated disk brakes.

Inside the car, the sober interior of the Montreal Expo was replaced with a new design, but it was to the exterior that the biggest changes were made. As a result of the bulky dimensions of the V8, the longitudinal louvres were eliminated with a noticeable bulge appearing in the form of a false NACA-style duct. The four circular headlights were grouped together beneath two finned eyelids that could be retracted using a pneumatic mechanism and sophisticated "millerighe" wheels made by Campagnolo replaced the Expo originals.

Teething troubles, the oil crisis and the need to completely redesign the bodywork caused severe delays in the production of the car and it only saw the light of day at the Geneva Motor Show in 1970. It stayed in the catalogue until 1977 with total sales of 3925 cars. In 1972 it was updated slightly, the most obvious change being the addition of a front spoiler.

Alfasud

NEW STYLE, NEW CLASS AND A NEW FACTORY.
"SHE'S THE VERY IMAGE OF HER AUNT GIULIA!"

Engine

Front, longitudinal, four horizontally opposed cylinders, block in cast iron, cylinder heads in light alloy, two valves per cylinder, single overhead camshaft per bank actuated by one toothed belt. One single-choke carburettor, distributor ignition, wet sump lubrication

Displacement

1186 cc (80x59 mm)

Power and torque

63 hp at 6000 rpm - 8.5 kgm at 3500 rpm

Transmission

Front-wheel drive, hydraulically actuated single dry-plate clutch, four speeds + reverse

Chassis

Sheet steel unitary construction

Bodywork

Hachback

Suspension

Front: independent, McPherson struts, wishbones, coil springs, hydraulic dampers, anti-roll bar

Rear: rigid axle, twin semi-trailing arms and Panhard rod, coil springs, hydraulic dampers

Brakes

Dual circuit, discs all round
floating at the front

Dimensions

Wheelbase: 2455 mm, length: 3890 mm, width: 1590 mm, height: 1370 mm

Weight (dry)

830 Kg

Maximum speed

150 kph

Cars produced

900,925 (Alfasud, 1972-1984)

Alfa Romeo's first attempt to enter a middle to low sector of the market had been in the Fifties when, in an attempt to maximise productivity at the Portello, many avenues were explored, before the firm decided on the Giulietta project. At the beginning of 1967, at a very positive moment for the company, IRI encouraged them to produce a new smaller and cheaper Alfa Romeo to be manufactured in a purpose-built factory at Pomigliano, a first attempt to enter a mithe generous financial benefits the State was offering to help the industrialisation of the "mezzogiorno" (south) of Italy.

The first step taken in an enterprise strongly supported by Giuseppe Luraghi, was to found SICA (Studi Impianti Consulenza Automobilistica) which, led by Rudolf Hruska, had the task of designing and building the car and the factory.

The technical specification was defined in a "cahier des charges" drawn up by Hruska even before they had appointed the design staff, who were later led by Domenico Chirico. The maximum length was to be no greater than 390 cm and the maximum weight 850 kg. The space available inside and the size of the boot had to be equal to that of a car in a higher class. All of these criteria had to be satisfied without neglecting the sporting appearance and performance that customers expected of an Alfa Romeo.

As for the engine, Hruska chose a four-cylinder boxer installed longitudinally, with front-wheel drive. This configuration took up very little space and allowed for a low bonnet, making the car more aerodynamic. Similarly, special McPherson front suspension was used with the shock absorber set laterally relative to the hub. At the rear, a rigid rear axle with a Panhard rod connected to two Watt's linkages was adopted. All four wheels were equipped with disk brakes, the front ones mounted inboard. Initially a 1.2 engine was used with a power output of 63 hp and a top speed of 152 kph, figures which placed the car firmly at the firmly top of its class.

The design of the bodywork was entrusted to Giorgetto Giugiaro Sirp, which later became Italdesign. In many ways ahead of his time, Giugiaro designed a hatchback with an attractive and youthful appearance that satisfied the brief in terms of interior and luggage space.

After the foundation stone laying ceremony at the factory on the 28TH of April 1968, the Alfasud was presented at the 1971 Turin Motor Show and the four-door 1.2 version with four gears was put on sale the following year. As early as 1974 the Alfasud range was updated — N and L trim versions of the saloon were offered, while a new and practical station wagon made its debut. The following year a five-speed gearbox was available (5m versions). However this was just the beginning of a long career that only came to an end with the presentation of the Alfa 33 in 1983.

Alfetta

A LEGENDARY NAME AND A GREAT PROJECT
CLASS-LEADING ARESE TECHNOLOGY

Engine

Front, longitudinal vertical straight-four, block and head in light alloy, two valves per cylinder, duplex chain driven double overhead camshafts. Two twin-choke vertical carburettors, distributor ignition, wet-sump lubrication

Displacement

1779 cc (80x88.5 mm)

Power and torque

122 hp at 5500 rpm — 17 kgm at 4400 rpm

Transmission

Rear-wheel drive, hydraulically actuated rear-mounted single dry-plate clutch, five speeds + reverse

Chassis

Pressed steel unitary construction

Bodywork

Saloon

Suspension

Front: independent, wishbones and oblique struts, longitudinal torsion bars, hydraulic dampers, anti-roll bar

Rear: De Dion rear axle, Watt's linkage, coil springs, hydraulic dampers, anti-roll bar

Brakes

Dual circuit with servo, discs all round, floating at the rear

Dimensions

Wheelbase: 2510 mm, Length: 4280 mm, Width: 1620 mm, Height: 1430 mm

Weight (dry)

1060 Kg

Maximum speed

180 kph

Cars produced

475,722 (Alfetta, 1972-1984)

In an age of great optimism, after the success of firstly the Giulietta and then the Giulia, the drafting tables at Alfa Romeo in the mid-Sixties were already filling up with plans relating to a completely new mechanical configuration, with the code name "Tipo 116 ", which would re-establish the superior performance that had always been a feature of the marque. A mechanical design that over the years was destined to replace all the rear-wheel drive vehicles but which was first introduced with the Alfetta, a car that should have been in segment 5, a step above the Giulia. The car made its official debut at Grignano on the 17TH of May 1972. The men in the experienced team led by Orazio Satta Puliga, in particular Giuseppe Busso, opted for an innovative transaxle layout — the engine was installed longitudinally at the front, while the clutch, gearbox, differential and in-board disk brakes were grouped together in a single unit, soon to be nicknamed "the little pig" by the workers, suspended from the body shell at the rear. The front suspension featured wishbones and torsion bars, while at the rear there was a sophisticated triangular De Dion transaxle with a Watt's parallelogram linkage, a layout long championed by Giuseppe Busso that he had at last managed to get into production. Excellent weight distribution, a reduction in unsprung weight and driven wheels that always stayed perpendicular to the ground were the main advantages of this layout, which translated into superb road-holding and very high-level performance, that made the car a pleasure to drive without sacrificing anything in comfort. The other side of the coin however, was a long and complicated assembly process that was to absorb much of the company's energy as they were not prepared to accept any compromises. One of the greatest difficulties was in developing the transmission with a driveshaft turning at the same speed as the engine and mounted directly on the body shell without the help of a torque tube that many competitors used in these situations. The engine was the 1.8 122 hp twin-cam, borrowed from the 1750 and simply adapted to the new mechanical arrangement. The overall weight was 1060 kg and the top speed was 180 kph. Just as with the mechanical configuration, the bodywork represented progress with respect to the previous generation. The upper body blended well with the lower part of the car and the interior was more modern. This was a layout that would continue to evolve over subsequent generations of the car. The name were not preparedced the legendary GP Tipo 158 and 159 cars that dominated the first two Formula 1 World Championships. They too had a transaxle layout and at the end of their career in 1951, also used a De Dion rear axle. It goes without saying that when the car was presented attention was drawn to the parallels between the two cars.

Alfa 75 2.0i TS A.S.N.

THE TRANSAXLE PAR EXCELLENCE.
THE LAST OF ITS GENERATION

Engine

Front, longitudinal vertical straight-four, block and head in light alloy, two valves per cylinder, duplex chain driven double overhead camshafts and variable valve timing. Bosch ME7-Motronic integrated electronic fuel injection and ignition, wet sump lubrication

Displacement

1962 cc (84x88.5 mm)

Power and torque

148 hp at 5800 rpm – 19 kgm at 4700 rpm

Transmission

Rear-wheel drive, hydraulically actuated rear-mounted single dry-plate clutch, five speeds + reverse

Chassis

Pressed steel unitary construction

Bodywork

Saloon

Suspension

Front: independent, wishbones and oblique struts, longitudinal torsion bars, hydraulic dampers, anti-roll bar

Rear: De Dion rear axle, Watt's linkage, coil springs, hydraulic dampers, anti-roll bar

Brakes

Self ventilating, rear floating

Dimensions

Wheelbase: 2510 mm, Length: 4330 mm, Width: 1660 mm, Height: 1440 mm

Weight (dry)

1120 Kg

Maximum speed

205 kph

Cars produced

386,773 (Alfa 75, 1985-1992)

With the 75TH anniversary of the founding of the marque falling in the May of 1985, the new sports saloon taking the place of the Giulietta could hardly be named anything other than the Alfa 75. Work began on the project code-named K1 in 1982, using the Alfetta's transaxle mechanical design, which although dated was still competitive in terms of performance. Alfa Romeo Styling Centre, then under the direction of Ermanno Cressoni, was commissioned to design the 75 and create a car with a modern image but which still used many of the Giulietta's body pressings, including the door-frames. As a result of these constraints, the Cx figure of 0.38 was no more than reasonable, but a reduced frontal area nonetheless made for excellent performance. However, greater attention was paid to production systems and quality control - welding methods were revised, as was the way the sheet metal was treated, the use of epoxy adhesive tape was adopted and new control systems were put in place, including the pilot plant that improved construction methods.

Compared to the Giulietta there was a significant improvement with regard to the power of the engines installed. Alongside the four-cylinder 1.6, 1.8, and 2.0 twin-cam engines and the 2.0 turbodiesel, the car was also available on its debut in 2.5i V6 Quadrifoglio Verde form, with 156 hp and a top speed of 205 kph. Increasingly powerful engines then succeeded one another, with the V6 eventually reaching a displacement of three litres; then there was the debut of the 1.8 Turbo, which was advertised with the phrase "finally, a Turbo engine deserves an Alfa Romeo".

Another Eighties trend were cylinder heads with four valves per cylinder: the drawing tables in Arese were crammed with plans for a new engine design. The company was then hit by the financial crisis and hard times and tight budgets led to the project being scaled down: a new "narrow" head, still with two valves per cylinder, fitted to the old engine block. Its strong suit was the ignition system with two spark plugs per cylinder providing for a widening of the flame face and the use of bigger valves. The power output was 148 hp with maximum torque of 19 kgm. These were high values that re-established the historical performance gap between Alfa Romeo and its rivals and gave the 75 2.0i Twin Spark a top speed of 205 kph making it the fastest two-litre on the market.

A model which stood out among the special versions was the ASN series (Allestimento Speciale Numerato) that on on certain markets was shared with the Turbo, equipped with special alloy wheels, Recaro upholstery and a different bodywork trim. The car on display, a 2.0i Twin Spark ASN is the car that was used for the photo-shoot at the presentation and was later assigned to the press office. Appreciated for its performance, personality and driving pleasure, the Alfa 75 was very successful — the production run ended after 386,773 cars had been produced.

164 3.0i V6

PININFARINA "CLOTHES" THE FRONT-WHEEL DRIVE FLAGSHIP

Engine

Front, transverse, 60° V6, block and cylinder heads in light alloy, two valves per cylinder, single overhead camshaft per bank and rockers actuated by a toothed belt. Bosch Motronic ML-4.1 integrated electronic fuel injection and ignition, wet sump lubrication

Displacement

2959 cc (93x72.6 mm)

Power and torque

188 hp at 5600 rpm – 25.5 kgm at 4400 rpm

Transmission

Front-wheel drive, hydraulically actuated single dry-plate clutch, five speeds + reverse

Chassis

Pressed steel unitary construction with front subframe

Bodywork

Saloon

Suspension

Front: independent, wishbones with McPherson struts, coil springs, hydraulic dampers, anti-roll bar

Rear: independent, trailing arms and control rods, coil springs, hydraulic dampers, anti-roll bar

Brakes

hydraulically actuated and assisted discs all round, front self-ventilated, ABS

Dimensions

Wheelbase: 2660 mm, Length: 4555 mm, Width: 1760 mm, Height: 1400 mm

Weight (dry)

1300 Kg

Maximum speed

230 kph

Cars produced

248,278 (164, 1987-1994)

Finished in bright red, one of the most distinguishing features of this model was the broad grey band encircling the lower half of the car.

The 164 3.0i V6 on display is the one used by the company in 1987 for the official photos that were included in the press pack Alfa Romeo used to launch its flagship model, the car fitted with the V6 3-litre (2959 cc) engine, which was directly descended from the engine of the same size designed by Giuseppe Busso for the Alfa 6 in the mid-Seventies. The company launched the 2.0i Twin Spark and 2.5 turbodiesel (made by VM of Cento) at the same time.

Presented at the Frankfurt Motor Show in 1987, the 164 was the first car to be launched after Alfa Romeo had been taken over by the Fiat Group, but in actual fact, the project to design a new flagship car with front-wheel drive had started a lot earlier. It had been Busso himself who had pursued such a design as early as the end of the Forties and by the time of the definitive acquisition of Alfa, working prototypes were already available which would lead to the new car being launched in little more than a year.

Even though the Type 4 platform of the 164 was shared by Lancia (Thema), Fiat (Croma) and Saab (9000), the input that came from Vittorio Ghidella at the head of the company, was very clear – the Biscione's new flagship was to be a refined car with a very strong personality in line with the established traditions of the Marque.

Pininfarina, to whom Alfa turned for the design of the new flagship car, took on the task and the designers from Turin did not disappoint them. They created a car that was very different from the other three by virtue of its low and streamlined profile, set off by the bodywork that in typical Pininfarina style was effectively the sum of two superimposed shells. However certain modifications to the original platform were necessary in order to achieve this. Specifically the angle of the windscreen and rear-window pillars was changed, changes were made to the front suspension, a "modified" McPherson set-up originally seen on the Alfasud, with coil springs and an anti-roll bar, which meant that a low bonnet height was possible that in turn gave a Cx of a mere 0.30.

The comfortable and sporting interior was very sophisticated thanks to its "hi-tech", simple styling. The 164 3.0i V6 matched the streamlined Pininfarina bodywork with the highest level of engineering with its V6 configuration, double overhead camshafts and Bosch Motronic electronic fuel injection. It had a maximum power output of 188 hp at 5600 rpm (25.5 kgm at 4400 rpm, 230 kph). Designed not just for the most demanding Italian customers but above all for a foreign market where engines larger than two litres did not face heavy tax penalties, the 164 V6 was immediately successful in Europe and the United States, a market for which specific versions would be produced.

Alfa 156

Alfa 156
Alfa 156

156

THE STYLE OF THE FUTURE LOOKS TO THE PAST.
A NEW ERA, A GREAT SUCCESS.

Engine

Front, transverse, straight-four, block in cast iron, cylinder heads in light alloy, four valves per cylinder, double overhead camshafts with electrohydraulic variable vale timing, toothed belt. Bosch Motronic M1.5.5 MPI integrated electronic fuel injection and ignition, two spark plugs per cylinder, wet sump lubrication

Displacement

1970 cc (83x91 mm)

Power and torque

155 hp at 6400 rpm — 19.1 kgm at 3500 rpm

Transmission

Front-wheel drive, hydraulically actuated single dry-plate clutch, five speeds + reverse

Chassis

Pressed steel unitary construction with front and rear subframes

Bodywork

Saloon

Suspension

Front: independent, double wishbones, coil springs, hydraulic dampers, anti-roll bar

Rear: independent, McPherson struts with lower lateral struts and reaction arms, coil springs, hydraulic dampers, anti-roll bar

Brakes

hydraulically actuated and assisted discs all round, front self-ventilated, ABS

Dimensions

Wheelbase: 2595 mm, Length: 4430 mm, Width: 1745 mm, Height: 1420 mm

Weight (dry)

1230 kg

Maximum speed

214 kph

Cars produced

Over 680,000 (156, 1997-2007)

The compact sports saloon sector had been one of the focal points of the Alfa Romeo range since the earliest days of its history. Hence when the moment came to launch a new model in the mid-Nineties, following the controversial 155, the company's resources were fully focussed on the new project and, as had been the case many times in Alfa Romeo's history, from the Giulietta to the Giulia, when the 156 was presented in Lisbon in the autumn of 1997, the automotive scene was turned upside down and the marque was resurrected. A resurrection which in terms of numbers was reflected in the production total of over 680,000 cars, in the record number of orders from day one of the car being put on sale and in the car being voted Car of the Year in 1998, all of which left a deep and lasting mark on the world of four wheels.

The most important element in this revolution was above all a radically seductive design, helped by the reorganisation of the Centro Stile Alfa Romeo, led at the time by Walter de' Silva, and a radically seductive design. However, the car marked a turning point from the mechanical point of view as well. The underlying platform, shared by many other cars from the Fiat Group, was thoroughly redesigned to improve handling. The rear suspension featured McPherson struts with unequal length transverse links and a high wishbone set-up at the front, this last being especially complex and sophisticated. On the engine front, four petrol units were available at the time the car was launched — the four-cylinder 16V 1.6, 1.8 and two-litre Twin Spark engines along with the new range-topping 2.5 V6 24V with its 190 hp. However, the true innovation came in the range of diesel engines: this was the world "premiere" of the common-rail system that allowed levels of performance which had hitherto been unimaginable and which was as smooth and silent as a petrol engine. There were two diesel versions of the 156: the four-cylinder 1.9 TTD and the five-cylinder 2.4 JTD, with power outputs of 105 and 136 hp respectively. The five-cylinder engine was also equipped with a variable geometry turbocharger. Five- and six-speed gearboxes were available, with the option of the electrically operated Selespeed on the 2.0 Twin Spark and the automatic Q-System on the 2.5 V6.

The excellence of the mechanical set-up was soon to be revealed in racing as well. In a career lasting ten years, a total of 13 championships were won by drivers, constructors and teams. Many different versions and developments of the car saw the light of day, from the Sportwagon to the GTA, from the 2003 restyling to the Crosswagon Q4.

The 2.0 Twin Spark on display is the car that was made available for the photo-shoot when the car was presented, with a "prototype" interior featuring various types of trim. The car is finished in Azzurro Nuvola, an iridescent paint, which was a new version of a blue that was very fashionable in the Thirties and was used on the stunning Nuvola concept car, presented at the Paris Motor Show in 1997.

8C Competizione

DESIGN, DRIVING PLEASURE, APPEAL. FOLLOWING A DREAM FROM CONCEPT TO LIMITED SERIES PRODUCTION

Engine

Front, longitudinal, 90° V8, block and cylinder heads in light alloy, four valves per cylinder, chain driven double overhead camshafts per bank. Electronic fuel injection and ignition, dry sump lubrication

Displacement

4691 cc

Power and torque

450 hp at 7000 rpm - 480 hp at 4750 rpm

Transmission

Rear-wheel drive, rear-mounted automated sequential gearbox, six speeds + reverse

Chassis

Pressed steel structural elements, carbonfibre panels

Bodywork

Coupé

Suspension

Front: independent, double wishbones, coil springs, hydraulic dampers, anti-roll bar

Rear: independent, double wishbones, coil springs, hydraulic dampers, anti-roll bar

Brakes

Perforated self-ventilating discs all round, ABS, ESP

Dimensions

Wheelbase: 2645 mm, Length: 4381 mm, Width: 1894 mm, Height: 1341 mm

Weight (dry)

1585 kg

Maximum speed

292 kph

Cars produced

500

8C. A number and a letter capable of bringing to mind extraordinary and glorious cars that in the 1930s secured some of the most important victories in the history of Alfa Romeo and motorsport in general. The 8C 2300's won the Le Mans 24 Hours four years in a row from 1931 to 1934, while the unforgettable 8C 2900 B "risked" winning the 1938 edition too, but it was the various 8C's that won the Mille Miglia between 1932 and 1938 that demonstrated a technical and sporting supremacy that had rarely been seen before. And then there is that "Competizione", another suffix that references the 6C 2500s that starred with alternate fortunes in the Mille Miglia between 1948 and 1950.

A fil rouge of success to which Alfa Romeo paid tribute in 2003 when presenting at the Frankfurt Motor Show a stunning concept car known as the 8C Competizione and styled by the German designer Wolfgang Egger. The sinuous forms of the aggressive coupé, which referenced in its trilobite front grille and faired headlights inspired by those of the 33 a number of the marque's most distinctive design motifs, allowed the car to achieve immediate consensus. And yet the powers-that-be at the company decided to produce the 8C Competizione in a limited edition of just 500 examples that only saw the light of day four years later, when sales (or rather deliveries as the entire batch was sold well before going into production) began in concomitance with the Frankfurt Motor Show in September 2007.

Providing the 450 hp (331 kW) at 7000 rpm (and maximum torque of 480 kgm at 4750 rpm) was a formidable 90° V8 of Maserati derivation, mounted longitudinally at the front with double overhead camshafts per bank, four valves per cylinder and variable valve timing and a displacement of 4691 cc (bore and stroke 94x84.5 mm). Following the consolidated transaxle layout also used on the cars of the Prancing Horse, the automated six-speed sequential gearbox and the limited-slip differential (also inherited from the Trident cars) were located at the rear, to the benefit of weight distribution with 49% bearing on the front axle and 51% on the rear.

The chassis of the 500 examples of the 8C Competizione (the example in the museum collection was the one made available to the press in 2007) that went into production was in steel (the concept car instead had a carbonfibre tub), while the bodywork was all carbonfibre, as was part of the cockpit, both produced by ITCA Colonnella. The seat frames produced by Sparco also used the same material. Mention naturally has to be made of performance when talking about a car such as the 8C Competizione: it was capable of a top speed of 292 kph and could sprint from 0 to 100 kph in just 4.2 seconds.

BELLEZZA

BELLEZZA

Lorenzo Ramaciotti

BELLEZZA

The halo surrounding the Alfa Romeo name that attracts public interest in countries where the company's cars have not been sold for decades and which has allowed the company to get through difficult times without losing the affection of anyone interested in cars, can only stem from something very special represented by its cars.

A quality that all Alfa Romeos have had during a journey lasting more than a hundred years and which has seen technical and production revolutions and social and technological upheavals. There has to be a continuous thread which connects the RL models of the Twenties, to the 6C's of the Thirties, to the Villa d'Este of the Forties, to the Giulias of the Sixties and so on up to the Alfettas, the 164's and the 156's.

This quality has to do with the way that Alfa Romeos correspond perfectly to most people's idea of the Italian car, the incarnation of the "bella macchina" an expression which is even more iconic abroad than here in Italy. "Bello" in this case refers of course to the bodywork, but in a broader sense to the mechanics of a car too, to the liveliness of its performance, in short, to the pleasure derived from travelling in an Italian car.

So the beauty of an Alfa Romeo stems from what you cannot see: from the engineering at the root of its performance and the way the car handles. Opening the bonnet and seeing the two overhead camshafts, the timing-chain case, the supercharger, seeing the way the cooling fins are cast in aluminium, the winding yet parallel path that the exhaust pipes take where they come out of the cylinder head, all of these things give as much pleasure as looking at the curves of the bodywork clothing the car.

An engineering design which is both pure and efficient, without any unnecessary frills or complications: the best that the technology of the moment can offer in order to attain the highest performance. Small capacity engines, less than three litres, because Alfa Romeo has always reasoned that performance derives from low weight and the quality of the engineering rather than the brute force of large displacement engines.

This school of design which has been followed down the ages by all Alfa Romeo engineers is the solid foundation underlying the legend. It has been the basis for the victories won by the "Biscione" racing cars on tracks around the world and for the road cars that have allowed the Italian automobile industry to compete on equal terms with the great French, English and German marques beyond the Alps.

In order to create true masterpieces based on this perfect engineering, forms are needed that complete and project its beauty. In the years when it was the customer's right to decide on the choice of bodywork, all the best ateliers had the chance to embellish Alfa Romeo chassis with the coachwork and this almost always produced outstanding results confirming the excellence of the basic mechanical structure. Most cars were made by coachbuilders in the Milan area: Sala, Castagna and above all Zagato and Touring.

Zagato was responsible for the iconic open-topped car produced with various displacements and dimensions around 1930, while Touring made the more refined road-going cars ranging from the Flying Star convertible to the series of small saloons and aerodynamic "spiders" that are considered to be the most beautiful and symbolic examples of the Italian school of coachbuilding from the mid-Thirties to the end of the Forties. It is worth remembering that both Zagato

BELLEZZA

and Touring were leading producers of lightweight aluminium bodywork which placedthem in perfect harmony with Alfa Romeo's philosophy of putting performance before everything else.

The situation changed completely in the post-war period with the arrival of mass production and the load-bearing body shells needed to satisfy the demands of a European population who now all wanted cars, bringing about a change in the relationship between the car manufacturer and the coachbuilder.

Alfa Romeo entrusted the design of its saloon cars (1900, Giulietta, Giulia) to the newly formed in-house Centro Stile, while maintaining a solid relationship with the Italian coachbuilders who completed the range with coupé, convertible and berlinetta versions.

With the specific aim of meeting Alfa Romeo's requirements, the more forward-looking coachbuilders, Bertone and Pininfarina, converted their workshops in the mid-Fifties into small-scale production lines capable of producing limited editions of vehicles which it would be impossible to build in the more inflexible plants designed to produce much larger numbers of cars. And it was Alfa Romeo again that, with its Alfasud project, invented a new player in the field of design, the service provider, a company created ad hoc that later became Italdesign. A further link between the Alfa Romeo story and that of Italian style.

The coachbuilders' creations served to drive sales of the saloon cars becoming objects of desire for whole generations of motorists: beautiful, fast, distant yet not unattainable. The Giulietta Sprint and Spider and later the Giulia GT and "Duetto" can be seen everywhere in films of the boom era. They represented a not too distant dream that could become reality with the necessary hard work, a few sacrifices and a little good luck.

Inspired by the name and the engineering of Alfa Romeo, the Italian designers came up with ever more daring ideas that took shape as the 'dream cars'.

Count Ricotti realised his dream as a rich pioneer in 1911, but it was in the post-war period that the exploration of futuristic forms to arouse the public's interest and give free reign to creativity became a constant. Touring continued to pursue its interest in aerodynamics and presented the Disco Volante. Bertone, with the creative input of Franco Scaglione, launched the futuristic BAT series of cars, which were more like three shapes in space rather than actual cars. Pininfarina worked on smooth, pure lines in a sequence of variations on the Superflow theme which was to lead to the production version of the Duetto.

Italian coachbuilders were to continue to produce prototypes for Alfa Romeo based on formal research inspired by innovations in mechanical design, like the mid-engined 33, which was a classic test bench for the style revolution of the Sixties. A number of the most important examples of this crop of prototypes have been acquired by Alfa Romeo and are now part of the Alfa Romeo historic collection.

In order to represent Bellezza or Beauty from various perspectives, four themes have been identified:

- The pure creativity of the 'dream cars', which is present throughout the history of the Biscione', from Count Ricotti's aerodynamics to the Nuvola and features some of the great names in Italian coachbuilding: Castagna, Touring, Bertone, Pininfarina, Italdesign and the Alfa Romeo Centro Stile.
- Cars from the golden age when Alfa Romeo worked with Touring, which also marks the transition from bodywork with separate mudguards to the integrated concept that became prevalent in the post-war years. These are considered to be the ultimate Italian cars among collectors and in Concours d'Elegance. They fetch dizzy sums of money in international auctions, in competition with the most prestigious marques.
- The Giulietta in its full range of versions – Berlina, Sprint, Spider, SS, SZ – as evidence of the success that Alfa Romeo enjoyed in creating a widely-sold medium-sized and medium cylinder capacity car that made speed and beauty available to the general public when both of these features would usually only be seen in much more prestigious models.
- The Giulia that, while following the rise in Italy's social and commercial evolution, displays classic Alfa Romeo engineering in an unconventional package from a functional and stylistic standpoint. Here again there are also various members of the Giulia's extended family – Sprint GT, "Duetto", GTA, TZ, Junior Z – displaying continuity in the variety of models on offer and the evolutionary development of style over the course of nearly a decade.

Speed and beauty as values to be pursued, lightness and simplicity as the means by which they are attained. This is the philosophy that lies behind Alfa Romeo's continuity and that continues to inspire all the people working there.

The masters **of style**

The great names pen great cars.
Dream cars in fact

Fabbricazione Castagna

A.L.F.A. 40/60 HP Aerodinamica

STYLING LIKE SOMETHING FROM A NOVEL BY JULES VERNE, BUT THE OBJECTIVE WAS PERFORMANCE

Engine

Front, longitudinal vertical straight-four, bock and fixed head in cast iron, two valves per cylinder, two gear-driven camshafts located in the crankcase. Carburettor, high tension magneto ignition, wet sump lubrication

Displacement

6082 cc (110x160 mm)

Power and torque

70 hp at 2200 rpm

Transmission

Rear-wheel drive, front mounted multiple dry-plate clutch, four speeds + reverse

Chassis

Pressed steel longerons and cross members

Bodywork

Closed, aluminium droplet (Castagna)

Suspension

Front: rigid axle, longitudinal semi-elliptical leaf springs

Rear: rigid axle, longitudinal semi-elliptical leaf springs

Brakes

Mechanically actuated rear drums

Front: absent

Dimensions

Wheelbase: 3200 mm

Weight

1250 Kg

Maximum speed

139 kph

Cars produced

1

Between the turn of the century and 1910, automotive engineering began to make a high level of performance possible, with top speeds of well over 100 kph, a record that was broken for the first time in 1899 by Camille Jenatzy at the wheel of the electrically-powered Jamais Contente, with its bullet-shaped bodywork that, by leaving the driver and chassis open to the air, showed a certain naivety as far as the science of aerodynamics was concerned. It was precisely for this reason that in 1914 Count Marco Ricotti of Milan commissioned special bodywork for the 40-60 HP chassis he had just bought, one of 25 produced.

Ercole Castagna, also from Milan, was the coachbuilder chosen to clothe the powerful machine, which at the time was the top model in the A.L.F.A. range. He was to establish an excellent working relationship with the Portello. The shape chosen, inspired by a drop of water and very fashionable with specialists of the time, was the "torpedo", all-metal and completely closed, with round portholes as windows, doors flush with the bodywork and with a broad wraparound windscreen. This was a very advanced approach for that time, as it already recognised the need to cover up as many parts exposed to the wind as possible. The bodywork was made of aluminium, mounted on a steel ladder frame. The only parts that were outside the bodyshell were the wheels, part of the suspension and the headlights, while the radiator, which was in its usual position on the chassis, was deeply embedded within the bodywork. Despite the imposing frontal section, the top speed achieved was 139 kph, compared to 125 kph of the version with standard bodywork and this was enough for the new shape to gain approval. However this positive outcome was not followed up; the following year the car was converted into a torpedo-type when the roof was removed, thereby losing all its efficiency — the noise, heat and fumes from the engine, which was not isolated but enclosed within the cockpit, probably made driving the car unbearable for the owner. This was proof that the golden age of aerodynamic research was still to come and that the coachbuilder's sense of aesthetics and the skills of the panel-beaters were not sufficient to ensure a follow-up for this concept car ante litteram, misunderstood in 1914 but still the object of study today.

As the original car was lost, in 1974 Luigi Fusi had a replica built that was based on the original drawings of the time as a way of reminding people of the extraordinary technical and stylistic achievement that Conte Ricotti's car represented. The replica was put on display in the company's museum that year.

1900 C52 Disco Volante

AVANT-GARDE MECHANICAL ENGINEERING, TIMELESS STYLING AND A LOOK TO THE FUTURE

Engine

Front, longitudinal vertical straight-four, block and removable head in light alloy, two valves per cylinder, two chain-driven overhead camshafts. Two twin-choke carburettors, distributor ignition, wet sump lubrication

Displacement

1997.4 cc (85x88 mm)

Power and torque

158 hp at 6500 rpm

Transmission

Rear-wheel drive, front mounted multiple dry-plate clutch, four speeds + reverse

Chassis

tubular with lateral longerons

Bodywork

Barchetta (Touring)

Suspension

Front: independent, wishbones, coil springs, hydraulic dampers

Rear: live axle, upper triangular element, trailing arms, coil springs, hydraulic dampers

Brakes

Hydraulically actuated drums all round

Dimensions

Wheelbase: 2200 mm, Length: 3950 mm, Width: 1780 mm, Height: 1064 mm

Weight

735 Kg

Maximum speed

Over 220 kph

Cars produced

5 (1 Spider, 1 Coupé, 1 "Fianchi Stretti" 2 Spider 6C 3000)

Alfa Romeo's commitment to racing was officially supposed to have ended when it withdrew at the end of the 1951 season, with the two world championship victories of Farina and Fangio to its credit. However, in the years that followed the firm continued development of a number of projects such as the revolutionary GP Tipo 160 with four-wheel drive and above all certain Sport class cars, in particular the CM and PR versions of the 6C 3000.

Another project, which came to life and caught the interest of Max Hoffman, the Alfa Romeo importer for the USA, was for an open two-seater sports car with a two-litre engine and a lightweight, extremely aerodynamic shape — in "aesthetic" as well as "scientific" terms. The prototype was immediately flown to the New York Motor Show but the agreement between Alfa Romeo and Hoffman was not taken any further.

The 1900 C52 Disco Volante, designed by Gioacchino Colombo, satisfied these requirements, starting with the name itself. 1900 C52, where the C stood for Competizione, is the typical Alfa Romeo way of naming competition cars, while the nickname Disco Volante is a nod in the direction of an overseas market with a fascination for flight and space travel.

Not much was left of the standard 1900 Sprint — the suspension was similar but mounted on a newly-designed tubular space frame; the 1997 cc twin-cam engine from the production car was completely redesigned with an engine block and head in light alloy, twin-cam valve gear and two twin-choke carburettors. The power output rose to 158 hp with a top speed of over 220 kph.

Using the tubular space frame as a starting point, Touring designed bodywork with a flattened lenticular shape that aimed to make the car extremely aerodynamically efficient. Innumerable tests in the wind tunnel and on the track confirmed the validity of the design. The testers' opinions were less flattering, as they complained that the body was too wide, extending beyond the wheel track and compromising handling. It was no coincidence that a "slimline" body, which took part in a number of Sport class races, was designed the following year. The Disco Volante Coupé, which was also produced in 1953, did not go beyond the prototype stage. With the bodywork and chassis from the Disco Volante Spider, two prototypes were produced with a 6-cylinder three-litre engine designed years before by Giuseppe Busso for the 6C 3000. The weight increased to 760 kg, compared to the 735 of the 1900 version, but the maximum power of 230 hp allowed the open version to reach a top speed of 240 kph.

2000 Sportiva

THE GENIUS OF THE DESIGNER AND THE SKILL OF THE CRAFTSMEN. JUST AROUND THE CORNER, HOWEVER, WAS THE GIULIETTA

Engine

Front, longitudinal vertical straight-four, block in cast iron and head in light alloy, two valves per cylinder, two chain-driven overhead camshafts. Two twin-choke carburettors, distributor ignition, dry sump lubrication

Displacement

1997.4 cc (85x88 mm)

Power and torque

138 hp at 6500 rpm

Transmission

Rear-wheel drive, front mounted multiple dry-plate clutch, five speeds + reverse

Chassis

Spaceframe in circular section tubing

Bodywork

Coupé (Bertone)

Suspension

Front: independent, wishbones, coil springs, hydraulic dampers

Rear: De Dion axle, Watt's linkage, coil springs, hydraulic dampers

Brakes

Hydraulically actuated drums all round, in-board at the rear

Dimensions

Wheelbase: 2200 mm, Length: 4160 mm

Weight

915 Kg

Maximum speed

220 kph

Cars produced

4 (2 spiders + 2 coupés)

With the intention of streamlining production, at the beginning of the 1950s two very ambitious projects, the 6C 3000 and the Disco Volante were dropped because they were too complex and too expensive. The two cars had a different styling and power outputs but shared the same tubular space frame; unfortunately although this last worked well in races, it was impossible to build economically if not in a small mainly hand-made series.

Under the leadership of Orazio Satta Puliga and with a team led by Giuseppe Busso, ideas for a new coupé began to gain ground. It was to have sparkling performance so that it could be used for racing as well, but it would share most of its mechanical design with the production 1900 in order to reduce production costs, while there would be a series intended for the most demanding clients and the gentleman drivers.

The end result was the 2000 Sportiva, which took to the road for the first time in August 1954. The twin-cam engine had the same cast-iron block as the 1900, but the displacement was increased right up to the two-litre limit (1997.4 cc) given its racing destination. The compression ratio was increased to 9:1 and it now had dry-sump lubrication and a power output of 138 hp. It had wishbone front suspension, while at the rear the same set-up was used that had appeared on the 6C 3000 CM: De Dion triangular axle with the upper element positioned towards the front, Watt's linkage with in-board helicoid-finned drum brakes, a configuration that had long been approved of and promoted by Busso and which not by chance, Alfa Romeo modified and used twenty years later on the Alfetta.

Four cars were made, two with a coupé body and two spiders, both types bodied by Bertone. With regard to the coupé, which is on display here, Franco Scaglione's pen traced sleek lines shaped by the wind with a few Baroque details, made possible by the skill of Bertone's craftsmen, making it even more fascinating. As did the performance: the top speed was 220 kph. The two spiders were given different bodywork.

Following the initial tests the project was put to one side, then in 1956 the 2000 Sportiva coupé was displayed at the Turin Motor Show before it was dropped for good because it was considered to be too expensive. Later, one of the coupés was preserved in perfect working order in the Testing Department's warehouse and was then transferred to the museum in 1965.

Giulia Sprint Speciale Prototype

MODERN, AMBITIOUS, ECCENTRIC AND STYLISH.
IT WAS TO REMAIN A PROTOTYPE

Engine

Front, longitudinal, vertical straight-four, block and head in light alloy, two valves per cylinder, duplex chain driven double overhead camshafts. Two twin-choke carburettors, distributor ignition, wet sump lubrication

Displacement

1570 cc (78x82 mm)

Power and torque

109 hp at 6000 rpm

Transmission

Rear-wheel drive, single dry-plate clutch five speeds + reverse

Chassis

Pressed steel unitary construction

Bodywork

Coupé (Bertone)

Suspension

Front: independent, wishbones, coil springs, hydraulic dampers, anti-roll bar

Rear: live axle, upper triangular element, trailing arms, hydraulic dampers

Brakes

Hydraulically actuated and assisted discs all round

Dimensions

Wheelbase: 2350 mm

Maximum speed

Over 185 kph

Cars produced

1

With the Giulietta Sprint Speciale project in 1957, Alfa Romeo wanted to offer their more sporting customers, including the many gentleman drivers, a more spartan and sporty alternative to the Sprint, aiming more specifically at an increase in aerodynamic efficiency. Franco Scaglione, who was working at Bertone at the time, successfully achieved this aim and the end result was a streamlined, slim and refined coupé in which much of the detail work, the finish and the eccentricities might even have had a Baroque inspiration. A body that was extremely interesting but was in some ways too refined to casually take to the track, despite its perfectly respectable performance. With regard to racing, the baton was soon passed to the less complex Giulietta SZ with Zagato bodywork and the Bertone's Sprint Speciale which opened a new chapter in the Alfa story. It was in fact to attract customers who were without doubt looking for more performance but who were also interested in a more eccentric and personal style of car.

With the launch of the Giulia , the bodywork of the Sprint Speciale, as was also the case with the Sprint and the Spider, was updated with the new mechanical assemblies to transform the car into the Giulia Sprint Speciale. In this case too, however, it was only a temporary solution, undertaken so as not to leave the range incomplete. While the Giulia Sprint GT and in 1966 the 1600 Spider Duetto were about to make their debuts, Bertone used the occasion to present a prototype that capable of reviving the philosophy the "old" SS had made its own. At the end of an era, on the strength of the extraordinary success the Giulia Sprint GT was enjoying at that time, Bertone decided to move on and look at things in a new way, with the resulting car being modern, ambitious and slim. It had very simple lines, with the low front end being dominated by four headlights recessed into the radiator grille and flanks by a prominent central pillar that partially prefigured the styling of the Montreal. Another special feature was the small roof panel in unpainted, brushed steel.

The prototype was certainly modern and in some ways futuristic, but its fate was sealed — Alfa Romeo's cautiousness, its two seats, and the looming presence of the Giulia Sprint GT cut short its career before it started with just one car being made.

Carabo

REVOLUTION. THE MOTOR CAR IS NO LONGER
A BUNDLE OF MUSCLES BUT A SHARPENED BLADE

Engine

Rear central, longitudinal, vertical 90° V8, block and heads in light alloy, four chain-driven overhead camshafts. Spica indirect fuel injection, two distributors, two coils, two spark plugs per cylinder, dry sump lubrication

Displacement

1995 cc (78x52.2 mm)

Power and torque

230 hp at 8800 rpm – 21 Kgm at 7000 rpm

Transmission

Rear-wheel drive, hydraulically actuated single dry-plate clutch, six speeds + reverse

Chassis

Welded tubular elements, bodywork in fibreglass

Bodywork

Coupé (Bertone)

Suspension

Front: independent, wishbones, coil springs, hydraulic dampers, anti-roll bar

Rear: independent, wishbones, coil springs, hydraulic dampers, anti-roll bar

Brakes

Dual circuit, discs all round

Dimensions

Wheelbase: 2350 mm, Length: 4170 mm, Width: 1780 mm, height: 990 mm

Weight

700 Kg

Cars produced

1

Among the most iconic cars in the history of Alfa Romeo and the automobile in general, a place on the front row of the grid has to be reserved for the 33 Stradale (1967), a road-going version of the 33/2, initially conceived for production in a limited run of 50 examples although only 18 of those were actually to the light of day. The muscular 90° V8 centrally located in a futuristic (for the time) spaceframe chassis and above all the lightweight fibreglass bodywork "sculpted" by the maestro Franco Scaglione, an authentic masterpiece of aggressive elegance, were the strong suits of this car. A year later, the same chassis was used by another great Italian stylist, Marcello Gandini, then working at Carrozzeria Bertone, as the basis for his Carabo, another milestone in Italian car design and one of the most evocative creations by the historic Turinese coachbuilder. Nuccio Bertone himself had recently created other concept cars on Alfa Romeo chassis such as the Canguro, based on the Giulia TZ in 1964 and the Montreal, displayed at the Montreal Expo in 1967.

With respect to these two cars, the Carabo was even more extreme, with the front section extremely taut and blending uninterruptedly into the large and sharply inclined windscreen. The rear section was equally spectacular and was dominated by the ventilation louvres cooling the engine compartment and a truncated tail. The hexagonal rear panel was covered with a rectangular grid set off by the bright green paintwork. The overtly wedge shape of the front section is even more clear in profile where the Carabo is also distinguished by the asymmetric wheel arches and the hydro-pneumatically actuated vertically opening doors that facilitate access to the cockpit (in a car that is just 99 cm high). Also worthy of mention are the headlight situated in bays concealed by swivelling blades.

The interior also features simple, square-cut shapes similar to those of the exterior: the futuristic dashboard and the central tunnel with the six-speed gearbox.

The scarab beetle that inspired the name of the car also gave rise to the colour of the bodywork, a brilliant green alternating with dark grey parts and the fluorescent orange of the sharp nose. The Carabo was one of the most interesting cars at the Paris Motor Show of 1968 where it made its debut.

Iguana

GIUGIARO AND THE 33 STRADALE.
THE PURITY OF EXPOSED METAL AND
THE GRAZE OF A UNIQUE PAINT FINISH

Engine

Rear central, longitudinal, vertical, 90° V8, block and heads in light alloy, four chain-driven overhead camshafts Spica indirect fuel injection, two distributors, two coils, two spark plugs per cylinder, dry sump lubrication

Displacement

1995 cc (78x52.2 mm)

Power and torque

230 hp at 8800 rpm – 21 Kgm at 7000 rpm

Transmission

Rear-wheel drive, hydraulically actuated single dry-plate clutch, six speeds + reverse

Chassis

Welded tubular elements, bodywork in fibreglass

Bodywork

Coupé (Italdesign)

Suspension

Front: independent, wishbones, coil springs, hydraulic dampers, anti-roll bar

Rear: independent, wishbones, coil springs, hydraulic dampers, anti-roll bar

Brakes

dual circuit, discs all round

Dimensions

Wheelbase: 2350 mm, Length: 4050 mm, Width: 1780 mm, Height: 1050

Weight

700 Kg

Cars produced

1

The rolling chassis of the 33/2 inspired another prestigious Italian car designer, Giorgetto Giugiaro who in 1969 presented this concept car baptised as the Iguana that first appeared unofficially at the Monza Sports Car Show and then at the Turin Motor Show in November that year in official form. At that show where the Italian coachbuilders always present a number of their best designs (Pininfarina boasted the prototype Ferrari 512 S and Bertone the Autobianchi A112), Italdesign displayed this two-seater coupé with linear, aggressive styling. The principal theme of the front section was again a wedge shape, with the slim front grille treated in minimalist fashion, with a slim chrome strip picking out a stylised version of the classic Alfa Romeo shield that had been used for years on the production cars. The front bonnet featured a chiselled central section creating a rectangular conspicuous air intake located just ahead of the large and sharply inclined windscreen that in its turn led into the large glazed sunroof. A third glazed section exposed the mechanical organs with the centrally located 90° V8 engine.

The treatment of the rear section was more complex and featured a large spoiler, which was electrically adjustable and acted as both an air-brake and an aerodynamic stabilizer, and conspicuous vents cooling the engine compartment (like those at the ends of the flanks). The composition was emphasised by the brilliant metallic colouring of the bodywork, a colour scheme repeated in the deliberately simple interior design. The main instruments were housed in a quadrangular binnacle set behind the steering wheel. The aluminium Campagnolo wheels were also eye-catching.

33/2 Speciale

THE AESTHETIC, AERODYNAMIC AND TECHNOLOGICAL RESEARCH OF PININFARINA

Engine

Rear central, longitudinal, vertical, 90° V8, block and heads in light alloy, four chain-driven overhead camshafts. Spica indirect fuel injection, two distributors, two coils, two spark plugs per cylinder, dry sump lubrication

Displacement

1995 cc (78x52.2 mm)

Power and torque

230 hp at 8800 rpm – 21 Kgm at 7000 rpm

Transmission

Rear-wheel drive, hydraulically actuated single dry-plate clutch, six speeds + reverse

Chassis

Welded tubular elements, bodywork in fibreglass

Bodywork

Coupé (Pininfarina)

Suspension

Front: independent, wishbones, coil springs, hydraulic dampers, anti-roll bar

Rear: independent, wishbones, coil springs, hydraulic dampers, anti-roll bar

Brakes

dual circuit, discs all round

Dimensions

Wheelbase: 2350 mm, Length: 4060 mm, Width: 1800 mm, Height: 980 mm

Weight

720 Kg

Maximum speed

260 kph

Cars produced

1

At the Geneva Motor Show of 1968, Pininfarina had presented the 250 P5, a futuristic berlinetta based around one of the most classic Ferrari engines: the three-litre 60° V12 delivering a maximum power output in the order of 400 hp.

In a season in which the response to any question regarding aerodynamics only appeared to be able to be resolved through the use of "modern" wings, the celebrated Turin stylist came up with absolutely clean, pure lines in which aerodynamics were the very essence of the forms themselves. The P5, which appeared in a highly original brilliant white livery with star-pattern blue wheels (only later was it finished in a classis Ferrari red) aroused much comment among those in the sector and the specialist press and certainly caught the attention of the Alfa Romeo chairman Giuseppe Luraghi. This last soon reached an agreement with Enzo Ferrari whereby Pininfarina would create a kind of "clone" of the P5 using the mechanical organs of the 33/2.

Out of this agreement was born in 1969 the 33/2 Speciale, which maintained the fundamental principles of the P5. Voluminous ogival wings dipping to the slim front grille, at the centre of which was the inevitable Alfa Romeo shield, characterised the front end of the prototype. While on the P5 there was an eye-catching single lighting cluster composed of eight halogen lamps under a fairing, on the 33/2 Pininfarina opted for much more traditional pop-up headlights buried in the wings themselves. At the centre of the nose, incised into the coachwork were two conspicuous air intakes. The upper body was virtually all glass and Perspex: in practice a transparent canopy that acted as a linking element between the front and rear sections of the car, permitting a particularly airy cockpit and leaving all the mechanical assemblies in full view. The flanks were a succession of solids and voids, with highly elegant central air intakes and scooped wheel arches, the sinuous curves of which helped with the cooling of the mechanical parts. The treatment of the rear end was significantly more conventional and less futuristic than the P where the horizontal louvres that constituted one of the major features of the Ferrari prototype were replaced with horizontal lighting clusters and black bumpers.

The white and then the red of the P5 were replaced here with a bright yellow that leant even greater emphasis to the lines of the coachwork. Almost as if to underline that, despite appearance, this was indeed an Alfa Romeo, the Biscione or serpent featured in the middle of the bonnet, while the green cloverleaf was applied to the centre of the gull-wing doors.

In the intentions of Alfa Romeo and Pinin Farina, this was to have been the prototype of a small batch of cars, but the project was shelved before production could begin.

Nuvola

A STUNNING CONCEPT CAR, THE FOUNDATION
FOR A NEW GENERATION OF ALFA ROMEOS

Engine

Front, longitudinal, vertical, 60° V6, block
and heads in light alloy, four valves per
cylinder, belt-driven double overhead
camshafts. Integrated electronic fuel
injection and ignition, turbocharger

Displacement

2492 cc (88x68.3 mm)

Power and torque

304 hp at 6000 rpm – 39.5 Kgm at 3000 rpm

Transmission

Four-wheel drive, hydraulically actuated
single dry-plate clutch, six speeds + reverse

Chassis

Steel spaceframe

Bodywork

Coupé (Centro Stile Alfa Romeo)

Brakes

Hydraulically actuated and assisted discs
all round

Dimensions

Wheelbase: 2600 mm, Length: 4286 mm,
Width: 1859 mm

Maximum speed

280 kph

Cars produced

1

In the early Nineties, the Centro Stile Alfa Romeo, under the guidance of Walter de' Silva, was undergoing a period of major renewal. Both from the material point of view with the modernisation of machine tooling, and from the creative point of view too, by looking at the history and tradition of the company and by looking at the most important elements which had made Alfa Romeo great in the past. The results were not slow in coming. The first signs of change came with the GTV and Spider by Pininfarina and with the 145, but the real turning point was the presentation of the Nuvola concept car at the 1996 Paris Motor Show.

This was a pure two-seater coupé, with lines that were both soft and muscular and which explored the principal elements of Alfa tradition while giving a taste of what was to come. The passenger compartment located over the rear axle made room for a low and elegant tail-section. The interior featured mixture of leather and hide with the metal of the bodywork.

The special characteristics of the Nuvola do not stop at form but have to do with substance too. On the contrary, in this case it was above all a question of substance, because the form that was officially presented was just one of an infinite number that could be fitted to the revolutionary chassis developed by Alfa Romeo.

The most important new feature was in fact a return to an old way of thinking about cars. A load-bearing rolling chassis that could be homologated and sold without bodywork and then be "clothed" by independent coachbuilders or by the company itself. This solution could potentially generate the most diverse bodies, from coupés to roadsters while also exploring brand new forms.

The chassis was a spaceframe made of high-strength steel sections, combining the torsional stiffness appropriate for a sports car with excellent levels of comfort, while still managing to respect ever more stringent safety regulations. Furthermore, the structure was open to low-cost modifications. A supercharged 2500 cc twin-turbo V6 engine was specified, but this too remained at the prototype stage.

The Nuvola project was distinguished by its decidedly pragmatic approach: even though it was a revolutionary concept, the chassis was designed so that it could be mass-produced and with a level of technology that would normally be available it could be built, sold and guaranteed, allowing the coachbuilders to offer exclusive but reasonably-priced versions while still providing the maker's guarantee on the mechanical parts.

Only one prototype of the Nuvola was assembled before the project was shelved: originally finished in red, the name of the car was intended to reprise the legend of Tazio Nuvolari. However, the Alfa management, hampered by copyright problems over the name, preferred the name Nuvola and very sophisticated iridescent paintwork, inspired by colours which were very common in the Twenties and Thirties: Azzurro Nuvola (Cloud Blue).

The Italian **school**

New, unique, sinuous forms The creativity
of the stylist and the talent of the panel-beater

8C 2900 B Lungo

TOURING'S MASTERPIECE
AND THE ULTIMATE ALFA ROMEO

Engine

Front, longitudinal vertical straight-eight, dual blocks and heads in light alloy, two valves per cylinder, two gear-driven overhead camshafts. Two carburettors, two superchargers, magneto ignition

Displacement

2905 cc (68x100 mm)

Power and torque

180 hp at 5200 rpm

Transmission

Rear-wheel drive, rear mounted multiple dry-plate clutch, four speeds + reverse

Chassis

Welded box section longerons and cross members

Bodywork

Berlinetta (Touring Superleggera)

Suspension

Front: independent, wishbones, coil springs, hydraulic dampers

Rear: independent, trailing arms transverse leaf spring, hydraulic and friction dampers

Brakes

Hydraulically actuated drums all round

Dimensions

Wheelbase: 3000 mm, Length: 5150 mm, Width: 1770 mm, Height: 1500 mm

Weight

1250 Kg

Maximum speed

175 kph

Cars produced

10 (Lungo)

It is said that the 8C 2900 originated at the end of 1934, when the GP Tipo B's career came to an end and the Portello's stores contained a lot of unused spare parts and about thirty engines, now obsolete in terms of GPs but still sufficiently modern and competitive for the hard-fought Sport class.

The engine in question was the well-proven 2905 cc eight-cylinder, with a power output of 220 hp, but with transaxle transmission unlike the Tipo B. The engine was at the front while the gearbox and differential were on the rear axle, as with the GP Tipo C introduced almost at the same time and which also inspired the independent suspension of the 8C 2900.

As a result of the 8C 2900 A's racing success during the 1936 and 1937 seasons, together with public interest in the spider prototype on show in Milan, Paris and Berlin, Alfa Romeo decided to make a small batch of very exclusive cars based on the same, slightly lengthened chassis, and with a power output reduced to 180 hp for road use.

Long and short chassis with lengths of 2800 and 3000 mm respectively were prepared. Their respective weights were 1250 and 1150 kg. Many coachbuilders tried their hand at providing bodywork for the illustrious chassis of the 8C 2900 and even Alfa Romeo's own elegant spider was shown again at the Paris Motor Show in 1937. The top speeds were 175 kph for the long chassis cars and 185 kph for the short chassis.

The 8C 2900 B, in this case with Touring bodywork, had its inevitable sporting competition debut in the 1938 Mille Miglia, filling the first three places. Pintacuda, driving with Severi, again triumphed in the Spa 24 Hours that same year, while the last great victory came as late as 1947 when Clemente Biondetti dominated the Mille Miglia with a Superleggera Touring berlinetta belonging to his co-driver Emilio Romano. This car, with the superchargers removed to satisfy to the new regulations, produced 137 hp, but was still able to get the better of the much more recent cars.

A total of 10 long and 20 short rolling chassis were assembled, along with the 8C 2900 B Speciale Le Mans. The queen of exclusive social circles the 8C 2900 B was appreciated above all for its mechanical engineering which allowed it to aspire to the title of "the fastest production car in the world", according to Cecil Clutton of *Motor Sport*. However, it was also popular because of the coachbuilders' glorious creations that enjoyed such success in the Concours d'Elegance. The car on display has elegant Touring Superleggera berlinetta bodywork, similar to that of the car driven by Biondetti and Romano in the 1947 Mille Miglia: found by Alfa Romeo in Switzerland without its engine, it was first restored and later fitted with an engine assembled from original parts.

ALFA ROMEO
6 C 2300 B
MILLE MIGLIA
6 C 2300 B 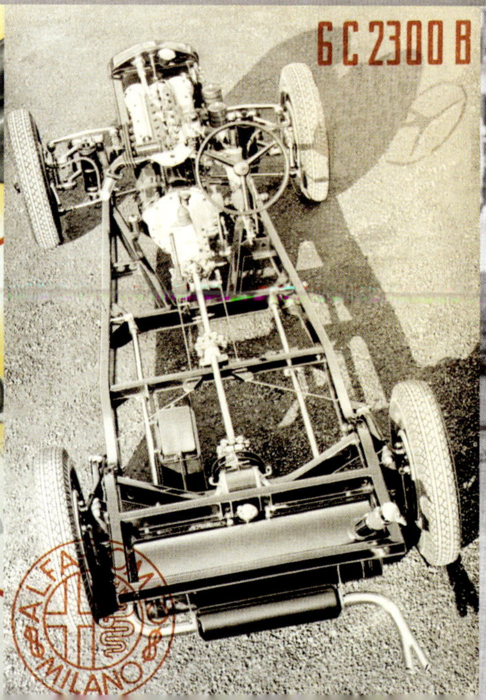 
ALFA ROMEO MILANO
119

6C 2300 B Mille Miglia

"SUPERLEGGERA".
BUT ALSO SEDUCTIVE AND AERODYNAMIC

Engine

Front, longitudinal, vertical straight-six, block and removable head in light alloy, two valves per cylinder, two chain-driven overhead camshafts. Two twin-choke carburettors, distributor ignition, wet sump lubrication

Displacement

2309 cc (70x100 mm)

Power and torque

95 hp at 4500 rpm

Transmission

Rear-wheel drive, front mounted single dry-plate clutch, four speeds + reverse

Chassis

Welded steel box section longerons and cross members

Bodywork

Berlinetta (Touring Superleggera)

Suspension

Front: independent, wishbones, coil springs, hydraulic dampers

Rear: independent, trailing arms longitudinal torsion bars, hydraulic dampers

Brakes

Hydraulically actuated drums all round

Dimensions

Wheelbase: 3000 mm, Length: 4640 mm, Width: 1680 mm, Height: 1550 mm

Weight

1380 Kg

Maximum speed

170 kph

Cars produced

106 (1938-1939)

The 6C 2300, produced in 1934 to replace the 6C 1900 GT, in its turn the heir to the legendary 6C 1750, made a name for itself from the moment it appeared as a refined and comfortable grand touring car, leaving the task of defending Alfa Romeo colours in the major races to the more extreme 8C 2300. Nonetheless, three cars, with a higher power output of 95 hp and a top speed of 145 kph, were developed and built for the 1934 Targa Abruzzo in Pescara. The chassis were fitted with slim, faux-cabriolet berlinetta bodywork made by Touring and named Aternum (after the river Aterno which flows near Pescara). Neither Pintacuda-Brivio's Lancia Astura, nor the extremely powerful 8C 2300's driven by Lord Howe, Tazio Nuvolari and Raymond Sommer were able to keep up with the fast and reliable six-cylinder cars that filled the first three places in the overall standings. After this success, Alfa Romeo decided to produce a batch of about 60 cars with this configuration, later baptised as the Pescara and replicated in 1935 on the basis of the improved 6C 2300 B. In the meantime, Alfa Romeo also prepared an even more powerful version using the short wheelbase chassis in time for the 1937 Mille Miglia. Ercole Boratto, Benito Mussolini's personal driver, and the experienced road-tester Giovanni Battista Guidotti managed an incredible fourth place overall and easily dominated their own class. The engine now produced 105 hp and improvements had also been made to the transmission and chassis, while Touring was responsible for the Superleggera aluminium bodywork. This model was sold directly by the company with the name 6C 2300 B Mille Miglia; replacing the Pescara at the top of the range it was intended for customers looking for a more sporting car, which in many cases they also used for racing. The car's success was not limited to the Apennine passes of the "Freccia Rossa" however, as Boratto again, paired with the young road-tester Gaboardi, dominated the Tobruk-Tripoli, the North African race organised by the Fascist regime to underline the power of the "empire" and inaugurate the new coast road. Despite the rather pompous style of the announcement, only 17 drivers took part, compared to the 123 in the Mille Miglia, and Boratto had more trouble coping the extremely severe conditions of the route than with the other competitors, although he managed to maintain an average speed of 133 kph, a record for a road race.

With the slender aluminium berlinetta bodywork fitted to the 6C 2300 Mille Miglia chassis, Carrozzeria Touring of Milan definitively established itself as one of the great names in coachbuilding on the strength of its Superleggera patent. The handcrafted aluminium body panels were attached to a tubular steel subframe. Weight was drastically reduced and the system also allowed for a design obviously inspired by aerodynamic research, a trend that was bursting onto the automotive scene in the mid-Thirties.

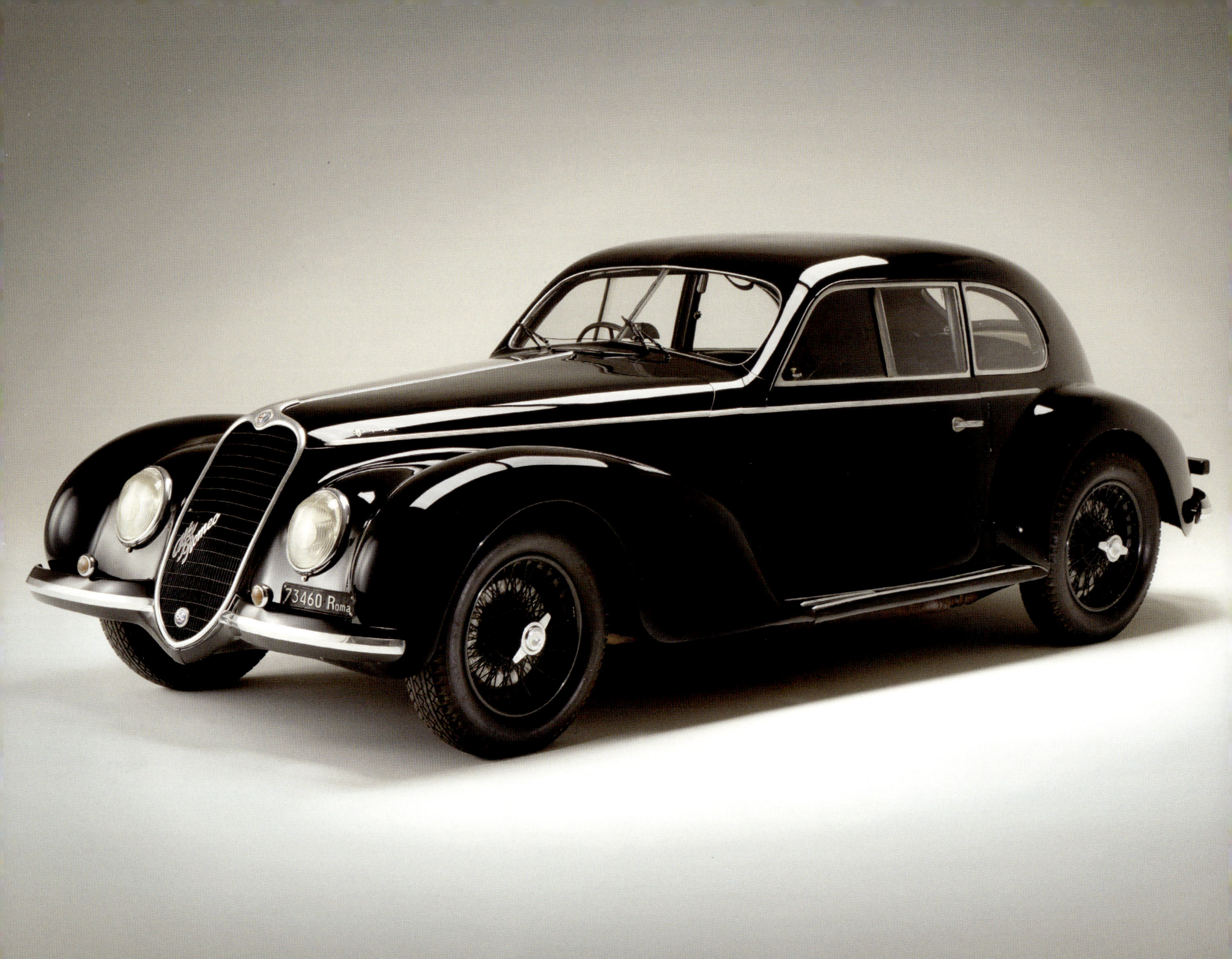

Alfa Rom
150
160
6C 2500 SPORT

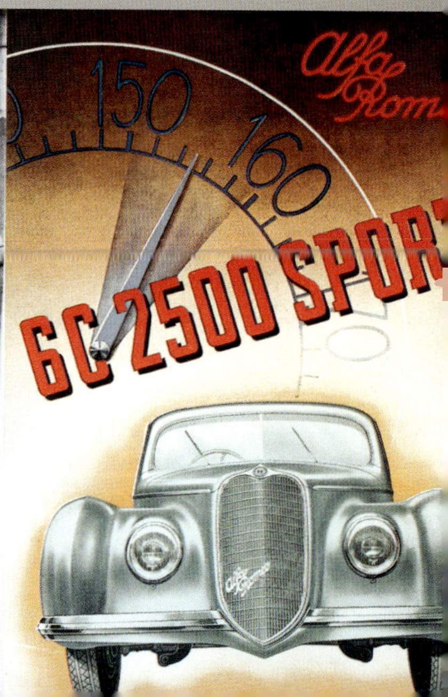

6C 2500 Sport

TOURING LOOKS TO THE FUTURE. UNDER THE COACHWORK, THE ULTIMATE EVOLUTION OF JANO'S SIX-CYLINDER

Engine

Front, longitudinal, vertical, straight-six, cast iron block and head in light alloy, two valves per cylinder, two chain-driven overhead camshafts. One twin-choke carburettor, distributor ignition, wet sump lubrication

Displacement

2443 cc (72x100 mm)

Power and torque

95 hp at 4600 rpm

Transmission

Rear-wheel drive, front mounted single dry-plate clutch, four speeds + reverse

Chassis

Welded longerons and cross members

Bodywork

Berlinetta (Touring Superleggera)

Suspension

Front: independent, wishbones, coil springs, hydraulic dampers

Rear: independent, trailing arms, longitudinal torsion bars, four hydraulic dampers

Brakes

Hydraulically actuated drums all round

Dimensions

Wheelbase: 3000 mm, Length: 5000 mm, Width: 1830 mm, Height: 1570 mm

Weight

1370 Kg

Maximum speed

155 kph

Cars produced

66 (1939)

With a view to replacing the 6C 2300 B, in the dual role of grand touring and sports saloon cars, two ambitious projects were initiated under the code names S10 – surprisingly to be equipped with a 60° V12 engine – and S11 (equipped with a 90° V8), which was supposed to have led to the manufacture of a two-light saloon with lines similar to those of the subsequent 6C 2500.

However, Alfa Romeo took neither of the cars any further, instead deciding to invest in a more traditional project resulting in 1939 in the 6C 2500, a logical development of the 6C 2300 B.

The engine, mounted in a chassis very similar to that of the preceding model, was a development of the classic straight-six with a total displacement increased to 2443 cc, thanks to the bore being increased to 72 mm while the stroke was left at 100 mm. A new fuel system brought an increase in the maximum power output to 87 hp at 4600 rpm.

In line with one of the firm's long-standing traditions, the new 6C 2500 Turismo was soon produced in Sport and SS (Super Sport) Corsa versions. The S model, as well as having a chassis with a wheelbase shortened to 3 metres (compared to the 3250 mm of the Turismo model) also boasted an engine with a power output increased to 95 hp at 4600 rpm. It had a top speed of 155 kph. External coachbuilders, in this case Touring, were asked to work on the cars.

One of the various models that prefigured the final version of the car was badged "Berlinetta Superleggera – interamente metallica – profilata al vento su telaio Alfa Romeo 6C 2500 Sport". The first 6C 2500 S's prepared by the famous Milanese coachbuilder appeared in the spring of 1939 and were added to the company's official catalogue as "production" cars.

Typical of Touring's repertoire of styles, the 6C 2500 Sport had a flowing and elegant line, marked by a prominent front end finished off with the classic radiator grille that had already been seen on the 6C 2300 B and had also been successful on the 8C 2900 B. The ample mudguards flowed into the inevitable running boards giving a sense of movement to the flanks of the car, while the upper body blended in perfectly with the rear section with the help of a sinuous tail fin. These were all enormously appealing and effective styling features that can be found on the car on display too.

This car had initially been purchased by the Alfa Romeo dealer in Novara and joined the collection in March 1971.

1939 also saw small-scale production (in all 8 open-topped examples of the so-called "ala spessa" or "thick wing" open type and a berlinetta) of the 6C 2500 SS Corsa, destined exclusively for competition. Further development work on the engine brought about an increase in power to 125 hp at 4800 rpm. Among the race victories, those that stood out were the Tobruk-Tripoli in 1939 (Boratto-Sanesi) and the Parma-Poggio di Berceto (Calamai), but also the overall second place in the Mille Miglia in 1940 (Farina-Mambelli).

6C 2500 Super Sport "Villa d'Este"

THE QUEEN OF THE CONCOURS D'ELEGANCE
AND THE END OF AN ERA

Engine

Front, longitudinal, vertical straight-six, cast iron block and head in light alloy, two valves per cylinder, two chain-driven overhead camshafts. Three single-choke carburettors, distributor ignition, wet sump lubrication

Displacement

2443 cc (72x100 mm)

Power and torque

105 hp at 4800 rpm

Transmission

Rear-wheel drive, front mounted single dry-plate clutch, four speeds + reverse

Chassis

Welded steel box section longerons and cross members

Bodywork

Berlinetta (Touring Superleggera)

Suspension

Front: independent, parallel trailing arms, coil springs, hydraulic dampers

Rear: independent, trailing arms, longitudinal torsion bars, hydraulic dampers

Brakes

Hydraulically actuated drums all round

Dimensions

Wheelbase: 2700 mm, Length: 1580 mm, Width: 1780 mm, Height: 1500 mm

Weight

1420 Kg

Maximum speed

165 kph

Cars produced

36

The career of the 6C 2500 Super Sport, born in 1939 and taking its place at the top of the 6C 2500 range, was brusquely interrupted by the outbreak of the Second World War, when car manufacturing ceased to make way for aeroplane engines and heavy goods vehicles. Nevertheless, as was the case with the other versions, it was to enjoy a second youth at the end of the war when, in an attempt to revive production, pre-war designs and projects were reprised, many of which proving to be still competitive despite being associated with the concept of exclusive and expensive cars that was living out its final days.

Through to 1946, the 6C 2500 Super Sport had been sold exclusively as a rolling chassis, allowing the customer the honour of their own bodywork, although there had been no lack of standard versions made by certain coachbuilders historically close to the company. When production started again, a body style designed and produced by Touring made its appearance in the official catalogue: even though the basic structure was still very close to the models made at the end of the Thirties, stylistic evolution was continuous and by the dawn of the 1950s, it had taken on a completely different appearance. Extremely high levels of quality were a constant, with workmanship and materials of the first order. The Aerlux version from this period was unusual, with its transparent Perspex roof, a result of aeronautical research into these synthetic materials carried out during the war, above all for use in the cockpit canopies of fighter planes. The principal contract for the construction of the cabriolet versions, a well-balanced and fascinating evolution of the cars built on the Sport chassis, and destined for considerable commercial success, with more than 150 built, was given to Pinin Farina, even though there was no lack of proposals from Touring and other coachbuilders, including a model designed by Mario Revelli di Beaumont for the nascent Carrozzeria Bertone.

The 6C 2500 Super Sport "Villa d'Este" designed by Carlo Felice Bianchi Anderloni in 1949, deserves special mention. It too had aluminium Superleggera bodywork and was mainly available in a coupé version, but sometimes also as a cabriolet. Elegant and sophisticated, its lines would become one the high points of the Italian coachbuilding school and a benchmark for Alfa Romeo. Here was a style that people found appealing at first glance, winning the Referendum Grand Prix at the Villa d'Este Concours d'Elegance organised as always at the well-known hotel in Cernobbio in September. About thirty cars were produced before it was removed from the catalogue in 1952, marking the end of an era and making way for a new generation of cars.

The example in the museum, a 1950 coupé, was bought in Rome in 1950 and first put on show in 1965.

Always **to the fore**

When the car is the star.
Firms, fashion, society

Giulietta Spider Prototipo

A PININFARINA DESIGN FOR THE USA.
A DREAM FOR WHOLE WORLD

Engine

Front, longitudinal, vertical, straight-four, block and head in light alloy, two valves per cylinder, two duplex chain-driven overhead camshafts. One twin-choke carburettor, distributor ignition, wet sump lubrication

Displacement

1290 cc (74x75mm mm)

Power and torque

65 hp at 6300 rpm – 11 Kgm at 4000 rpm

Transmission

Rear-wheel drive, front mounted single dry-plate clutch, four speeds + reverse

Chassis

Pressed steel unitary construction

Bodywork

Spider (Pinin Farina)

Suspension

Front: independent, wishbones, coil springs, hydraulic dampers, anti-roll bar

Rear: live axle, upper triangular element, trailing arms, hydraulic dampers

Brakes

Hydraulically actuated drums all round

Dimensions

Wheelbase: 2250 mm, Length: 3860 mm, Width: 1580 mm, Height: 1310 mm

Weight

860 Kg

Maximum speed

155 kph

Cars produced

14,300 (+ 2,796 Spider Veloce)

The ties between Alfa Romeo and Max Hoffman, a Californian importer of the majority of European makes of car, had already led to the 1952 Disco Volante project, which was later abandoned. Given the success that a few small English open cars were having on the North American market and given the performance of the Giulietta Sprint, it was Hoffman once more who put forward the idea of a spider version.

Although initially hesitant, Alfa Romeo later asked both Bertone and Pininfarina to design a prototype: for the former Franco Scaglione designed a sporting, futuristic car with unusual lines. Pininfarina on the other hand presented a car with sober, elegant bodywork, the synthesis of a stylistic approach that aimed to achieve a perfect balance between form and function, bringing it in line with other models produced around that time.

Although Hoffman preferred Bertone's offering, foreseeing its potential appeal to eccentric Californian buyers, Alfa Romeo's desire to sell the spider on the European market as well, meant that the choice fell on the Pininfarina prototype, the very car on display in the museum today.

The chassis and engine were from the Sprint, albeit with the wheelbase shortened by 18 cm. While the prototype still had roadster bodywork, a panoramic windscreen, removable side windows, a minimalist interior and no door handles, the production version was more mature with greater attention to detail, while still retaining the freshness and dynamism of the prototype.

The Giulietta Spider had a long and richly satisfying career, quickly becoming one of the symbols of the Fifties and was the model in the range that could best be described as "Italy's sweetheart". The second series came out in 1959, while in 1961 another update introduced the third series, which hinted at the styling changes that would later appear on the 1600 Giulia Spider.

Between 1956 and 1957 a special Giulietta Spider was produced in a batch of 24 cars with single-seater bodywork and an engine producing 95 hp. Called the Sebring, even though it had never taken part in the famous 12 Hours, it only saw the chequered flag a few times: it took part in the 1956 Mille Miglia with Consalvo Sanesi a the wheel with disastrous results, ending in a terrible accident. Nor did the Californian single-marque championship for which Hoffman had originally intended the car take off either.

What was more significant but of course unofficial was the duel in 1961 from Milan to Rome between Sanesi at the wheel of a Giulietta Spider Veloce and Gianni Mazzocchi, owner of *Quattroruote*, aboard the brand new Settebello, pride and joy of the Italian Railways. The driver arrived in Via Veneto a good 38 minutes ahead of Mazzocchi's taxi, even though he had a puncture and there was no motorway from Florence onwards.

A total of 17,096 cars were made, figures that fail to reflect the impact the Giulietta Spider had on society and the collective imagination at that time.

1600 Spider "Duetto"

UNIQUE STYLING, A REMARKABLY LONG CAREER AND TIMELESS APPEAL

Engine

Front, longitudinal, vertical, straight-four, block and removable head in light alloy, two valves per cylinder, two duplex chain-driven overhead camshafts. Two twin-choke carburettors, distributor ignition, wet sump lubrication

Displacement

1570 cc (78x82 mm)

Power and torque

109 hp at 6000 rpm

Transmission

Rear-wheel drive, single dry-plate clutch, five speeds + reverse

Chassis

Pressed steel unitary construction

Bodywork

Spider (Pinin Farina)

Suspension

Front: independent, wishbones, oblique arms, coil springs, hydraulic dampers, anti-roll bar

Rear: live axle, upper triangular element, trailing arms, hydraulic dampers

Brakes

Hydraulically actuated and assisted discs all round

Dimensions

Wheelbase: 2250 mm, Length: 4250 mm, Width: 1630 mm, Height: 1290 mm

Weight

990 Kg

Maximum speed

185 kph

Cars produced

6,325

The success of the Giulietta Spider, which had proved capable of dominating both the market and the collective imagination, made it very hard to design a successor based on the mechanical design of the new Giulia, introduced in 1962. Initially, the new mechanical assemblies were installed in Giulietta Spider bodies, giving birth to the Giulia Spider. Subsequently, after the presentation of the Giulia Sprint GT by Bertone, an attempt was made to produce an open-topped version by simply removing the roof and upper body, a procedure carried out by Touring, but which came to an end after only 1000 cars were made.

The real turning point came in 1966, when at last a completely new car debuted, the 1600 Spider, known to most as the "Duetto", with Pininfarina bodywork. The styling was based on the Super Flow prototype, presented at Turin in 1956, using 6C 3000 CM mechanicals and designed by Aldo Brovarone. The new car boasted an unusual, unconventional design that was very different to the other models in the Giulia range, with a low front end and the famous "Osso di Seppia" (cuttlefish bone) tail, which was almost the antithesis of the truncated rear that was such a strong feature of the saloon.

The mechanical design was based on that of the Giulia Sprint GT, but with the power output increased to 109 hp and the wheelbase shortened to 225 cm: performance and the driving experience placed it firmly at the top of its class. Its top speed of 182 kph (5 kph less with the roof down), was only a little slower than the 185 kph of the Giulia Sprint GT Veloce introduced at the same time and with the same mechanical specification.

The car was shown to the public at the Geneva Motor Show in 1966, and the following May it was loaded onto the Raffaello, a cruise liner bound for New York from Genoa and stopping off at Cannes for the Film Festival. Alfa Romeo organised a spectacular presentation aimed at the North American market: a circuit was even set up on deck, where Consalvo Sanesi gave a demonstration to VIPs and the press, issuing a fancy sounding "High Seas Licence". As a means of deciding on a name it was decided to organise a competition open to all: out of the 140,000 participants who sent in a postcard with their suggestion, seven people chose the name "Duetto". Once they had drawn the winner, Guidobaldo Trionfi, he was presented with a white example as a prize. However, a copyright issue with the name and Alfa Romeo's opinion that "Duetto" was not aggressive enough for this type of car, meant that they gave up the idea in favour of the simple name Spider.

The promotional activities invented by the Public Relations Department, led by Camillo Marchetti, ended in a brilliant piece of product placement which saw the Spider 1600 appear in the film "The Graduate" with Dustin Hoffman, securing its place on the international market and making it a synonym for Alfa Romeo. The "Duetto" had a remarkably long career: there were four series and several versions and it was produced until 1994.

ALFA ROMEO
MILANO
sprint

Giulietta. **Italy's sweetheart**

Mirror of an era: insuperable technology
and fabulous coachwork

Giulietta Sprint

AVANT-GARDE ENGINEERING, BERTONE STYLING AND CLASS-LEADING PERFORMANCE. AN ITALIAN-STYLE COUPÉ

Engine

Front, longitudinal, vertical, straight-four, block and head in light alloy, two valves per cylinder, two duplex chain-driven overhead camshafts. Twin-choke carburettor, distributor ignition, wet sump lubrication

Displacement

1290 cc (74x75 mm)

Power and torque

65 hp at 6000 rpm

Transmission

Rear-wheel drive, front mounted single dry-plate clutch, four speeds + reverse

Chassis

Pressed steel unitary construction

Bodywork

Coupé (Bertone)

Suspension

Front: independent, wishbones, coil springs, hydraulic dampers, anti-roll bar

Rear: live axle, upper triangular element, trailing arms, hydraulic dampers

Brakes

Hydraulically actuated drums all round

Dimensions

Wheelbase: 2380 mm, Length: 3980 mm, Width: 1540 mm , Height: 1320 mm

Weight

880 Kg

Maximum speed

165 kph

Cars produced

24,084

The car that marked the transformation of Alfa Romeo into a major car manufacturer was without doubt the Giulietta, "Italy's sweetheart". As the 1900 was the only car in the catalogue at the time, in 1952 the idea of a more modern car with a smaller displacement began to gain ground.

The initial ideas for a small 350 cc mini-car or another with a 750 cc engine and front-wheel drive were abandoned (although the 750 code was used as a name for the projects which followed). In August 1952, it became clear that the car would have a traditional layout (front-engined, rear-wheel drive). Less than a year later, the first prototype took to the road. It was a compact coupé, made by Ivo Colucci's coachwork department and it was fitted with a four-cylinder twin-cam 1100 cc engine made of lightweight alloy. The displacement was later increased to 1290 cc (1300). With a single-choke carburettor, it produced 65 hp and had a top speed of 165 kph, but at the end of its lifetime, the last version in 1958 had a twin-choke carburettor, more power — 79 hp — and a top speed of 170 kph. The gearbox and the differential, both made of aluminium, were also new. The drum brakes with helical finning were derived from those fitted to the 1900.

Early in 1954, the mechanical side of the car was very nearly ready, but there were only sketches and some very basic prototypes of the body. Despite this, Finmeccanica announced that they would be delivering a batch of cars to a number of shareholders and this created a difficult and dangerous state of affairs. It was Rudolf Hruska who resolved the dilemma. He had recently been asked to reorganise the factory by Giuseppe Luraghi to get it ready to achieve the output of 50 cars a day planned for the Giulietta. An external coachbuilder assembled a limited batch of coupés to be delivered to the shareholders while the saloon version was readied. Initially sceptical, the IRI eventually accepted the proposal. The sketches (which were apparently inspired by Colucci's first coupé) were presented by Boneschi, Boano and Bertone. The latter, making use of Franco Scaglione's drawing skills, proposed a car that was compact and well proportioned, with spare, refined and sporting lines. The Giulietta Sprint was born.

The car was presented at the Turin Motor Show on the 21ST of April 1954, but two weeks previously, in the courtyard at the Portello authorized personnel and the management had been given a preview when two Shakespearian actors were lowered from a helicopter wearing the costumes of Romeo and… Juliet. The Giulietta dominated the market from the moment it was presented. After very few days orders had to be suspended because the factory was unable to produce enough cars. The reason for its success, apart from its attractive, dynamic lines, was its performance, which put the car on a level which was unheard of for cars of this class and which threatened competitors in much higher categories. This was the turning point for Alfa Romeo and the birth of a major automotive manufacturer.

Production of the Giulietta and various versions of it continued for 11 years during which time a total of 177,513 cars were made.

Giulietta TI

THE EVOLUTION OF THE SPECIES:
THE GIULIETTA COMES OF AGE

Engine

Front, longitudinal, vertical, straight-four, block and head in light alloy, two valves per cylinder, two chain-driven overhead camshafts. One twin-choke carburettor, distributor ignition, wet sump lubrication

Displacement

1290 cc (74x75 mm)

Power and torque

65 hp at 6150 rpm

Transmission

Rear-wheel drive, front mounted single dry-plate clutch, four speeds + reverse

Chassis

Pressed steel unitary construction

Bodywork

Saloon

Suspension

Front: independent, wishbones, coil springs, hydraulic dampers, anti-roll bar

Rear: live axle, upper triangular element, trailing arms, hydraulic dampers

Brakes

Hydraulically actuated drums all round

Dimensions

Wheelbase: 2380 mm, Length: 4106 mm, Width: 1550 mm, Height: 1500 mm

Weight

908 Kg

Maximum speed

155 kph

Cars produced

92,658

When the Giulietta saloon was presented in 1955 its overwhelming success gave rise to a long waiting list for buyers: performance, driving pleasure and handling were of the highest levelorder. However, the company continued to update its products and just two years later, in September 1957, the first variation of the saloon car was presented at the Monza racetrack. As with the version of the 1900 with the same name, It was called the Giulietta TI (Turismo Internazionale) which, as in the case of the 1900 version with the same name, offered even better performance and a more sporting appearancestance. Only minor changes were made to the bodywork to do with the rear lights and the, instruments, and while appearance of more marked pronounced tail-sections of the mudguardsend sections to the rear wings were introduced. Greater attention was paid devoted to the engine: thanks to a higher compression ratio and the use of a twin-choke carburettor, power was increased to 65 hp giving a maximum speed of 155 kph.

In 1958, the mechanical specifications were further improved. The "unpredictable" gearbox with its Werner synchronizers was replaced by with a more modern Porsche synchronized gearbox using the Porsche system. The following year the bodywork was given a slight facelift focussing mainly on the radiator grille, which was given two chrome "moustaches" on the air intakes in place of the single piece of trim. The headlights were also recessed and the bumpers were given rubber-faced overriders and indicators on each side. Inside, the dashboard was reworked revised with newly redesigned instruments. This set series of improvements, aimed mainly at improving ride comfort, had a negative effect on the overall weight, which increased slightly with a corresponding drop in performance. This was one of the reasons why the Giulietta TI was updated again in 1961, in both in mechanical and styling terms of mechanics and aesthetics. The engine now had a new crankcase which is shared with the imminent Giulia which was about to be presented. Thanks to different tuning work on the engine and a new carburettor, the power output increased to 74 hp giving a maximum speed of 155 km/hph. The gear lever stayed on the steering wheel column until the end of 1962 when a floor-mounted gear-lever was fitted once and for all.

The main differences in the bodywork were to be seen at the front of the car, where the shape of the air intakes was modified and they were closed with a chrome-plated grille. On the inside of the car, separate and reclining seats were now standard.

Production of the Giulietta TI came to an end in 1964, but it stillremained on sale for a few months. The warehouses stocks were effortlessly "emptied" of the remaining with and more than 90,000 examples were eventually having been sold. In fact, even though the much more modern Giulia was on sale, the Giulietta was still popular, thanks to a much lower list price and lower running costs.

alfa romeo
MAGGIO - AGOSTO 1961
ANNO II N. 3-4

Giulietta Sprint Speciale

SCAGLIONE SETS HIS SIGHTSFOCUSES ON AERODYNAMICS. REFINED AND EXCLUSIVE, IT BECAME MORE AT HOME IN SALONS THAN ON THE TRACK

Engine

Front, longitudinal, straight-four, block and head in light alloy, two valves per cylinder, two duplex chain-driven overhead camshafts Two twin-choke carburettors, distributor ignition, wet sump lubrication

Displacement

1290 cc (74x75mm mm)

Power and torque

97 hp at 6500 rpm

Transmission

Rear-wheel drive, front mounted single dry-plate clutch, five speeds + reverse

Chassis

Pressed steel unitary construction

Bodywork

Coupé (Bertone)

Suspension

Front: independent, wishbones, coil springs, hydraulic dampers, anti-roll bar

Rear: live axle, upper triangular element, trailing arms, hydraulic dampers

Brakes

Hydraulically actuated triple-shoe drums all round

Dimensions

Wheelbase: 2250 mm, Length: 4120 mm, Width: 1660 mm, Height: 1280 mm

Weight

950 Kg

Maximum speed

183 kph

Cars produced

1,252

The immediate success of the Giulietta Sprint encouraged many independent racing drivers to use it for racing, and their enthusiasm for Alfa Romeo cars became even greater after the launch of the Sprint Veloce. However at the beginning of 1957 their the car's success in racing had its ups and downs as the competition had gradually become fiercer. This competition was not just from other manufacturers, but also from Alfa Romeo itself as the superlight particularly light Zagato-bodied Sprint Veloce cars with Zagato bodyworkhad started to push their way to the front on the track. Alfa Romeo was quick to respond to the challenge and they gave Bertone — a company very close to them after the unexpected and overwhelming success of the Giulietta Sprint — the task of designing a more extreme and race-orientated car based on the Sprint Veloce to be used above all for racing.

The 1290 cc twin-cam was prepared with a higher compression ratio, two twin-choke carburettors and slightly more "extreme" valve-timing, all of which helped to increase the power output to 97 hp. A five-speed gearbox was fitted and the track was shortened to 2250 mm. The prototype of the Giulietta SS, without even the Alfa badge, was presented at the Turin Motor Show in October 1957. Using a short track wheelbase chassis Franco Scaglione produced one of his most appealing works designs — the Giulietta Sprint Speciale was long and wide, even wider than the saloon. It was an extremely low and swept-back coupé, distinguished by sleek, rounded lines. No bumpers and a radiator grill shaped like a shark's mouth made it clear that this was a dream car. However, beneath the refined sophisticated styling design was hidden some very thorough aerodynamic research, that could be seen in the low front section and the a pronounced truncated tail.

The performance was very respectable with a top speed approaching and often exceeding the wall of 200 kph. These were figures that had hitherto been absolutely unimaginable for a 1300 and were a benchmark that proved very difficult to improve on for a long time afterwards. The linestyling, which had a rather "baroque" flavour, the pronounced changes of overhangs which that make made it less agile, and above all its 950 kg weight made the SS a car more suited to social occasions than the race track. And, as regards with regard to racing, the baton was soon passed to the lighter and more compact Giulietta SZ, that which in the meantime had come out from the limbo of made-to-measure craft productions to be included in the official Alfa Romeo price lists. The company's intention for with the SS too was just that, to offer a high-performance product that was rigorously a production car at the same time (the exception to this was a limited number of handmade cars with aluminium bodywork). Proof of this was came at the official presentation on the 24TH of June 1959 at the Monza race track: several dozen SS's lined up on the track to bear witness to the "standardization" of the model. Six colours were available. During its three years in the catalogue, 1,252 were sold, after which the Giulia Sprint Speciale, with a 1600 engine, a few modifications to the dashboard and, at a later date, disk brakes, took over. The example in the collection was the first one produced, in 1963.

Giulietta SZ "Coda Tronca"

COMPACT, LIGHT AND SUCCESSFUL
WITH THE "Z" ON THE FLANK.
THE TRUNCATED TAIL WAS TO MAKE IT INVINCIBLE

Engine

Front, longitudinal, vertical, straight-four, block and head in light alloy, two valves per cylinder, two duplex chain-driven overhead camshafts. Two twin-choke carburettors, distributor ignition, wet sump lubrication

Displacement

1290 cc (74x75 mm)

Power and torque

98 hp at 6500 rpm

Transmission

Rear-wheel drive, front mounted single dry-plate clutch, five speeds + reverse

Chassis

Pressed steel unitary construction, aluminium panels

Bodywork

Coupé (Zagato)

Suspension

Front: independent, wishbones, coil springs, hydraulic dampers, anti-roll bar

Rear: live axle, upper triangular element, trailing arms, hydraulic dampers

Brakes

Front: disc, rear: drum

Dimensions

Wheelbase: 2250 mm, Length: 4000 mm, Width: 1500 mm, Height: 1230 mm

Weight

840 Kg

Maximum speed

200 kph

Cars produced

840 (Giulietta SZ, 1960-1962)

Despite the racing sporting success of the Giulietta Sprint Veloce, Alfa Romeo soon began to think about building a more "racing" version. This ended up as the Giulietta SS, with its Scaglione bodywork. It was certainly aerodynamic but maybe a little too baroque and extravagant for the tarmac of the tracks. In the meantime, via an unusual path, the first steps were taken by the Giulietta Sprint Zagato, the well-known SZ, had taken its first steps. Its history was firmly rooted in an episode associated with the world of racing: Dore Leto di Priolo (he andtogether his brothers Carlo and Massimo were amongo the best known Italian gentlemen drivers) destroyed his own Sprint Veloce during the 1956 Mille Miglia. On taking it to be repaired Dore asked Elio Zagato to not just to rebuild it but to make it as light as possible even if the work would be complex and expensive. The chassis was therefore stripped of its body panels and given a framework of steel tubes which was then covered panelled in aluminium bodywork. The result was a car that clearly showed its origins – many of the details like the radiator grille or the headlights lighting clusters were unchanged – but it now had a more rounded and shapely line. Furthermore, the overall weight came down by as much as 145 kg. Racing success came quickly for the SVZ and at the Coppa Intereuropea on the 2ND of September Massimo Leto di Priolo dominated the under 1300 class, thrashing the production Sprint Veloce's. The first effect of this success was that orders for the Zagato increased rapidlymultiplied: a matter of months dozens of private owners had SVZ's made to measure. They were all different from each one another, with each one becoming more extreme in terms of aerodynamics and weight-saving.

At first Zagato had to fall back on the uneconomical solution of working as a private builder, which meant that he had to dismantle and rebuild cars purchased at full list price. Things changed in 1959 and the Milanese coachbuilder was at last able to build the definitive official version of the Sprint Zagato with its very rounded shape. It weighed just over 850 kg and the level of performance was very high, with a top speed of nearly 190 kph. Almost immediately the validity of the project was confirmed by a series of race victories. At least this was true until the end of 1960 at least, when the ever fiercer competition led them to work on a new version without making changes to the engine but adding disk brakes to at the front and completely redesigning the bodywork. It had a more taperinged front end, minimalist side-panels sides, and more especially, a longer truncated tail section. Maximum speed was greater now: over 200 kph km/h although and legend has it that during testing Zagato himself was timed at 227 kph by the designer Ercole Spada. Elio Zagato was at the wheel for the first race, which was the Coppa Sant'Ambroeus in June 1961. He won took pole position and won the race itself, the first in a long series of victories. In 1962 there wasbrought a minor update which included headlights covered faired in plexiglas and more weight-saving. Some "coda tonda" or "round tail" models were produced alongside the standard production cars.

Giulia. **Designed by the wind**

Just one word: innovation.
Immediately after the launch, the legend begins

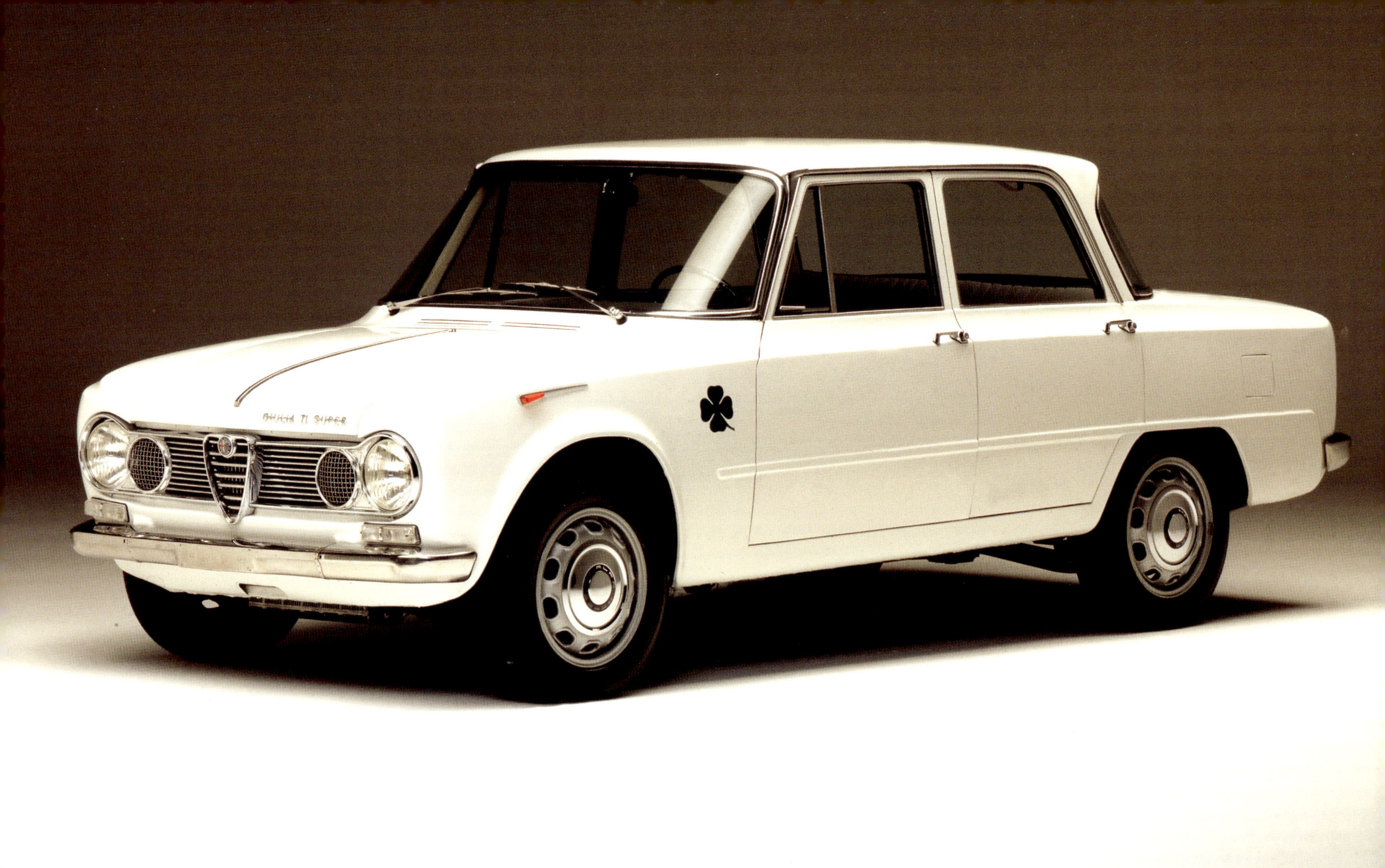
GIULIA TI SUPER

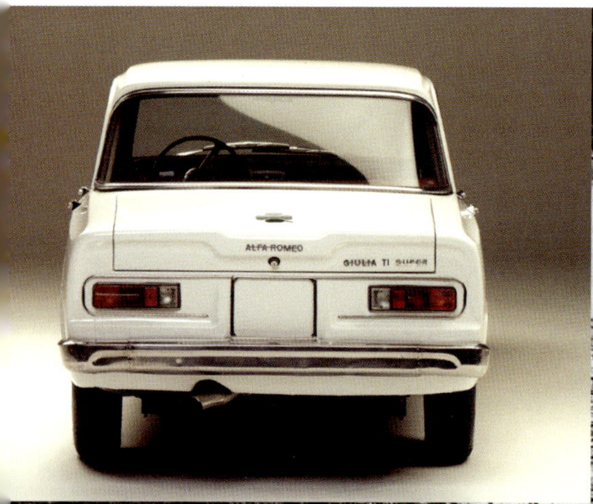
ALFA ROMEO
GIULIA TI SUPER

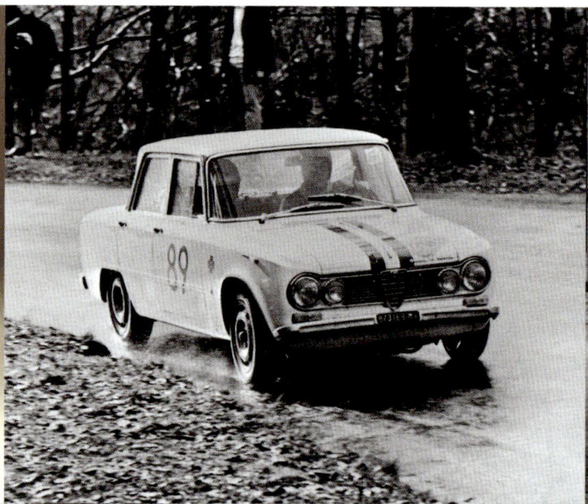
89

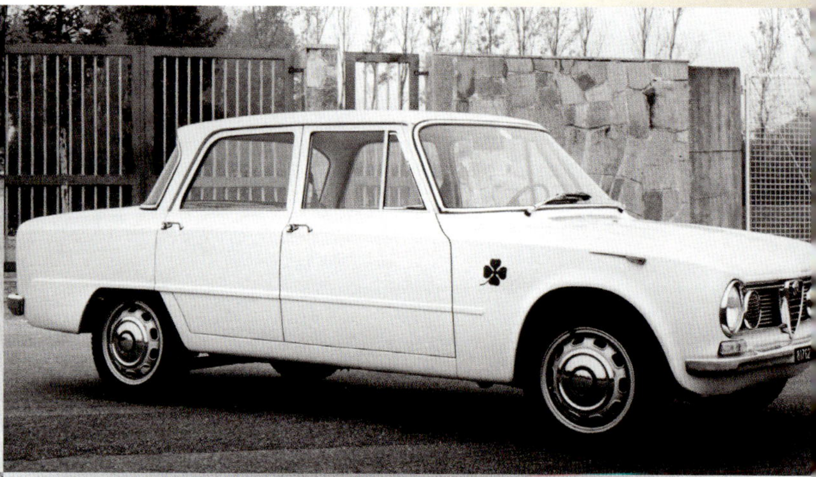

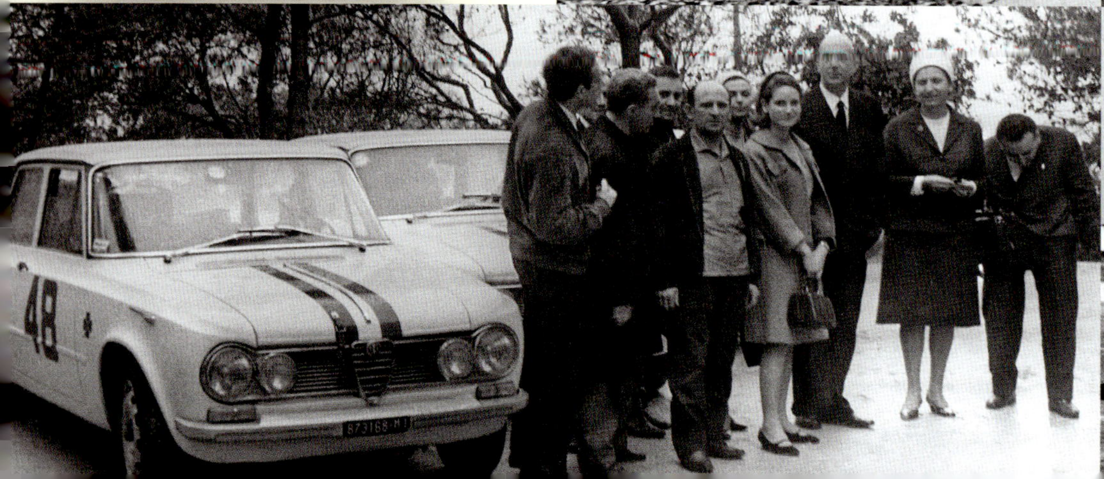
48

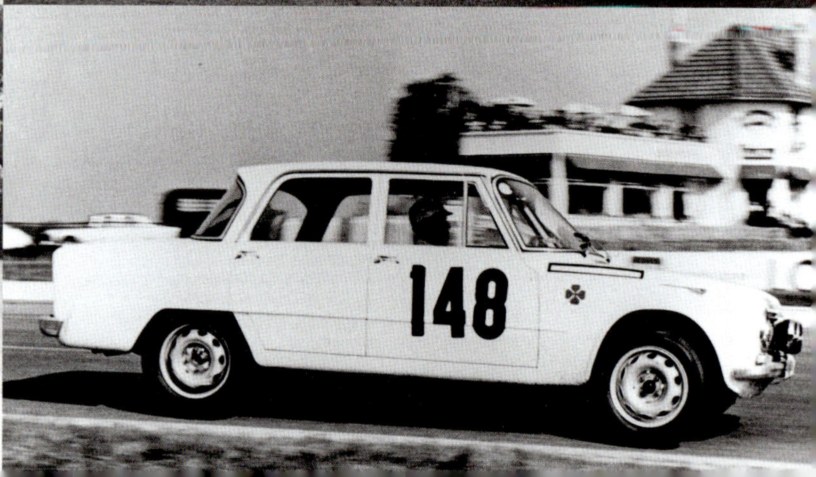
148

Giulia TI Super

TUBULAR CHASSIS, RACING MECHANICALS AND BESPOKE ZAGATO "CLOTHING"

Engine

Front, longitudinal, vertical, straight-four, block and head in light alloy, two valves per cylinder, two duplex chain-driven overhead camshafts. Two twin-choke carburettors, distributor ignition, wet sump lubrication

Displacement

1570 cc (78x82 mm)

Power and torque

112 hp at 6500 rpm

Transmission

Rear-wheel drive, single dry-plate clutch, five speeds + reverse

Chassis

Pressed steel unitary construction

Bodywork

Saloon

Suspension

Front: independent, wishbones, coil springs, hydraulic dampers, anti-roll bar

Rear: live axle, upper triangular element, trailing arms, hydraulic dampers

Brakes

Hydraulically actuated discs all round

Dimensions

Wheelbase: 2510 mm, Width: 4115 mm, Width: 1560 mm, Height: 1430 mm

Weight

960 Kg

Maximum speed

189 kph

Cars produced

501

The 27TH of June 1962 is another historic date for Alfa Romeo. The Giulia TI made its debut at Monza racetrack. Heiress to the Giulietta, it had the same mechanical configuration but wore an all-new "dress". The unitary construction steel body was the most innovative part of this car. It was big, roomy and aerodynamic, as shown by the minimal front overhang, tapering slightly near the radiator grille and the high, truncated tail section, initially "misunderstood" by the marque's devotees.

Less than a year later, on the 24TH of April 1963, the Brianza circuit witnessed the baptism of the Giulia TI Super, a more powerful and lighter variant, of which only 500 + 1 examples were made so that it could be homologated for the Turismo class. The "sporting heart" of the Alfa enthusiasts did not take long to realise that a sports version of the Giulia was essential and Alfa satisfied these expectations. From an aesthetic point of view, certain important details help observers realise that they are looking at a TI Super rather than a "normal" Giulia: the absence of rubber over-riders on the bumpers, Campagnolo Elektron magnesium wheels, the use of plexiglas rear windows and two circular steel grilles protecting the headlights (these were not fitted at the time the car was presented), a dynamic air intake for the fuel supply and another to direct the airflow onto the exhaust manifold. And of course there was the badging with the distinctive mark of "genuine" racing Alfas — three conspicuous green four-leafed clover decals on the sides and the boot.

Beneath the bonnet was the straight-four twin-cam from the Giulia SS, fed by two twin-choke Weber DCOE 14 carburettors with a power output of 112 hp at 6500 rpm and a power to weight ratio of 7.84 kg/hp. Other important features of the Super's technical specification included the floor-mounted gear change for the five-speed + reverse gearbox, lowered suspension, disk brakes from September 1963 onwards and an overall unladen weight of 910 kg, which is to say 90 kg less than the TI, achieved thanks to some thorough lightening of the interior as befits a true sport car — the dashboard was simplified with just the four main circular instruments.

The competition career of the TI Super was rather short (within a few years it was the Giulia Sprint GTA's turn to reap further success), partly because it was not homologated in the Turismo class until January 1964. For the whole of the 1963 season the TI Supers were obliged to race in the Gran Turismo class, competing with the likes of the Lotus Cortina and Mini Cooper S. Most of the time the TI Supers raced in the colours of the Scuderia Milanese Jolly Club, an unmistakeable Biancospino or hawthorn white, but with an Italian flag on the boot. Thanks to tuners such as Bosato, Conrero, Baggioli and Facetti, there was no shortage of success both on the track and in hillclimbs.

Giulia TZ

TUBULAR CHASSIS, RACING MECHANICALS AND BESPOKE ZAGATO "CLOTHING"

Engine

Front, longitudinal, vertical, straight-four, block and head in light alloy, two valves per cylinder, two duplex chain-driven overhead camshafts. Two twin-choke carburettors, distributor ignition, wet sump lubrication

Displacement

1570 cc (78x82 mm)

Power and torque

113 hp at 6500 rpm

Transmission

Rear-wheel drive, single dry-plate clutch, five speeds + reverse

Chassis

Welded tubular spaceframe

Bodywork

Coupé (Zagato)

Suspension

Front: independent, wishbones, coil springs, hydraulic dampers, anti-roll bar

Rear: independent, wishbones, coil springs, hydraulic dampers, anti-roll bar

Brakes

Hydraulically actuated and assisted discs all round, in-board at the rear

Dimensions

Wheelbase: 2500 mm, Length: 3950 mm, Width: 1510 mm, Height: 1200 mm

Weight

660 kg

Maximum speed

215 kph

Cars produced

117

Two letters, T and Z, Tubolare-Zagato, identify one of the most fascinating cars in Alfa Romeo's history that, as the years went by, became a true icon of the marque. Even before the Giulietta SZ had made its competition debut in the Coppa Sant'Ambroeus in June 1961, Alfa Romeo was already thinking about its successor and in 1959 they started to work on a car that would race in the Gran Turismo class.

Never was it truer than in this case that a car was literally born around... its chassis. The Alfa Romeo Design Department under the direction of Orazio Satta and Giuseppe Busso, who had already tackled this theme with the 6C 3000 PR and Alfa-Abarth 1000, decided on a modern spaceframe of welded tubes, a basis for one of Zagato's masterpieces. A low, sloping front end, a fierce-looking radiator grille that once again had the typical Alfa three-lobed motif, and shrouded headlights were the main features of the front of the car. The TZ boasted slim, flowing flanks ending in the characteristic feature of this car, its cut-off rear end with the tail dropping away steeply relative to the line of the body. The designers paid equal attention to the suspension, with the front equipped with wishbones of Giulietta/Giulia derivation, while at the independent rear layout featured multiple arms and with the swinging half-shaft making up the upper arm of the wishbone. This brought about a significant reduction in unsprung weight but created one of the greatest obstacles to the car's development as initially a mistake in the adjustment caused the suspension to bottom out to the detriment of its efficacy. It was only during a test session on the Raticosa circuit on the 24TH of October 1963 that Sanesi discovered the problem and the TZ started to... fly.

Looking after the mechanical side of the TZ and the well-proven 4-cylinder twin-cam 1570 cc engine from the Giulia SS, which now produced 113 hp at 6500 rpm and maximum torque of 14.4 kg/m at 4200 rpm, was the Delta company of Udine. Founded by Carlo Chiti and Ludovico Chizzola in 1963, the firm subsequently moved to Settimo Milanese (1964) under the name of Autodelta and later become a subsidiary of Alfa Romeo from 1966 on. And it was Autodelta that took over preparation of the TZ for private owners, soon becoming the "semi-works" Biscione racing department and then taking over the marque's racing activity from the beginning of 1966. After the first season, 1963, during which the TZ took part in a few minor races (worthy of note was the success of Lorenzo Bandini in the Coppa Fisa at Monza), in 1964 the "Tubolare Zagato" achieved a number of significant class wins in international races: the Sebring 12 Hours, the Targa Florio, the Nürburgring 1000 Km, the Le Mans 24 Hours, the Tour de France, the Coupe des Alpes (1ST overall) and the Tour de Corse (1ST and 2ND overall). In 1965 it won at Sebring and the Targa Florio again.

833982 MI
GIULIA GT

Giulia Sprint GT

GIUGIARO CREATES THE COUPÉ FOR BERTONE.
AFTER THE PRESENTATION, A PLACE IN THE ALFA LEGEND

Engine

Front, longitudinal, vertical straight-four, block and head in light alloy, two valves per cylinder, duplex chain driven double overhead camshafts, two twin-choke carburettors, distributor ignition, wet sump lubrication

Displacement

1570 cc (78x82 mm)

Power and torque

103 hp at 6000 rpm – 14.2 kgm at 3000 rpm

Transmission

Rear-wheel drive, single dry-plate clutch, five speeds + reverse

Chassis

Pressed steel unitary construction

Bodywork

Coupé (Bertone)

Suspension

Front: independent, wishbones, coil springs, hydraulic dampers, anti-roll bar

Rear: live axle, upper triangular element, trailing arms, hydraulic dampers

Brakes

Hydraulically actuated and assisted discs all round

Dimensions

Wheelbase: 2350 mm, Length: 4080 mm, Width: 1580 mm, Height: 1290 mm

Dry Weight

950 Kg

Maximum speed

180 kph

Cars produced

22,671

When the Giulia TI was presented in 1962, the "old" Giulietta bodies were immediately made available in Sprint and Spider forms updated with the 1600 engine. This temporary solution meant that the full range was maintained while the new cars were being developed. Three was not long to wait, at least for the coupé: ahead of its official launch at the Frankfurt Motor Show, the Giulia Sprint GT was presented to the press on the 9TH of September 1963 in the new Arese factory, in which it was to be the first car to be assembled.

The starting point was the Giulia TI, but the wheelbase was shortened to 2350 mm and the power output of the 1570 cc twin-cam was increased to 6000 rpm, sufficient to propel the slim car to 179 kph. The principal modification consisted of the adoption of individual induction with two twin-choke carburettors. This feature allowed outright performance to be improved along with greater flexibility and better pick-up. Thanks to long testing sessions, the suspension configuration was uprated in line with the improved performance, as were the brakes, with discs being fitted all round from the outset. Another major novelty was the bodywork, designed by the very young Giorgetto Giugiaro for Bertone: a sleek and sporting coupé with a high, aggressive front end, characterised by an unusual "scalino" or step along the leading edge of the bonnet, a kind of long, thin air intake with an unmistakeable appearance. The tail was truncated, but perfectly integrated with the lines of the car. The Cx value was slightly higher than that of the record-breaking saloon, but the reduced frontal compensated for the inferior drag coefficient, guaranteeing class-leading performance. The interior was spacious and airy, with a simple design and a very low and sporting seating position. The car was homologated as a 2+2 and offered a high level of comfort. Among the aspect that attracted most criticism were the noise level, despite the enticing sound of the engine, and the excessive simplicity of the trim, which was redressed to a point with the "Lusso Bertone" version that boasted perforated leather upholstery and metallic paint.

The role of the car went well beyond that of the single model: the Giulia Sprint GT was the forefather of a line of versions that only drew to a close in the mid-Seventies with the 2000 GTV and was to range from the economical GT 1300 Junior to the legendary Giulia Sprint GTA. The merit lay with the sporting and elegant coachwork and excellent driveability, with performance that in many respects was well ahead of that of many rivals.

The subsequent presentation of the GTA, more suited to competition, greatly restricted the sporting career of the Sprint GT, over 22,000 examples of which were to be produced.

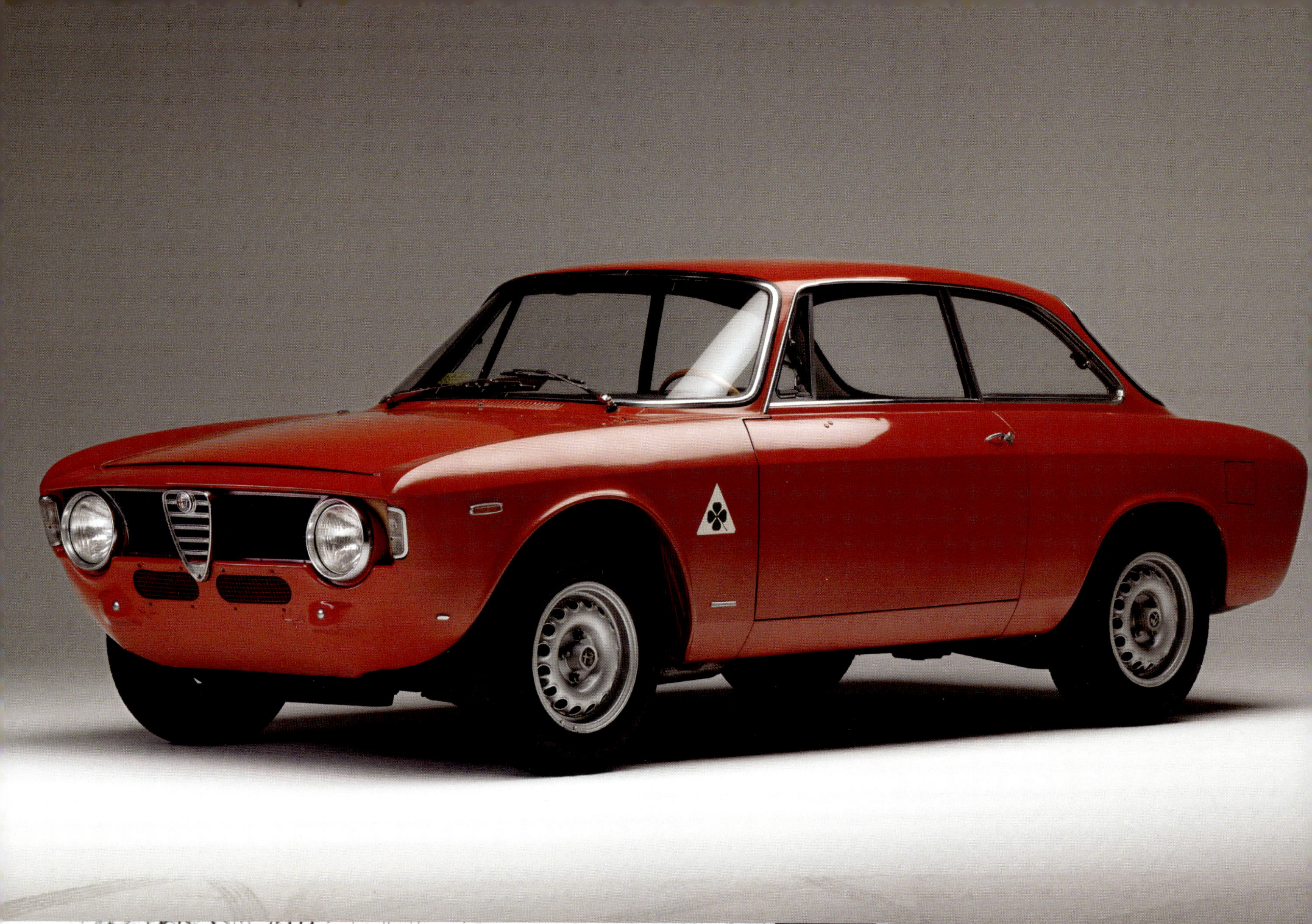

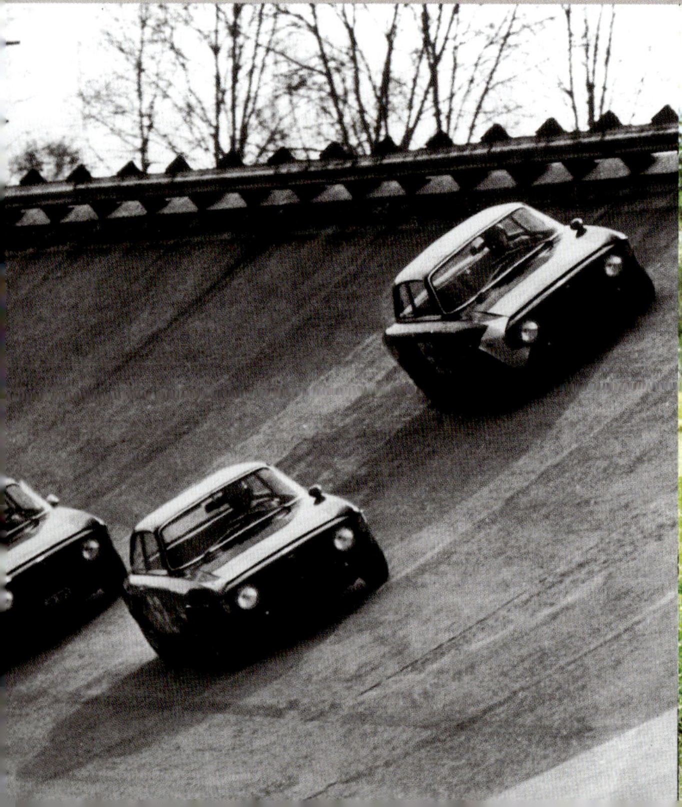

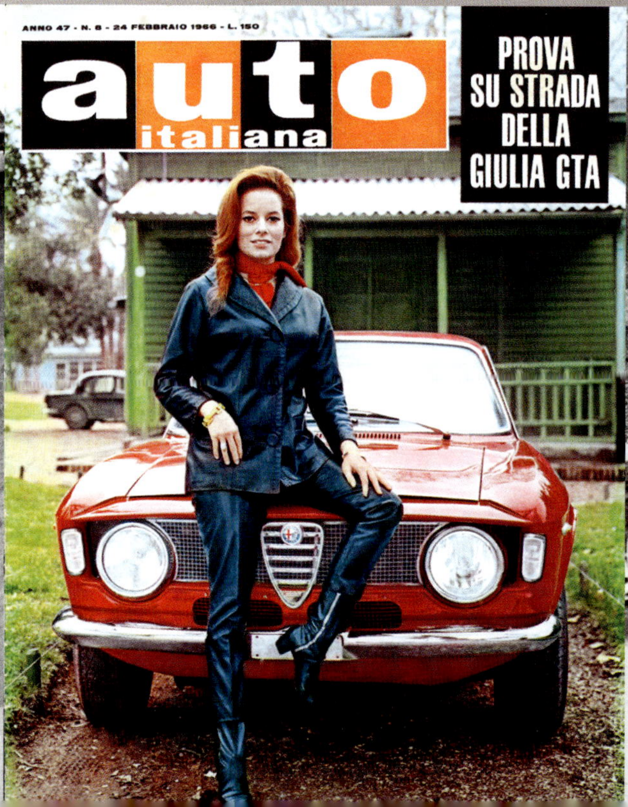
ANNO 47 - N. 8 - 24 FEBBRAIO 1966 - L. 150
auto italiana
PROVA SU STRADA DELLA GIULIA GTA

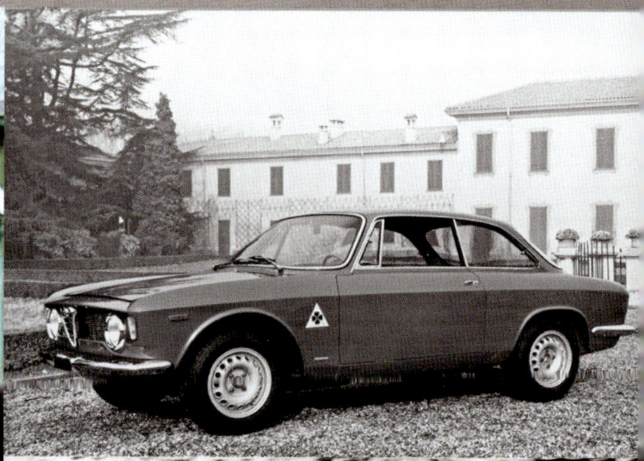

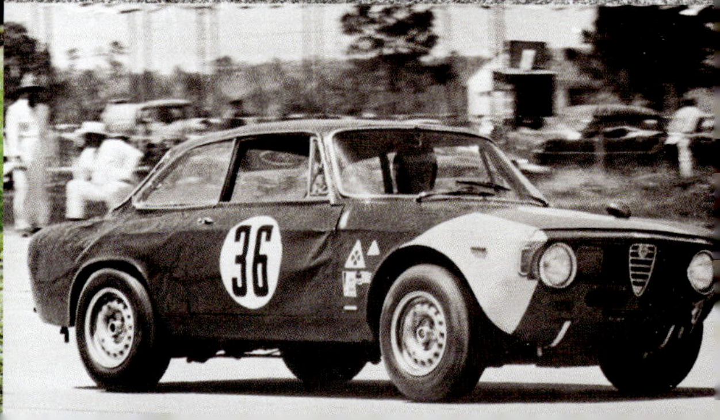
36

Giulia Sprint GTA

"A" FOR "ALLEGGERITA": A WIN EVERY DAY FOR THE EVERYDAY CAR.

Engine

Front, longitudinal, vertical, straight-four, block and head in light alloy, two valves per cylinder, two duplex chain-driven overhead camshafts. Two twin-choke carburettors, distributor ignition, wet sump lubrication

Displacement

1570 cc (78x82 mm)

Power and torque

115 hp at 6000 rpm

Transmission

Rear-wheel drive, single dry-plate clutch, five speeds + reverse

Chassis

Pressed steel unitary construction, lighy alloy panels

Bodywork

Coupé (Bertone)

Suspension

Front: independent, wishbones, hydraulic dampers, anti-roll bar

Rear: live axle, upper triangular element, trailing arms, hydraulic dampers

Brakes

Hydraulically actuated and assisted discs all round

Dimensions

Wheelbase: 2350 mm, Length: 4080 mm, Width: 1580 mm, Height: 1315 mm

Weight

745 Kg (dry)

Maximum speed

185 kph

Cars produced

500

Among the Alfa Romeos of the 1960s that left the longest-lasting memories in the minds of enthusiasts, the Giulia Sprint GTA is probably one of the most important. It annihilated its rivals in races and was a highly important advertising tool, with its lines that were almost identical to those of the production GT. And it was precisely for this reason that the powers-that-be decided, despite their success, to stop development work on the Giulia TZ and TZ2 in favour of a new car. While the TZ and TZ2 were in fact prototypes, designed purely for racing, the GTA on the other hand looked very similar to the cars that customers could find at their local dealers. Thus every win was immediately associated with the "everyday car" with obvious benefits in terms of advertising.

So the choice fell on the Group 2 Touring class, for which the manufacture of at least 500 road cars was necessary to obtain homologation. The Giulia Sprint GTA was presented at the Amsterdam Motor Show in 1965. The "A" in GTA stood for "Alleggerita" (lightened) to remind people of the most significant modification that had been made to the production Sprint GT: the steel bodywork was replaced with extremely light alloy panels (Peraluman 25). Thanks also to the removal of sound deadening material, the simplification of the trim and the use of 14" Campagnolo magnesium wheels, a weight saving of 205 kg was made for a total of 745 kg compared to the 950 kg of the road-going Sprint GT.

Another modification concerned the engine: the twin-cam 1570 cc was given a twin spark head, a design that made use of the largest possible valves without the inconvenience of a spark plug at the centre of the combustion chamber. The adoption of two side-mounted spark plugs allowed the engineers to go from the 35 and 31 mm diameter valves used on the Giulia Sprint GT to diameter of 40.5 and 36.5 on the GTA, which at the same time brought an improvement in the propagation of the flame front. The power output increased to 115 hp with a top speed of over 185 kph.

These figures were just a starting point however: after the official race tuning carried out by Autodelta, the maximum power increased beyond 170 hp. The GTA was immediately successful in races and boasts a remarkably impressive palmares, with victories for both the works team and the privateers who often turned to external tuners: as well as the three consecutive wins in the European Touring Car Challenge series from 1966 to 1968, there were dozens of National Championship wins and hundreds of individual races in every corner of the world against rivals often using cars powered by much bigger engines.

The car on display in the Museum is still set up for road use and only differs from the Sprint GT in certain details: simpler door handles, a lighter shield grille, air intakes at the front, alloy wheels and purpose made interior trim are the main ones. The modifications carried out by the tuners were much more conspicuous: first and foremost the removal of the bumpers.

GT 1600 Junior Z

VARIATION ON A THEME: A SLEEK AND SIMPLE ZAGATO SPECIAL

Engine

Front, longitudinal, vertical, straight-four, block and head in light alloy, two valves per cylinder, two duplex chain-driven overhead camshafts. Two twin-choke carburettors, distributor ignition, wet sump lubrication

Displacement

1570 cc (78x82 mm)

Power and torque

109 hp at 6000 rpm

Transmission

Rear-wheel drive, hydraulically actuated single dry-plate clutch, five speeds + reverse

Chassis

Pressed steel unitary construction

Bodywork

Coupé (Zagato)

Suspension

Front: independent, wishbones, oblique arms, coil springs, hydraulic dampers, anti-roll bar

Rear: live axle, upper triangular element, trailing arms, coil springs, hydraulic dampers, anti-roll bar

Brakes

Dual circuit with servo, discs all round

Dimensions

Wheelbase: 2250 mm, Length: 4000 mm, Width: 1550 mm, Height: 1280 mm

Weight

950 Kg

Maximum speed

190 kph

Cars produced

402

Alfa Romeo and Zagato, two names, two marques that together created some of the most emblematic cars in the history of Alfa and motoring in general. Milestones in this long partnership were the unbeatable 6C 1500's and 1750's in their various guises, which appeared during the Twenties and Thirties, the 1900 SS Zagato in the second half of the Fifties and last of all the various Giulietta SZ, 2600 SZ, Giulia TZ and TZ2's of the Sixties. Right at the end of that decade, at the Turin Motor Show in 1969, Zagato decided to make a more sporty and aggressive version of the GT 1300 Junior (1966) and after working on the shortened wheelbase chassis of the Junior 1300 produced a nimble and feisty coupé, a 2-seater, distinguished by a radiator grille and four headlights covered in a single piece of Plexiglas but in particular by the upper body connected directly to the rear end by means of a steeply inclined rear window in the so-called fastback manner. Zagato added the inevitable Z to the name of the car but Zagato's real signature was the rigorously truncated tail section where conspicuous rectangular rear lighting units were fitted.

The GT 1300 Junior Z was not as successful as had been hoped with only 1100 being sold in three years, but in 1972, once again at the Turin Motor Show, Zagato reprised the theme with the GT 1600 Junior Z. At first sight it looked as though the new model was just an update of the previous one, but in fact this was a completely new car. The new coupé was no longer based on the Spider's chassis, as had been the case with the earlier car, but on that of the GT and now had an overall length of 4 metres (10 cm more than the 1300 Junior). If there were fewer differences at the front end of the car (although more prominent wheel arches and heftier bumpers could be seen) the rear end featured a less drastically truncated tail, lighting units of a different size and shape, and the end of the exhaust pointing downwards as on the Alfetta of the same period.

Even though it would be true to say that according to Zagato's longstanding tradition, in the case of this car too, comfort and convenience were sacrificed in the name of sports performance, it has to be recognised that the interior fittings of the GT 1.6 Junior Z were less spartan than before, the wooden three-spoked steering wheel being an example.

The main innovation from a mechanical perspective was the use of the four-cylinder, twin-cam 1570 cc engine, which gave 110 hp at 6000 rpm. With this extra power, the car could now reach 190 kph, a 7-8 kph improvement over the Bertone with standard bodywork. The perhaps excessively futuristic lines and the improved performance were not a sufficient trade-off against a considerably higher price (2,620,000 Lire compared to 2,110,000) and the two fewer seats, which restricted sales of the 1600 to only 402 cars.

VELOCITÀ

VELOCITÀ

Nino Vaccarella

MY ALFA

My first race was at the wheel of a Fiat, then came Lancias, Maseratis, many Ferraris, Abarths and a few drives with foreign works teams such as Porsche and Matra. However, in my career as a driver there is a special place for Alfa Romeo and its men, first and foremost the engineer Carlo Chiti, the Tuscan with blood as hot as a Sicilian.

I won a lot with Alfa Romeo and, perhaps, we could or should have won even more. It is not this this that I regret, as what I carry with me from my years in "rosso Alfa" is above all the atmosphere of the group, of a team, of men with whom I worked and got on well. When racing and otherwise.

Neither has the knowledge that I raced for one of the most important manufacturers in automotive history ever left me. When I was still very young, the Portello had already produced the beautiful Alfettas of the first two Formula 1 World Championships with drivers of the calibre of Nino Farina and Juan Manuel Fangio. That marque which other champions before them had carried to success around the world: Campari, Nuvolari, Varzi. Italians like me, with that Italian pride that at a certain point in my career I decided to display on my white helmet with a simple but unmistakeable tricolour stripe. Look, it's Nino Vaccarella, the Italian driver in the Alfa. This was the message I was trying to transmit to the people who saw me racing, distinguishing myself through the helmet rather than the number of my car. White, red and green, a simple of belonging, for both me and for Alfa.

And I also proud to have had the privilege of writing unforgettable chapters in the sporting history of Alfa Romeo. Chapters written in red ink and narrating victories such as those in two editions of the Targa Florio in 1971 and 1975. The last of a wonderful era and no longer possible in the motorsport of today.

For that win in '71, one of the last that was valid for the World Championship, I was paired with a Dutchman who grew up on bread and GTAs, Tonie Hezemans, sent to make his bones in sports car racing with me. My first three laps were the first hammer blows in a charge to victory in a race that I hadn't made my own for all too many years (I had won my last Targa in 1965 with the Ferrari 275 P2 and many others had escaped me in the years that followed). When I got back behind the wheel of the 33/3 however, I didn't find it where it should have been, out in front, where I'd left it, but we nonetheless managed to snatch victory.

And yet, many years after the fact, I think that my contribution to Alfa was not so much in gear-changing speed, driving

VELOCITÀ

talent and, in the Targa at least, a perfect knowledge of the circuit. Chiti and his group were for me fellow adventurers, men to be helped in any way I could. And that included searching out the best accommodation for the entire team when we were racing in Sicily. It was not part of my contract, but that way we would all be winners. And, as ever, with a little luck this too would help us to keep on winning.

Just as when, four years later in 1945, at over 40 years of age and a father two years earlier, Alfa came calling again and I was ready. There was also the curiosity of experiencing first hand the latest evolution of a project born many years earlier and to which I had also made my contribution. The final version of the 33, the TT 12 was no disappointment and I won again together with Arturo Merzario.

That was, however, the last, glorious episode in a story that had begun long before, in the late spring of 1966 when the young Enrico Pinto and I left Sicily for Trieste with a robust GTA 1600 to take part in the Jolly Hotels Rally. Taking turns at the wheel according to a programme developed with Ingegnere Chiti, who saw me driving on tracks such as Siracusa, Vallelunga and Monza, the first victory with Alfa soon arrived.

The GTA was an excellent car, but clearly the Biscione's sports cars and prototypes I was to have the opportunity to drive in later years were something else entirely. The 33/2, 33/3 and 33 TT12 were unforgettable cars for me, not just in the Targa Florio but also at Le Mans, the Nürburgring, Daytona, Sebring and Zeltweg and in victories at Pergusa, Imola and the Mugello.

Thinking about those years it is not just the cars and the machinery that come to mind, but also the names of drivers and friends with whom I shared joys and sorrows: from Ignazio Giunti to Nanni Galli or Andrea De Adamich to "foreigners" such as Rolf Stommelen, Tonie Hezemans and Udo Schutz.

All people who, like me, made their own contributions to making Alfa Romeo great over the course of those great years, weaving stories that would be difficult to repeat today.

I run through my memories and recollections still as vivid today as the events had happened yesterday and I find myself in the company of men who were all true professionals and were all very fast. Drivers who you would come up against the following Sunday on different tracks and with different marques but still with the same respect. They too, I am sure, conserve a piece of their stories consecrated to the shield with the Biscione.

CARROZZERIA TOURING MILANO
Superleggera

Birth of the **legend**

The heroic era of motoring: birth of the legend.
Under the insignia of the Quadrifoglio

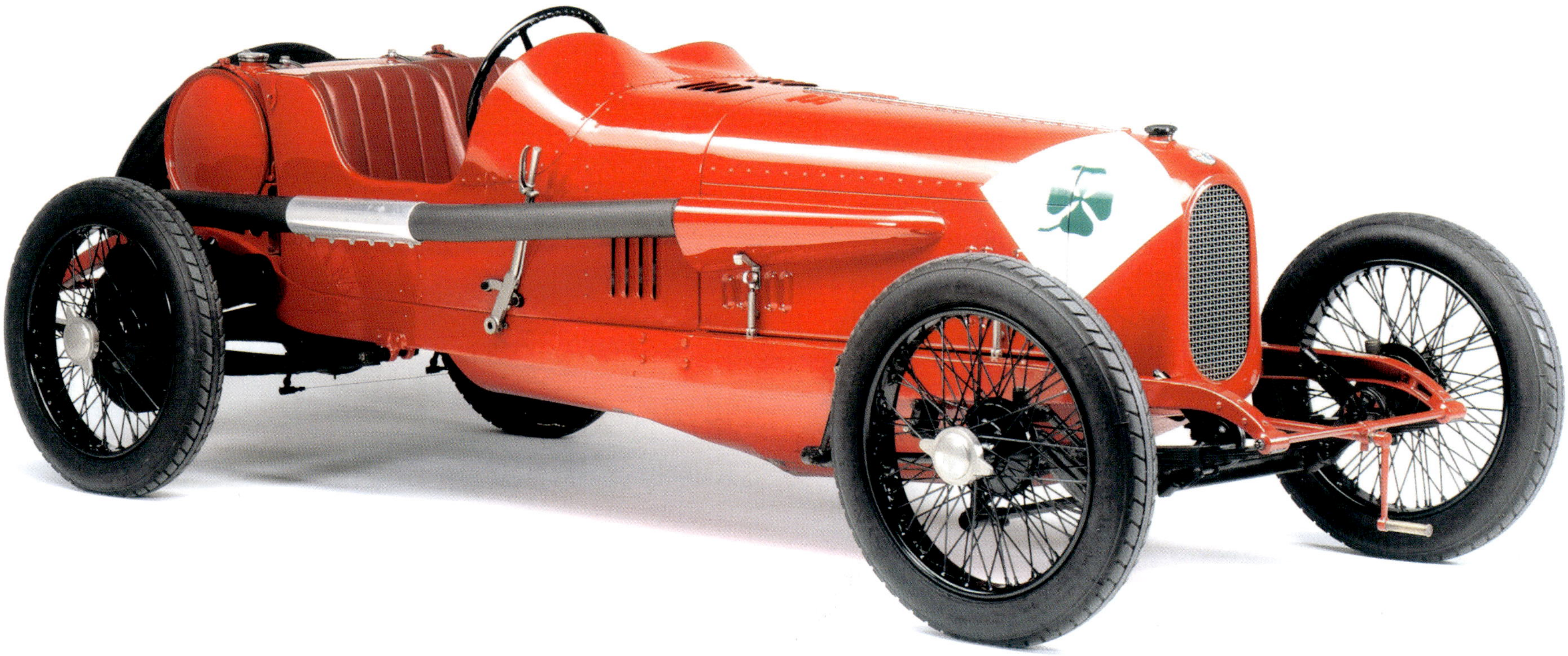

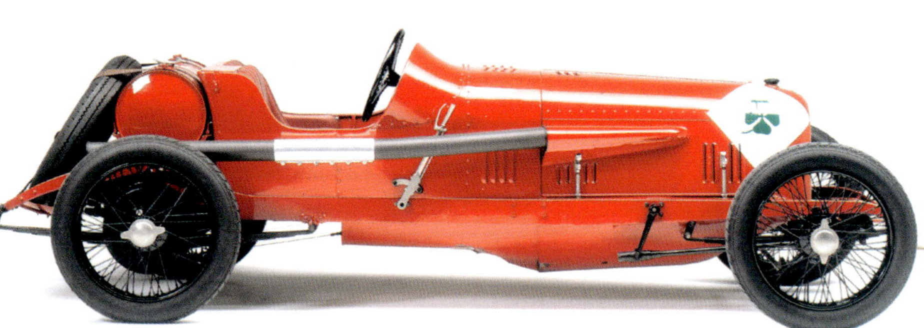

RL Targa Florio
A STUNNING VICTORY CONSECRATES THE MARQUE. UNDER THE INSIGNIA OF THE QUADRIFOGLIO

Engine

Front, longitudinal, vertical straight-six, block and cylinder head in cast iron. Two valves per cylinder, gear-driven lateral camshaft. Two carburettors, magneto ignition

Displacement

3154 cc (78x110 mm)

Power and torque

95 CV a 3800 rpm

Transmission

Rear-wheel drive, front –mounted, multiple dry-plate clutch, four speeds + reverse

Chassis

Pressed steel longerons and cross members

Bodywork

Spider corsa

Suspension

Front: rigid axle, semi-elliptical leaf springs, friction dampers

Rear: live axle, double semi-elliptical longitudinal leaf springs, friction dampers

Brakes

Mechanically actuated drums on the rear wheels

Dimensions

Length: 4050 mm - Wheelbase: 2880 mm
Height: 1200 mm

Weight

980 Kg

Maximum speed

157 kph

Cars produced

2

As early as 1922, shortly after the model's launch, work began on the definition of a version of the RL destined exclusively for competition, with motorsport once again enthusing the masses and stimulating constructors after the horrors of the First World War. The most evident modifications were the shortening of the wheelbase, the dual dampers at the rear, the spider open bodywork with two staggered seats to allow a narrower body and a barrel fuel tank. Under the skin the novelties were more substantial: diverse engines were developed for the various categories: the Sport version produced 90 hp and permitted at top speed of 150 kph. The block was also bored out to a displacement of 3154 cc, giving a power output of 95 hp that propelled the car's 980 kg to a maximum speed of 157 kph.

Following Ugo Sivocci's brilliant debut at the autumn GP in 1922, the marque had a major opportunity to catch the eye in the 1923 edition of the Targa Florio. Sivocci dominated the race, followed home by Ascari in a twin car to give Alfa Romeo the first of its 10 victories in the Sicilian race. In reality, Sivocci's feat was not without its unexpected episodes, as Vincenzo Florio himself recounted: "…on the fourth lap there 10 of the 17 cars that started were still in the race and at least five could aspire to victory. The excitement of the crowd for the arrival of the winner was at its height when Ascari's car appeared out of the hills. At the Cerda station corner Ascari's Alfa came to a stop with mechanic and driver desperately rummaging amongst the mechanical organs, trying to breathe life into the moribund engine. Dramatic minutes passed, mechanics arrived and finally the car restarted, but it was to cross the line with four extra people aboard. The stewards felt that this was inappropriate and Ascari was obliged to turn back. Not finding his own riding mechanic he grabbed a spectator who had found a way into the refuelling area, threw him into the car, set off again as far as the point where he had stopped and then crossed the line once again. By that time a number of minutes had passed and Ascari missed out on victory as Sivocci had swooped in to steal first place." A series of fortuitous circumstances that were to do justice to the decision to paint a Quadrifoglio, a four-leafed clover, on the bonnet. The car was immediately renamed as the "RL Targa Florio": the didactic reconstruction on display will be assembled with original mechanical components, together with an engine that was used in the 1923 Targa Florio, obtained in 1953 by Milan Polytechnic in exchange for a Giulietta Sprint power unit. The model was to enjoy many more major sporting triumphs. In 1924, two new engines were built with displacements of 3617 cc (125 hp, 180 kph), this time fitted in chassis with four disc brakes. Ascari was again to miss out on victory in the Targa Florio when he spun just a few metres from the finish.

Grand Prix Tipo P2

ALFA ROMEO - WORLD CHAMPION.
THE DAWN OF THE VITTORIO JANO ERA

Engine

Front, longitudinal vertical straight-eight, dual blocks and fixed heads in steel, two valves per cylinder, two gear-driven overhead camshafts. Twin carburettors, supercharger, magneto ignition

Displacement

1987 cc (61x85 mm)

Power and torque

155 hp at 5500 rpm

Transmission

Rear-wheel drive, front mounted multiple dry-plate clutch, four speeds + reverse

Chassis

Pressed steel longerons and cross members

Bodywork

GP

Suspension

Front: rigid axle, longitudinal semi-elliptical leaf springs, friction dampers

Rear: live axle, oblique semi-elliptical leaf springs, friction dampers

Brakes

Mechanically actuated drums

Dimensions

Wheelbase: 2630 mm, Length: 3950 mm (pointed tail), Width: 1550 mm, height: 1180 mm

Weight

750 Kg

Maximum speed

225 kph

Cars produced

6

In the early Twenties the public at races was wildly enthusiastic, with huge crowds attending the GP, and as a result this had a substantial effect on sales. So and after the meteoric success of the GPR, Vittorio Jano left Fiat and joined Alfa Romeo in October 1923. He was personally appointed by Nicola Romeo to design the P2. "Listen, I am not expecting you to make a car which will beat all others, but I'd like one which will make us look good, so that we can make an identity card for this factory, then later, when it has a name, later we'll make the car."

Jano's first move was to make design a two-litre inline straight eight cylinder engine, with a double crankcase, fixed steel heads and a gear-driven twin-cam valvetrain gear. The obvious superiority of supercharged engines, of which Jano's Fiat had been one of the first, encouraged the designer to fit a Roots supercharger to the P2, now fitted equipped with an ante-litteram intercooler to stop prevent the petrol of the day catching fire, a finned "lung", fitted to the bottom of the car which that was able to reduce the temperature by a further 7-8°C. The power output was 140 hp at 5500 rpm. The chassis was much more traditional, consisting of a ladder-type layoutwith longerons and cross-members, while the bodywork, with two staggered seats, could be fitted with an aerodynamic tail section or a trunk with two spare wheels. The overall weight of the car was 750 kg.

The first car example was assembled on the 2ND of June 1924 and was immediately tested at the Portello by Campari and Ascari, after which it was painted and taken to Monza. A few days later, the car had made its debut in the Circuito di Cremona, won by Ascari at an average speed of 158 kph. The victory at Lyons in the European GP in 1924 was the beginning of a long period when the car was virtually unbeatable, culminating at the end of 1925 with winning the first World Championship for Grand Prix cars.

The P2 was relegated to minor races as a result of changes to the rules in 1926 that limited engine displacement to 1.5 litres. The P2 car started to compete at the top againreturned to competition during the 1930 season when the pragmatic manager Prospero Gianferrari bought back three of the cars examples and thoroughly redeveloped them, employing some of the new technical innovations used on the 6C 1750. The result was an extremely powerful but ill-tempered car. It was so bad that Campari, after a few test laps refused to drive it as he was exhausted and had even torn the seat of his trousers too.

The ageing P2's greatest success came in the Targa Florio in 1930, won by Varzi, despite the fact that a bracket supporting the spare wheel (fixed to the petrol tank) caused a leak and the beginnings of a fire which was extinguished by the co-driver during the race using the seat cushions! The glorious P2 took part in a race for the last time in Brno on the 28TH of September 1930. It then became part of the legend.

Alfa Romeo was to keep two examples in the Experimental Department, one a 1925 model and the other in 1930 trim. The latter was subsequently donated to the Museo Nazionale dell'Automobile in Turin while the former was on show at the Museo della Scienza e della Tecnica in Milan through to 1958 and before being restored and added to the Alfa museum's collection in 1964.

6C 1500 Super Sport

THE FIRST MILLE MIGLIA.
THE FIRST OF VITTORIO JANO'S LEGENDARY STRAIGHT-SIXES

Engine

Front, longitudinal, vertical straight-six, block and head in cast iron, two valves per cylinder, twin overhead camshafts, layshaft and bevel gear drive. Carburettor, supercharger, distributor ignition, wet sump lubrication

Displacement

1487 cc (62x82 mm)

Power and torque

76 hp at 4800 rpm

Transmission

Rear-wheel drive, front mounted multiple dry-plate clutch, four speeds + reverse

Chassis

Pressed steel longerons and cross members

Bodywork

Spider corsa

Suspension

Front: rigid axle, longitudinal semi-elliptical leaf springs, friction dampers

Rear: rigid axle, longitudinal semi-elliptical leaf springs, friction dampers

Brakes

Mechanically-actuated drums

Dimensions

Wheelbase: 2920 mm, Length: 4000 mm, Width: 1630 mm, height: 1350 mm

Weight

860 Kg

Maximum speed

140 kph

Cars produced

31 (6C 1500 SS, 1928-1929)

In the mid-Twenties Alfa Romeo recognised the need to create a model that would open up new market segments and interest the middle class motorists who were not necessarily seeking an elite car but rather an "easier" vehicle that still offered sparkling performance. The ever prolific Vittorio Jano responded to these demands with the 6C 1500, the chassis of which with oppressed steel longerons and cross members was previewed at the Paris Motor Show in 1925. Customers had to wait for the new car to go into production equipped with a 1487 cc straight-six (44 hp at 4200 rpm) until 1927, but success was assured despite this delay.

The 6C 1500 immediately proved to be a versatile car that in just a few years gave a whole new look to the Portello-based company's catalogue. As early as 1928, in concomitance with the launch of the second series, the 6C 1500 Sport made its debut as an uprated version of the base model, with the straight-six now delivering 54 hp at 4400 rpm. That same year, the Super Sport, the Super Sport Compressore and the Super Sport Compressore Testa Fissa all made their debuts. The first offered 60 hp at 4800 rpm (125 kph) thanks to a higher compression ratio and a different carburettor. When a Roots-type supercharger was added to this same mechanical configuration the power output rose to 76 hp at 4800 rpm, with a maximum speed of 140 kph. On the basis of this last version, a variant was developed with a fixed cylinder head and a power output of 84 hp at 5000 rpm (155 kph).

The second Coppa delle Mille Miglia was held on the 31ST of March and 1st of April 1928. Alfa Romeo had taken part in the 1927 edition and the Portello team returned with six cars for drivers and mechanics of the calibre of Giovan Battista Guidotti and, above all, Giuseppe Campari who shared with Giulio Ramponi the cockpit of a 6C 1500 MMS (Mille Miglia Speciale). This model was equipped with the 1487 cc straight-six with a Roots-type supercharger that allowed it to deliver a maximum power output of over 80 hp 5000 rpm. It was to be this very car, specially prepared for the Brescian race and initially destined for Marinoni and Guidotti, that dominated the second edition of the Mille Miglia. With the threat of the three works Bugattis driven by Gastone Brilli Peri, Pietro Bordino and Tazio Nuvolari having evaporated in the early stages, by the Rome checkpoint Campari and Ramponi were in the lead, a position they were to retain through to the chequered flag in Brescia, finishing the race in first place overall at an average speed of 84.128 kph.

As well as being a successful racing car, between 1927 and 1929 the 6C 1500 in its various guises brought Alfa Romeo considerable commercial satisfaction with no less than 1,064 examples being sold, a very respectable figure for the time.

The 6C 1500 Super Sport was added to the museum's collection in 1966.

Pronti per la 1000 Miglia
1930

6C 1750 GS

AN AVERAGE OF OVER 100. AN ICONIC CAR FOR A TIMELESS FEAT

Engine

Front, longitudinal, vertical straight-six, block and fixed head in cast iron, two valves per cylinder, twin overhead camshafts, layshaft and bevel gear drive. Single twin-choke carburettor, supercharger, distributor ignition, wet sump lubrication

Displacement

1752 cc (65x88 mm)

Power and torque

102 hp at 5000 rpm

Transmission

Rear-wheel drive, front mounted multiple dry-plate clutch, four speeds + reverse

Chassis

Pressed steel longerons and cross members

Bodywork

Spider Corsa

Suspension

Front: rigid axle, longitudinal semi-elliptical leaf springs, friction dampers

Rear: rigid axle, longitudinal semi-elliptical leaf springs, friction dampers

Brakes

Mechanically actuated rear drums

Dimensions

Wheelbase: 2745 mm, Length: 3652 mm, Width: -, Height: -

Weight

840 Kg

Maximum speed

170 kph

Cars produced

6

The 6C 1750 was the logical next step after the 6C 1500 that had been such a commercial and sporting success for Alfa Romeo. The new car was as versatile as the model that had come before and would become one of the cornerstones not just of the history of the company but of the Italian car as well. The car was presented in three versions, Turismo, Sport and Super Sport when it made its debut at the International Motor Show in Rome in 1929.

The straight-six fitted to the basic model now had a displacement of 1752 cc (65x88 mm) while the maximum power output was now 46 hp at 4000 rpm. A power output that in the Sport version, equipped with double overhead camshafts, rose to 55 hp at 4400 rpm and reached no less than 64 hp at 4500 rpm with the Super Sport and 85 hp with the SS, which was equipped with a Roots supercharger. The six Super Sport cars that were supplied with a fixed cylinder head, cast in one piece with the cylinders developed an impressive 95 hp at 5000 rpm. Between 1929 and 1933, 2,579 examples of the 6C 1750 were sold in various versions. Some of the best-known coachbuilders of the time clothed the chassis, from Castagna to the Stabilimenti Farina, from Touring to Zagato. However the top of the range was the 6C 1750 Gran Sport, introduced in 1930 as a sports derivative of the 1750 Gran Turismo, replacing the Super Sport model. The main difference with the GS lay in the fuel supply, where a Roots supercharger made by Alfa Romeo was fitted coaxially to the crankshaft and a twin-choke carburettor was fitted to the left-hand side. The power output was once more about 85 hp at 4500 rpm, increasing to 102 hp at 5000 rpm on the Testa Fissa or Fixed Head version of which once again only 6 were made.

As was the case with the 6C 1500 Super Sport, for the 1750 Gran Sport too the Mille Miglia proved to be the ideal place for the car to show off its talents. After the second consecutive win by the well-established Campari-Ramponi pairing in the 1929 edition aboard a 6C 1750 SS, for the fourth Mille Miglia in 1930 Alfa Romeo fielded an even more impressive line-up of men and machines including Campari-Marinoni, Pirola-Guatta, Varzi-Canavesi, Ghersi-Cortese and Mazzotti-Maggi. As if that were not enough, alongside the works Alfas there were other cars entered by the new Scuderia Ferrari team.

The main interest in the race was the closely-fought struggle between Nuvolari and Varzi, with the former setting off ten minutes behind his rival and therefore able to check his progress at the various timing points. This undoubted advantage helped Nuvolari establish an overall lead by the Florence checkpoint.

Legend has it — and it really is just a legend — that Nuvolari overtook Varzi with his headlights off (to trick his rival) near Peschiera at dawn on the 13TH of April 1930. By then they were racing in daylight and not having headlights on would have served no useful purpose, but this hardly detract from Nuvolari and Guidotti's extraordinary endeavour as they swooped into the finish in Brescia after racing for 16 hours 18.59 minutes at a spectacular average speed of over 100 kph, 100.450 to be precise. A triumph.

The car in the collection today is similar to the 1750 GS that won the Mille Miglia in 1930. It was partly rebuilt with original spares of the period and was added to the museum's collection in 1971.

Esso le super carburant  
28
23ª TARGA FLORIO
8 MAGGIO 1932
PIRELLI
PNEUS PIRELLI

8C 2300 Monza

BORN AS A GT, GOES ON TO CHALLENGE THE GRANDS PRIX. CAMPARI AND NUVOLARI CONFIRMS ITS PLACE AMONG THE GREATS

Engine

Front, longitudinal vertical straight-eight, dual blocks and heads in light alloy, two valves per cylinder, two gear-driven overhead camshafts. Twin carburettors, supercharger, magneto ignition, wet sump lubrication

Displacement

2336 cc (65x88 mm)

Power and torque

165 hp at 5400 rpm

Transmission

Rear-wheel drive, front mounted multiple dry-plate clutch, four speeds + reverse

Chassis

Pressed steel longerons and cross members

Bodywork

GP

Suspension

Front: rigid axle, longitudinal semi-elliptical leaf springs, friction dampers

Rear: rigid axle, longitudinal semi-elliptical leaf springs, friction dampers

Brakes

Mechanically-actuated drums

Dimensions

Wheelbase: 2650 mm, Length: 3840 mm, Width: 1380 mm, Height: 1200 mm

Weight

920 Kg

Maximum speed

210 kph

Cars produced

10

Another model destined over the years to become one of the marque's most symbolic cars appeared in the 1931 edition of the Portello's catalogue: the 8C 2300, fitted with a new straight-eight 2336cc engine. This car, which inherited the 6C 1750's chassis, was available in a Lungo (3100 mm) and Corto versions (2750 mm) and principally owed its fame to its success in competitions.

The 8C 2300's in fact dominated the classic Sarthe 24 Hours from 1931 to 1934 unchallenged, while in the same period they also achieved impressive results in the Grand Prix class. A case in point was the 1931 Italian Grand Prix at Monza, when Giuseppe Campari, assisted by Tazio Nuvolari (who in fact started the race in another Alfa Romeo shared with Baconin Borzacchini, but after the car was forced to retire, shared the driving with Campari until the finish) won the race in their 8C 2300 which, in honour of that victory, was henceforth called the Monza.

In the Monza the straight-eight engine, composed of two blocks of four cylinders with a light alloy fixed cylinder head and double overhead camshafts, gave a maximum power output of 165 hp at 5400 rpm and a top speed of around 210 kph. Compared to the 8C 2300 with the short 2750mm chassis, the Monza's chassis was shortened by a further 10 cm and on this was built a "almost" two-seater body (the unfortunate passenger's seat was, to say the least, makeshift) and it was intended to use the car both in the Sport category (where it was equipped with narrow cycle-wings) and in the Grands Prix (stripped of the mudguards).

In that first season's racing, 1931, the 8C 2300 Monzas, together with the 8C 2300 MM's secured a number of major victories, including Tazio Nuvolari's win in the Targa Florio on the 10TH of May. However, in 1932 Alfa's top model for racing was now the new Tipo B, again fitted with a straight-eight 2654 cc engine, which soon became the car to beat in Grands Prix. At that point it seemed as though the racing career of the 2300 Monza had come to an end, but partly as a result of Alfa Romeo deciding to withdraw from competitions, as least as a works team, at the beginning of the 1933 season, both the Monza and the Tipo B had a new lease of life racing under the Scuderia Ferrari banner. The former, with the engine bored out to 68 mm, became the 2600 Monza and continued to race and of course, to win.

A good example was the 1934 Mille Miglia when the Scuderia Ferrari fielded several 8C 2600 Monzas driven, amongst others, by Louis Chiron, but above all by Achille Varzi paired with Amedeo Bignami. It was they who won the race that finished with eight Alfa Romeos in the first ten places: four 8C 2600 Monzas, two 2300 Monzas, one standard 8C 2300 and one old but still competitive 6C 1750. Not bad at all for cars that were supposed to have been pensioned off two seasons before.

The 8C 2300 Monza on display in the Alfa Romeo museum was partially rebuilt using original spares in the mid-Seventies.

8C 2300 Le Mans

LONG WHEELBASE, FOUR SEATS AND CORSA MECHANICALS FOR THE QUEEN OF LE MANS

Engine

Front, longitudinal vertical straight-eight, dual blocks and heads in light alloy, two valves per cylinder, two gear-driven overhead camshafts. Carburettor, supercharger, distributor ignition, wet sump lubrication

Displacement

2336 cc (65x88mm)

Power and torque

155 hp at 5200 rpm

Transmission

Rear-wheel drive, front mounted multiple dry-plate clutch, four speeds + reverse

Chassis

Pressed steel longerons and cross members

Bodywork

Torpedo

Suspension

Front: rigid axle, longitudinal semi-elliptical leaf springs, friction dampers

Rear: rigid axle, longitudinal semi-elliptical leaf springs, friction dampers

Brakes

Mechanically-actuated drums

Dimensions

Wheelbase: 3100 mm, Length: 4400 mm, Height: 1350 mm

Weight

1000 Kg

Maximum speed

200 kph

Cars produced

9

1931. The great adventure, promoted by the energetic director Prospero Gianferrari, began when the team "occupied" the Hotel Moderne, the historic headquarters of the "Bentley Boys" who for years had been unbeaten at Le Mans: three 8C 2300 cars, two practice cars, a lorry, seven drivers, thirteen mechanics and one race director.

A special version of the 8C 2300 was made specifically with the French marathon in mind: a long wheelbase and four-seater bodywork as specified in the regulations, a 155 hp engine derived from the Spider Corsa and racing mechanicals.

That first year the cars that lined up were the Campari-Marinoni and Minoia-Zehender works cars plus the privately-owned but works-assisted example belonging to Lord Howe, who was paired with Sir Henry Birkin. Lord Howe, to show that he was competing with the official Alfa Romeo team, even had his car painted red, keeping just his overalls blue, his favourite racing colour. A red carnation on his cap matched the colour of the 8C that, at the end of the 24 Hours, won the race, a good 112 km ahead of Ivanowski-Stoffel's Mercedes, at a record average speed of 125.74 kph.

In 1932, there were a grand total of six 8C 2300's on the grid out of the 9 that had been built: the race was hard fought from the very first hour, entrancing the crowd and exhausting the cars, which over the course of the race started to shed pieces, including the mudguards and the windscreen, but managed to hold on for a one-two victory with Cortese-Guidotti finishing second to the victorious Sommer-Chinetti crew. In reality, the feat was all the more remarkable because Raymond Sommer had had to drive for 21 hours after his partner had been taken ill.

Paired with Nuvolari, Sommer dominated the race in 1933 too, at least until a leak in the petrol tank forced him to make an unforeseen stop. It was the mechanics of the Lewis-Rose-Richards team who, under the orders of Arthur Fox, solved the problem and repaired the leak with chewing-gum allowing the 8C 2300 not just to win the race, but to raise the record average speed to 137 kph.

In the 1934 edition too, an 8C 2300 by now officially called the Le Mans and driven by Phi-Phi Etancelin and Luigi Chinetti, was first across the finishing with a lead of 180 km over the second-placed car. In the meantime the car had been thoroughly updated, to the extent that it now developed 180 hp.

The example on display is the one that won at Le Mans in 1931 driven by Lord Howe and Sir Henry Birkin. After that Le Mans win it was bought by a private owner from Birkin's father. Birkin died as the result of an infection after he was burned on the arm by his car's exhaust pipe during the Tripoli Grand Prix in 1933. Kept for years in a tin mine in Nigeria, it was bought by Alfa Romeo and added to the museum's collection in 1966.

Gran Premio Tipo A

TWO CARS IN ONE. JANO'S FASCINATING
AND IMPOSSIBLE SINGLE-SEATER

Engine

Two front, longitudinal, vertical straight-sixes, block and fixed head in cast iron, two valves per cylinder, twin overhead camshafts, layshaft and bevel gear drive. Single twin-choke carburettor, supercharger, distributor ignition, wet sump lubrication

Displacement

1752 cc (65x88 mm) x 2

Power and torque

2 x 115 hp (230 hp) at 5200 rpm

Transmission

Rear-wheel drive, two front mounted multiple dry-plate clutches, 2 x three speeds + reverse

Chassis

Pressed steel longerons and cross members

Bodywork

GP

Suspension

Front: rigid axle, longitudinal semi-elliptical leaf springs, friction dampers

Rear: rigid axle, longitudinal semi-elliptical leaf springs, friction dampers

Brakes

Mechanically-actuated drums

Dimensions

Wheelbase: 2800 mm, Length: 4100 mm, Width: 1590 mm

Weight

930 Kg

Maximum speed

240 kph

Cars produced

4

In 1931, the International Racing Committee set up a European Formula Libre Championship with no limit on engine size and three races in the calendar, each lasting 10 hours. The newly-appointed director Prospero Gianferrari immediately announced Alfa's participation and at the same time asked Vittorio Jano to work out the best technical specification: unfortunately neither the 6C 1750 nor the new 8C 2300 were good enough for the level of a Championship that, according to Jano, would require cars capable of 210-220 kph.

Putting aside the idea of designing a new engine and mechanical parts from scratch, Jano suggested the bizarre solution of a car powered by two 6C 1750 GS supercharged 115 hp engines. The transmission was composed of two gearboxes in-unit with the engines, two transmission shafts and two differentials. The right-hand engine was to transmit power to the right wheel with the same set up on the left without any mechanical connection between the two.

Although it had a traditional chassis, the bodywork was unusual, fully faired around the cockpit with only the driver's head protruding through a circular opening as on an aeroplane. This feature was contested by the drivers, who complained that they were unable to see the front wheels while they were secretly afraid of being imprisoned in the car if it caught fire.

With its top speed of 240 kph and initial instability problems solved, the Tipo A was entered for the Italian Grand Prix. Unfortunately, during Saturday's practice session Luigi Arcangeli was killed in a dramatic accident: the car was unusable but a telegram from the fascist government ordered them to "race and win", obliging the engineers to prepare the spare car during the night. Tazio Nuvolari was able to start the race but was then forced to retire when one of the engines developed a fault.

Campari raced the Tipo A again on the 5TH of July in the Susa-Moncenisio: in the hairpin bends he had to turn off one of the engines and turn it on again on the straights. The advantage gained was immediately obvious, but during one of the off-on operations both of the engines flooded and the car had to be bump started, relegating Campari, who said diplomatically that he had had a "problem with the spark plugs", to fifth place.

In view of the 7TH Coppa Acerbo in Pescara scheduled for the 16TH of August, modifications were made to the Tipo A's lubrication system and it was fitted with two freewheels downstream of the gearboxes: Nuvolari and Campari set off and dominated the race, conquering the car's one and only victory laurels.

The four cars built in 1931 having been lost, in the early Seventies Luigi Fusi, the first curator of the museum, obtained funding to build a didactical replica: the two 6C 1750 engines were purchased at Asmara, other components were found in the Alfa stores, while all those parts which could not be found were made using the original drawings.

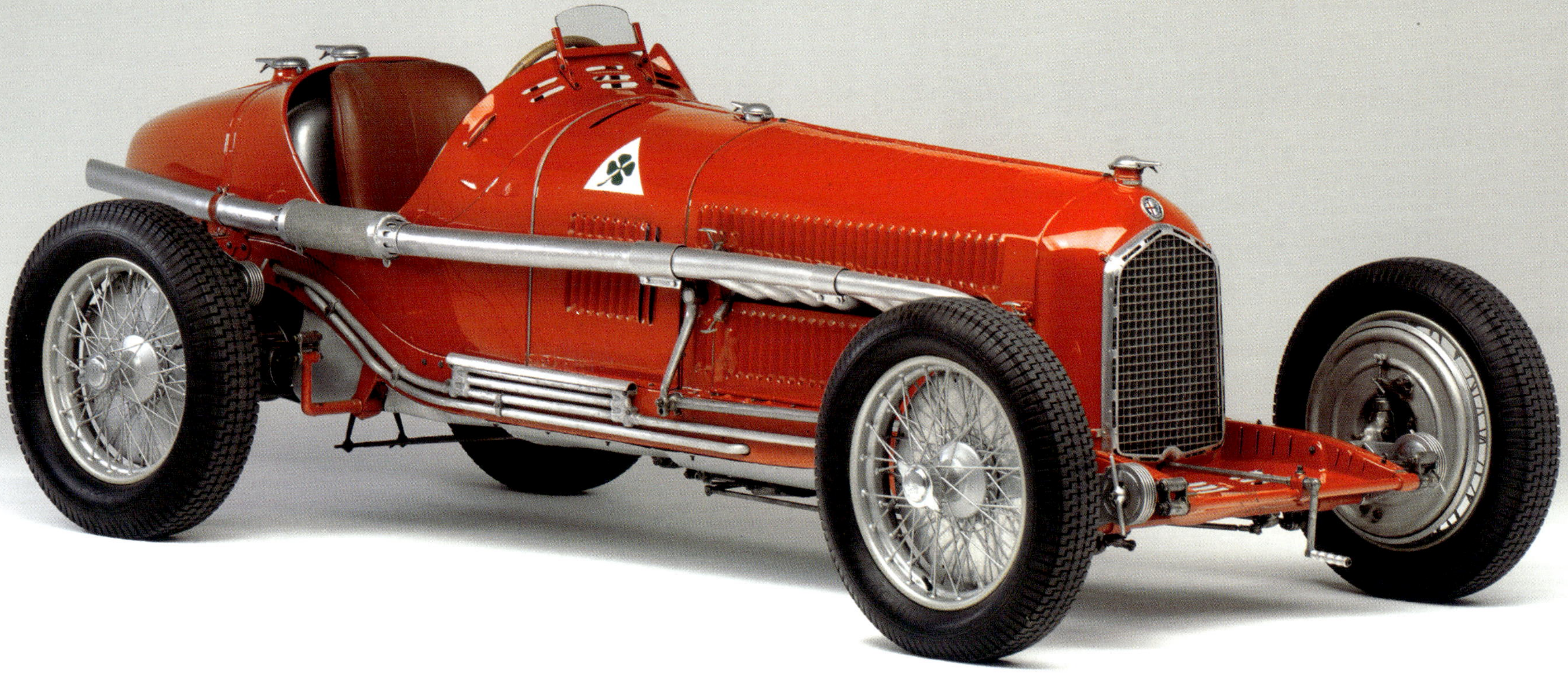

Gran Premio Tipo B

SLIM, NIMBLE AND UNBEATABLE. THE SINGLE-SEATER OF THE GREAT, FREQUENTLY IMPOSSIBLE CHALLENGES

Engine

Front, longitudinal vertical straight-eight, dual blocks and fixed heads in light alloy, two valves per cylinder, two gear-driven overhead camshafts. Two carburettors, two superchargers, magneto ignition

Displacement

2654 cc (65x100 mm)

Power and torque

215 hp at 5600 rpm

Transmission

Rear-wheel drive, V-configuration half-shafts, front mounted multiple dry-plate clutch, four speeds + reverse

Chassis

Pressed steel longerons and cross members

Bodywork

GP

Suspension

Front: rigid axle, longitudinal semi-elliptical leaf springs, friction dampers

Rear: rigid axle, longitudinal semi-elliptical leaf springs, friction dampers

Brakes

Mechanically-actuated drums

Dimensions

Wheelbase: 3840 mm, Length: 3840 mm, Width: 1380 mm, Height: 1165 mm

Weight

700 Kg

Maximum speed

232 kph

Cars produced

6

While the eccentric Tipo A had been a temporary solution to ensure that Alfa Romeo had a racing presence, the major project that Vittorio Jano was working on at the dawn of the 1930s was destined to leave an indelible mark on the history of the marque: the GP Tipo B.

The chassis with pressed steel longerons and cross members could be said to have been developed from the Tipo A, but the mechanical assemblies were all new: the engine was a straight-eight with a double engine block and light alloy fixed heads. Its double overhead camshafts were gear-driven with the gear train mounted between the blocks. The fuel system was fitted with two laterally mounted twin-lobe Roots superchargers and two single-choke carburettors. The unit had a displacement of 2654 cc and delivered a maximum power output of 215 hp, good for a top speed of 232 kph.

The transmission had a particularly unusual layout too: the differential was located immediately behind the gearbox, sending power to the rear wheels through two long half-shafts arranged in a V with two bevel gear pairs. This configuration meant that Jano was able to lower the car's centre of gravity by allowing the driver to sit lower in the car.

The car's debut came in the 1932 Italian Grand Prix, won by Nuvolari in what was becoming a tradition. That very was restored in 1966 and is on display in the museum today. Wins followed in the French Grand Prix, the first three places in the German Grand Prix, the Coppa Ciano, Coppa Acerbo, Circuito Principe di Piemonte and Monza. In 1933, Alfa Romeo, which had been sold to the IRI, withdrew from competition, the official reason being the Tipo B's "demonstrable invincibility". The cars did not race again until the Coppa Acerbo when they were handed over to the Scuderia Ferrari as the 8C 2300 Monzas were by then uncompetitive.

In 1934, the rules were changed and at the same time the field was expanded with the return of Mercedes and Auto Union to racing. The Tipo B was updated and given a wider body, a strengthened chassis and a revised engine, which now had a displacement of 2905 cc and gave 255 hp for 262 kph. After a positive start to the season, the team enjoyed alternating fortunes, while a new special aerodynamic body was created specially for the AVUS Grand Prix. It was designed by the engineer Cesare Pallavicino and tested on the Milano-Laghi autostrada and driven to victory by Guy Moll.

In 1935, the now dated Tipo B had its engine enlarged to 3165 cc, giving 265 hp and 275 kph; it was fitted with hydraulic brakes and Dubonnet independent front suspension. However, it was above all Nuvolari's courage that allowed it one last incredible win in the 1935 German Grand Prix at the legendary Nürburgring. The Flying Mantuan managed to snatch an impossible victory, so unlikely that the organizers, convinced that there would be a German winner, which they had already decided as form of propaganda, had trouble finding a record with the Italian national anthem.

Bimotore

TWO ENGINES NOT ENOUGH FOR VICTORY.
BUT EVERY RECORD IS BROKEN

Engine

One front and one rear longitudinal vertical straight-eight, dual blocks and fixed heads in light alloy, two valves per cylinder, two gear-driven overhead camshafts. Two carburettors, two superchargers x 2, magneto ignition

Displacement

3165 cc (71x100 mm) x 2

Power and torque

2 x 270 hp (540 hp) at 5400 rpm

Transmission

Rear-wheel drive, V-configuration half-shafts, front mounted multiple dry-plate clutch, three speeds + reverse

Chassis

Pressed steel longerons and cross members

Bodywork

GP

Suspension

Front: independent, wishbones, trailing arms, coil springs, hydraulic and friction dampers

Rear: independent, semi-elliptical longitudinal lea springs, dual friction dampers

Brakes

Hydraulically actuated drums all round

Dimensions

Wheelbase: 2800 mm, Length: 4200 mm, Width: 1510 mm, Height: 1290 mm

Weight

1030 Kg

Maximum speed

325 kph

Cars produced

2

During the first part of the 1935 season Tazio Nuvolari had his ups and downs. At the wheel of the Tipo B Alfa Romeo he won the Pau GP in February, then he handed over the car to his teammate Trossi in the following Monaco GP (22ND of April), who was forced to retire on the 53RD lap. He also had to retire in Tunis (5TH May) but secured two admirable wins in the first Coppa Città di Bergamo on the 19TH of May and in the Belgian Grand Prix on the 9TH of June.

During those first few months however, the man from Mantua found the time to take the wheel of a car as "monstrous" as it was brilliant, the legitimate heir to the Tipo B, designed by the ingenious Luigi Bazzi "on behalf of" the Scuderia Ferrari. This was know as the "Bimotore" because the car had a classic straight-8 placed in front of the cockpit, with a second unit added behind the driver in place of the traditional fuel tank (of which there were now two, positioned along the sides of the body). Two versions of the car were constructed in Modena: one with 2905 cc engines, intended for Louis Chiron, and another fitted with two eight-cylinder engines for Nuvolari with displacements of no less than 3165 cc that were able to generate a maximum power output of 540 hp.

The setting for the debut of the two cars could hardly be anywhere other than the Tripoli Grand Prix, scheduled for the 12TH of May. The immense straights of the Mellaha circuit in Libya seemed to be the ideal place to give a free rein to a similar herd of wild horses but the Bimotores turned out to be (as might have been imagined...) cantankerous and difficult to tame. "Nivola" and Chiron had to settle for 4TH and 5TH places respectively behind the Mercedes-Benz W25B's of the winner Rudolf Caracciola and Luigi Fagioli and the Auto Union driven by Achille Varzi who was second.

Alfa Romeo tried its luck again at Avusrennen, on the 26TH of May with Chiron who managed to steal an encouraging second place overall while Nuvolari failed to qualify for the finale.

Just when it looked like the Bimotore's star was waning before its time, on the 15TH of June 1935 on the Altopascio-Lucca section of the Firenze-Mare autostrada, Nuvolari climbed into the cockpit of the Bimotore again to make an attempt on the flying kilometre and flying mile records.

There were many imponderables: a mechanical failure, a burst tyre or even just a gust of wind could be fatal at those speeds and there would have been a catastrophe. "Nivola" set off and here are the timers' results: an average speed of 321.428 kph with an average time of 11.02 seconds and an average of 323.125 kph for the mile, with a time of 17.093 seconds and a terminal speed of approximately 364 kph. Mission accomplished.

When he got out of the Bimotore, Nuvolari was congratulated by the President of the RACI, Prince Aimone di Savoia-Aosta, Duke of Spoleto, but also by his greatest rival, Achille Varzi, who had not wanted to miss the occasion and paid a well-earned tribute to the record man, the same Tazio, to whom, three years earlier, the "Vate" D'Annunzio had given an amulet, a gold turtle, inscribed "To the fastest man, the slowest animal".

The car on show in the Alfa Romeo Museum today was reconstructed by the company itself and the "Biscione" badge features on the radiator grille instead of the Prancing Horse.

GP Tipo C 12 C

A NEW V12 AND NUMEROUS VICTORIES.
THE GREATEST IN AMERICA

Engine

Front, longitudinal vertical 60° V12, block and fixed heads in light alloy, two valves per cylinder, two gear-driven overhead camshafts. Two twin-choke carburettors, two superchargers, magneto ignition, wet sump lubrication

Displacement

4064 cc (70x88 mm)

Power and torque

370 hp at 5800 rpm

Transmission

Rear-wheel drive, front mounted multiple dry-plate clutch, four speeds + reverse

Chassis

Pressed steel longerons and cross members

Bodywork

GP

Suspension

Front: independent, wishbones, oblique arm, coil springs, hydraulic dampers

Rear: independent, trailing arms, transverse leaf spring, hydraulic and friction dampers

Brakes

Hydraulically actuated drums all round

Dimensions

Wheelbase: 2750 mm, Length: 4200 mm, Width: 1520 mm, Height: 1215 mm

Weight

820 Kg

Maximum speed

290 kph

Cars produced

6

From the earliest phases of its development, the chassis of the Tipo C could be used with both the tried and trusted straight-eight engine based on that of the Tipo B and a new V12, another of Jano's projects, which was just about to see the light of day. A ladder-type chassis composed of pressed-steel longerons and cross-members and above all independent suspension on all four wheels — oblique arms and transverse leaf-springs with hydraulic friction dampers at the rear, and one oblique and one transverse arm, and coil springs, encased in a cylinder with an integral hydraulic damper at the front. While efficient, this solution was bulky and its fairing defined the unmistakable front end of the car. Another innovative feature was the transmission with the gearbox was mounted on the rear axle in-unit with the differential with the aim of improving weight distribution.

While the 330 hp of the Tipo C 8C allowed it to reach a top speed of 275 kph and above all in the hands of the fearless driver Tazio Nuvolari to win a lot of races, the decisive turning point was to be the debut of the V12 in 1936.

This engine featured a monoblock and cylinder heads in light alloy, a crankcase and sump cast in Elektron, a 60°V and a displacement of more than four litres (4064 cc). The valve train had two valves per cylinder, two gear-driven camshafts per head and a Roots-type supercharger coaxial with the crankshaft. Maximum power was now 370 hp at 5800 rpm with a top speed of 290 kph.

Despite these performance figures, on its debut in the very fast GP di Tripoli the car failed to live up to expectations and the beautiful Tipo C 12C's — which only differed from the 8C by the use of a double exhaust pipe — proved to be more suitable for winding courses than the notorious "rings". Its best results were obtained in Barcelona, Budapest, Milan and a second place at the Nürburgring. However, the most significant win of all was in the Vanderbilt Cup at Roosevelt Field on Long Island. At the wheel of the car on display today (extensively restored at the beginning of the 1970s) Nuvolari dominated the race, winning the coveted trophy and stunning the American spectators with the performance of his Tipo C. This was a victory that would become part of the Alfa legend, from the moment the team crossed the Atlantic wearing Scuderia Ferrari colours aboard the transatlantic liner Rex, to the photos of Tazio Nuvolari smiling while sitting inside the impressive silver cup donated by the American tycoon. Nuvolari may have been smiling in public, but on the outward journey he had been told that his eldest son had died.

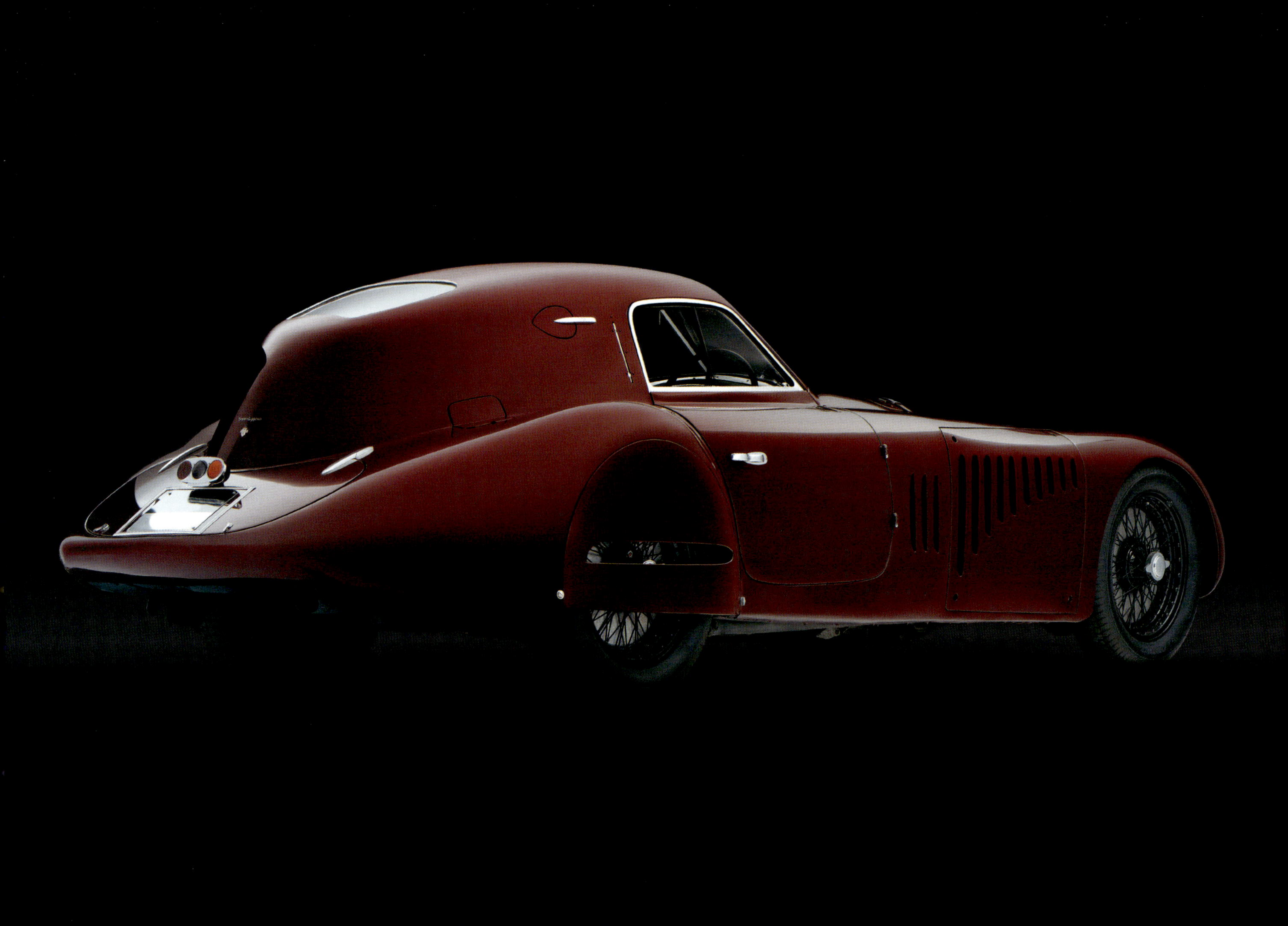

8C 2900 B Speciale Le Mans

AERODYNAMIC, ADVANCED, VERY, VERY FAST.
AND UNFORTUNATE. A HAIR'S BREADTH FROM GLORY

Engine

Front, longitudinal vertical straight-eight, dual blocks and heads in light alloy, two valves per cylinder, two gear-driven overhead camshafts. Two carburettors, two superchargers, magneto ignition, pressurised lubrication

Displacement

2926 cc (68.25x100 mm)

Power and torque

220 hp at 5500 rpm

Transmission

Rear-wheel drive, front mounted multiple dry-plate clutch, four speeds + reverse

Chassis

Welded box section longerons and cross members

Bodywork

Berlinetta (Touring Superleggera)

Suspension

Front: independent, wishbones, coil springs, hydraulic dampers

Rear: independent, trailing arms transverse leaf spring, hydraulic and friction dampers

Brakes

Hydraulically actuated drums all round

Dimensions

Wheelbase: 3000 mm, Length: 5150 mm

Weight

1250 Kg

Maximum speed

220 kph

Cars produced

1

While the 8C 2900 B had already become one of the symbols of its age, the Touring saloon car prepared for the 1938 Le Mans 24 Hours race deserves a chapter of its own.

The starting point was the chassis from the Mille Miglia model with lowered longerons and the gearbox/differential assembly cast in Elektron, as on the 8C 2900 A. The engine was enlarged from 2905 to 2926 cc, developed 220 hp and provided a top speed of 240 kph.

The Touring Superleggera bodywork had aluminium alloy panels of varying thicknesses depending on where they were fitted on the car and boasted sinuous, aerodynamic styling. It was tested on the 25TH of June 1987 in the Pininfarina wind tunnel, which confirmed that Touring had intuitively got the design right. With the air-intakes sealed, the Cx of 0.42 actually came down to an amazing 0.37.

The race: at 4.00 AM on the 18TH of June 1938, the starter dropped the flag to get the Le Mans 24 Hour race underway. Raymond Sommer and Clemente Biondetti's 8C 2900 B with number 19 had a slow start, but after five hours they were already a lap ahead of the second-placed car and after sixteen hours they were eleven laps ahead with a total distance between them and the next car of 148 km. They also posted the fastest average lap speed of 154.783 kph before being struck by bad luck: the front right-hand tyre lost its tread at high speed. Sommer managed to regain control of the car after a series of skids and drive slowly back to the pits where interminable repairs were made. The car restarted the race still in first place, its average speed remained the same and its lead even increased. Then came a dramatic turn of events. Biondetti's car spluttered to a halt and he vainly tried to push it to the pits. The official version was that a valve had broken, but in 1986 the driver stated that the differential had failed.

Very probably, whatever the damage was, it was caused by the stresses generated by the tyre bursting. Victory went to Chaboud-Tremoulet's Delahaye. The saloon's second life began on the 25TH of February 1939 when it was sold by the Modena dealership to Count Michelangelo Leonardi, complete with an official Alfa Corse certificate signed by Enzo Ferrari guaranteeing the car's authenticity. In July 1942, the car was sold to Gaetano Magno and on the 28TH of April 1946 the racing driver Inico Bernabei won the Flying Kilometre in Rome, followed by Venturi's win in the Coppa del Mare. Subsequently, the car was sold to Prince Sforza Ruspoli, then to Eliseo Linuzzi and finally to Franco Venturi. When the great collector died, the car was offered to Alfa Romeo for the paltry sum of three million lire, but Luigi Fusi was unable to raise the money for the purchase. In 1968, Giovannino Lurani and Corrado Cupellini restored the car and it was immediately sold to Colin Crebbe who broke one of the cylinder heads while attempting to drive it to England. Lord Doune bought the car and it was on display in a private museum until 1982 when it was bought and restored by Mike Sparken, whose real name was Michel Poberejsky. On show at the Mille Miglia and at Villa d'Este in 1986, it was then acquired by Alfa Romeo who "swapped" it for some parts for a Tipo 158 Alfetta.

World **Champion**

The birth of Formula 1, with Alfa Romeo immediately to the fore.
The Alfetta's two titles

GP Tipo 512

A REMARKABLE, AMBITIOUS AND INNOVATIVE PROJECT, STOPPED ONLY BY THE WAR

Engine

Rear, longitudinal, 12-cylinder boxer, crankcase in–unit with the blocks in Elektron and removable heads in light alloy, two valves per cylinder, four gear-driven overhead camshafts. One triple-choke carburettor, two two-stage superchargers in series, two magnetos, dry sump lubrication

Displacement

1490 cc (54x54.2 mm)

Power and torque

335 hp at 8600 rpm

Transmission

Rear-wheel drive, rear-mounted multiple dry-plate clutch, with sprung hub, five speeds + reverse

Chassis

Welded tubular longerons and cross members

Bodywork

GP

Suspension

Front: independent, wishbones, coil springs, hydraulic dampers, anti-roll bar

Rear: De Dion axle, upper triangular element, trailing arms, hydraulic dampers

Brakes

Hydraulically actuated and assisted discs all round

Dimensions

Wheelbase: 2350 mm, Length: 4080 mm, Width: 1500 mm, Height: 1050 mm

Weight

710 Kg

Maximum speed

300 kph (theoretical)

Cars produced

3, assembled 2

Wifredo Ricart was a fascinating and controversial character from a well-known upper-class Spanish family. Educated, refined and gifted, he was summoned to the Portello in 1936 by Ugo Gobbato who was looking for a "strong man" to manage the avionics section, which was becoming more and more important in a company that now had strong links with the military. In 1940, he was made head of the Special Research Department — which Alfa Corse was also part of — and the Design Department. If Wilfredo Ricart's masterpiece at Alfa Romeo was the 1101 aeroplane engine, the 512 is without doubt its automotive equivalent by virtue of the modernity and daring of the thinking behind it. And its bad luck too. The car was created for the "Voiturettes" class with supercharged 1.5-litre engines. This was a class in which the Germans did not compete and it was to become Formula 1 after the war. It was the alternative to Gioachino Colombo's 158 (a car which, according to Giuseppe Busso, the sarcastic Ricart had described as being "fit for a museum").

This was the first Alfa Romeo with mid-rear engine, a 1.5-litre, virtually square (54x54.2 mm), magnesium alloy, 12-cylinder boxer fitted with a two-stage supercharger. All these refinements contributed to a power output of 335 hp at 8600 rpm, with a record specific power output of 225 hp/litre, which was enough to trounce the previous year's record of 186 hp/litre established by the Mercedes-Benz M165, which had been considered to be an unsurpassable figure. The chassis had a De Dion rear axle and wishbones at the front, while the drum brakes were the extremely efficient triple-shoe type, which Alfa Romeo continued to use even after the War as they considered them to be more efficient than the early disk brakes.

The first car was assembled on the 10TH of September 1940 and took to the track for its first test runs two days later. By then, however, Italy already had been at war for three months. In the meantime, trials had been conducted using various test cars, including the one in which Attilio Marinoni died during a test on the Milano-Laghi autostrada. Testing continued into 1941 with Sanesi and Canavesi, but without much success. The chassis was not stiff enough and the roll axis of the rear axle had the wrong angle of inclination. These were problems that could be resolved and could be put down to the designers' lack of experience in the automotive field but they were blown out of all proportion by the animosity between the Scuderia Ferrari's "old hands" and Ricart's "new blood" who were now forced to live under the same roof.

The war then began to make itself felt more intensely and it was time for the slender single-seaters to hide away and wait for better times. Unfortunately this did not work out. After the war Ricart left the Portello and it was easier for Alfa Romeo to improve the 158's and abandon the beautiful dream of the 512. Both prototypes were hidden at a property on the outskirts of Milan and were later stored in the warehouses of the Experimental Department. In 1965, one of the cars was put on display in the Arese museum while the second was donated to the Museo della Scienza e della Tecnica in Milan.

PNEU ENGLEBERT
NOMBRE DE TOURS A PARCOURIR 35
NOMBRE DE TOURS PARCOURUS
NOMBRE DE TOURS PARCOURUS
IMPERIA
ALFA-ROMEO

GP Tipo 158 Alfetta

FROM THE BEGINNINGS TO THE GREAT POST-WAR VICTORIES. THE FIRST FORMULA 1 WORLD CHAMPIONSHIP

Engine

Front, longitudinal, vertical straight-eight, dual block and heads in light alloy, two valves per cylinder, gear-driven double overhead camshafts. One triple-choke carburettor, one two-stage supercharger, two magnetos, dry sump lubrication

Displacement

1479 cc (58x70 mm)

Power and torque

350 hp at 8500 rpm

Transmission

Rear-wheel drive, front-mounted multiple dry-plate clutch, four speeds + reverse

Chassis

Tubular longerons and sheet metal cross members, welded

Bodywork

GP

Suspension

Front: independent, trailing arms, transverse leaf spring, hydraulic and friction dampers

Rear: independent, trailing arms, transverse leaf spring, hydraulic and friction dampers

Brakes

Hydraulically actuated drums all round

Dimensions

Wheelbase: 2500 mm, Length: 4150 mm, Width: 1570 mm

Weight

700 Kg

Maximum speed

620 kph

Cars produced

4

Towards the end of the Thirties, Alfa Romeo's industrial fortunes picked up, thanks to aviation products, heavy goods vehicles and cars that were becoming increasingly popular. Ugo Gobbato decided that the decisive factor was racing success, not so much in the Sport category, where Alfa Romeo was practically unbeatable, but rather in Grands Prix where the German builders' superiority encouraged the management to abandon the inefficient Alfa Romeo-Scuderia Ferrari partnership and set up Alfa Corse. In the meantime, the company's designers were concentrating on a project to build a new "vetturette" with a 1.5-litre supercharged engine. This category had been left untouched by the German companies but it was to become the leading class in 1940. The team, led by Gioachino Colombo, sketched out the lines of the GP Tipo 158, soon to be nicknamed "Alfetta".

The engine was an innovative straight-eight design in light alloy with screw-in steel bores, twin-cam valve train and a fuel system featuring a Roots supercharger. The gearbox was in-unit with differential and mounted on the rear axle. The power output of the first version was 195 hp but this had increased to 225 hp by 1939.

With its top speed of 232 kph, the lean single-seater made its debut at the Coppa Ciano in 1938, taking first and second place before an enthusiastic crowd. Next there was the Milan GP and a series of wins that were only brought to a halt with the outbreak of war that put a stop to all competitions and forced Alfa Romeo to hide all their cars in Melzo, near Milan, under a fake wood-pile on a pig farm.

At the end of the war racing slowly started up again but there was no overall classification. In 1947, the Alfetta's, now making 275 hp with a top speed of 270 kph thanks to their two-stage superchargers, were overwhelmingly superior to other cars. Their triumphant charge was halted in 1949 when the team was decimated. Jean-Pierre Wimille, Achille Varzi and Carlo Felice Trossi all lost their lives and Alfa Romeo withdrew from Grand Prix racing. This was not just as a result of the tragedy but above all to allow them time to prepare for the 1950 season when the first World Formula 1 Championship would be contested. The power output increased to 350 hp with a top speed of 290 kph.

1950 was the year of the "Fa-Fa-Fa" team: Nino Farina, Juan Manuel Fangio and Luigi Fagioli. According to Giuseppe Busso, "the main problem was deciding which of the three drivers should win the race." The 158 won six of the seven official Championship races. Like the other European teams, Alfa snubbed the Indianapolis 500 Mile race but dominated five other non-championship Grands Prix. From its debut at the Silverstone GP, the Alfa Romeo remained unbeaten and occupied the top three places in the classification. Giuseppe "Nino" Farina became the first World Champion of the new Formula 1 series.

One of the single-seaters was restored in 1969 — just the chassis to start with — and was put on display in Arese before the bodywork was finished in 1975.

GP Tipo 159 "Alfetta"

THE HIGHEST EXPRESSION OF THE ALFETTA. WORLD CHAMPION AGAIN

Engine

Front, longitudinal, vertical straight-eight, dual block and fixed heads in light alloy, two valves per cylinder, gear-driven double overhead camshafts. One triple-choke carburettor, two two-stage superchargers in series, two magnetos, dry sump lubrication

Displacement

1479 cc (58x70 mm)

Power and torque

425 hp at 9300 rpm

Transmission

Rear-wheel drive, front-mounted multiple dry-plate clutch, four speeds + reverse

Chassis

Tubular longerons and sheet metal cross members, welded

Bodywork

GP

Suspension

Front: independent, trailing arms, transverse leaf spring, hydraulic and friction dampers

Rear: independent, De Dion axle, trailing arms, transverse leaf spring, hydraulic and friction dampers

Brakes

Hydraulically actuated drums all round

Dimensions

Wheelbase: 2550 mm, Length: 4280 mm, Width: 1620 mm, Height: 1150 mm

Weight

710 Kg

Maximum speed

305 kph

Cars produced

4 (existing cars modified)

Following the overwhelming success of 1950, when Giuseppe "Nino" Farina won the World Championship at the last race, ahead of two teammates Fangio and Fagioli, for the 1951 season Alfa Romeo decided to continue using the Alfetta, albeit under the new name Tipo 159 reflecting the depth of changes that had been made.

Over the course of the season, the Alfettas proved to be faster than the Ferraris, with Maranello trying various cars and various technical features, but very high petrol consumption forced the Alfas to make frequent stops to refuel. Of the eight championship races, the first three were won by Alfa Romeo, excluding the Indianapolis 500 Miles which was regularly ignored by the European teams even though it was part of the World Championship. Fangio won the first race in Switzerland, while his teammate Farina won in Belgium. The French Grand Prix, which was also the European GP, was run on the extremely fast Reims circuit and on this occasion the Alfa Romeo team entered Luigi Fagioli, the third "Fa" in 1950, in the race as well. When Fangio's 159 retired it was Fagioli who gave him his own car during a pit-stop, allowing him to go on to win the race and earn points which would prove to be invaluable at the end of the season. In fact, in the next race, the British Grand Prix, José Froilán González managed to lead Fangio across the finish line, giving Ferrari its first Formula 1 victory, after which Enzo Ferrari himself wrote a famous letter to Alfa Romeo confessing: "Today I killed my mother". The Cabezon's was, however, just the first of Maranello's victories: in the Grands Prix which followed victory went to Alberto Ascari, son of the late Antonio, the great Alfa Romeo champion at the time of the P2.

The outcome of the Championship was uncertain through to the last race, the Spanish Grand Prix, where Fangio and Alberto Ascari started with the same number of points, with the Italian in the Ferrari in pole position. However, the Pedralbes street circuit proved to be treacherous, especially for the tyres: Ferrari decided to fit one type of tyre while the Alfa Romeo men, having noticed that Fangios's car had a suspicious lack of grip during practice, opted for another. It was this decision that allowed Fangio to win, as the Ferraris were constantly troubled by problems with their tyres. Thus the Argentinian won his first World Championship, the first of the five that made him a motorsport legend.

For Alfa Romeo it marked the successful conclusion to a period of exhaustive development that had begun as early as 1938 with the Tipo 158. After careful consideration on the part of the engineers and management the team decided to retire from motor racing's blue ribbon series: the 159 had reached its limit of its potential and in order to carry on winning the team would have needed a new car which Alfa Romeo, with its commitments to road car production, could not afford.

159 chassis

BEHIND THE WORLD CHAMPIONSHIP SCENES, A GREAT PROJECT AND ITS DEVELOPMENT

Engine

Front, longitudinal, vertical straight-eight, dual block and fixed heads in light alloy, two valves per cylinder, gear-driven double overhead camshafts. One triple-choke carburettor, two two-stage superchargers in series, two magnetos, dry sump lubrication

Displacement

1479 cc (58x70 mm)

Power and torque

425 hp at 9300 rpm

Transmission

Rear-wheel drive, front-mounted multiple dry-plate clutch, four speeds + reverse

Chassis

Tubular longerons and sheet metal cross members, welded

Bodywork

GP

Suspension

Front: independent, trailing arms, transverse leaf spring, hydraulic and friction dampers

Rear: independent, De Dion axle, trailing arms, transverse leaf spring, hydraulic and friction dampers

Brakes

Hydraulically actuated drums all round

Dimensions

Wheelbase: 2550 mm, Length: 4280 mm, Width: 1620 mm, Height: 1150 mm

Weight

710 Kg

Maximum speed

305 kph

Cars produced

4 (existing cars modified)

While the 1950 season had been easily dominated by Alfa Romeo, by 1951 the Alfetta's advantage was gradually being eroded. It was not only that Alfa's rivals were becoming more competitive by the day, first and foremost Ferrari, but that the car itself, designed in 1938 and continuously developed, was approaching the limit of its potential. Both in terms of design and the wear on certain components, some of which had accompanied the car throughout its career without ever having been replaced. It was not so much outright performance that felt the weight of the years, quite the contrary, as the continual development guaranteed it a place at the head of the grid. And neither was reliability a problem, the experience accumulated by engineers and mechanics in the aviation field during the Second World War helping keep the cars running. Where the Alfettas were beginning to suffer was in terms of fuel consumption that had increased exponentially as every expedient was tried to get the utmost out of the small supercharged straight-eight.

Working on the superchargers, now two-stage units, on the materials and on the tolerances, the 1.5-litre engine was coaxed to produced no less than 425 hp, with peaks of 450 hp, good for maximum speeds in excess of 305 kph. These results were in part obtained thanks to the use of specially developed fuels and lubricants. The vast power output dictated improvements to the transmission and brakes too, but the most eye-catching modification was actually the adoption of larger fuel tanks that during the course of the season were gradually increased in capacity in an attempt to limit the need for pit stops during which the cars would lose all the time they had previously gained thanks to their performance. A number of competitors, opting for less powerful, naturally aspirated 4.5-litre engines benefitted from fuel consumption that was up to four times lower, allowing them to adopt a less aggressive but certainly profitable race strategy. The new fuel and lubricant tanks were located on the sides of the car, as well as in the tail, forcing modifications to be made to the coachwork. The cars now had wider underbodies which lent them an unmistakeable appearance. So different were they to the 1950 car that the name was changed to Tipo 159, "betraying" the origins of the 158 denomination that stood for 1.5 litres and eight cylinders. Further modifications were made to the suspension: during the course of the season, Gioachino Colombo replaced the rear swinging axle he had himself designed in 1938 with an efficient de Dion layout. This was used only on a limited number of occasions but represents the final evolution of the Alfetta prior to its victorious retirement at the end of the season. The example displayed in the museum, stripped of its bodywork, represents the pinnacle of this long evolutionary process.

Agip
GOODYEAR
GOODYEAR

CAMPARI

CAMPARI
GOOD YEAR
KONI
GOODYEAR
Agip
GOODYEAR

The 33 **project**

A ten-year career: a grandiose dream
and two world titles

33
COUPE
500

33 Stradale prototype

FROM RACING TO THE STREET.
SCAGLIONE PENS A REMARKABLE PROJECT

Engine

Rear, longitudinal, vertical 90° V8, block and cylinder heads in light alloy, two valves per cylinder, two chain-driven overhead camshafts. Spica indirect fuel injection, two distributors, two coils, two spark plugs per cylinder, dry sump lubrication

Displacement

1995 cc (78x52.2 mm)

Power and torque

230 hp at 8800 rpm

Transmission

Rear-wheel drive, hydraulically actuated rear-mounted single dry-plate clutch, six speeds + reverse

Chassis

Welded tubular elements, fibreglass bodywork

Bodywork

Coupé (Franco Scaglione)

Suspension

Front: independent, wishbones, coil springs, hydraulic dampers, anti-roll bar

Rear: independent, wishbones, coil springs, hydraulic dampers, anti-roll bar

Brakes

Dual circuits, discs all round

Dimensions

Wheelbase. 2350 mm, Length. 3970 mm, Width: 1710 mm, Height: 990 mm

Weight

700 Kg

Maximum speed

260 kph

Cars produced

18 (chassis)

Destined to become one of Alfa Romeo's most symbolic icons, the 33 Stradale was produced in a small batch of 18 chassis between November 1967 and March 1968. The original idea had been to make full use of the enormous sum of money that had been made available for the racing car and build a limited edition of 50 cars that would share a considerable number of the mechanical components. The specialist magazines greeted the idea with enthusiasm: "Now you can drive the star of Le Mans." A waiting time of just one month was given, the cars being assembled by Autodelta, but it soon became clear that development would be extremely complex.

The chassis retained the racing configuration of the Tipo 33 Sport, with the same capacious tubular H-shaped assembly housing the fuel tanks and a front subframe made of magnesium. The main difference was above all a 10 cm increase in the wheelbase designed to provide acceptable interior space. This modification required the chassis to be reinforced with sheet-steel around the cockpit. Equipment and trim were also added to make the car more suitable for road use — from the seats to the upholstery, from the dashboard to the instruments. The engine of the 33/2, a two-litre V8 was also detuned and with power dropping to 230 hp from the 270 hp of the prototype version. The car had a dry weight of 700 kg and the resulting performance was such that no other two-litre car on the market came anywhere close.

The bodywork that Alfa Romeo offered at the presentation in Monza in September 1967 was sleek aluminium berlinetta penned by Franco Scaglione and made by Marazzi. The designer had to personally monitor the production of every single example because of the inexperience of the coachbuilder's workforce.

As a result of the unanimous approval with which the prototype was received, the definitive version was put into production with just minor modifications that did not compromise Scaglione's captivating lines. However, the 9,750,000 lire price tag was extremely high, easily exceeding that of prestigious and sophisticated supercars with engines three times the size. That astronomical price for a car that could hardly be used on an everyday basis together with production issues contributed to just 18 cars being produced. Only 12 with the official Scaglione bodywork were sold to private owners. The remainder, apart from the prototype on display in the museum, which is different from the production models in a number of details, especially at the front of the car, were chosen by many famous coachbuilders as a basis for concept cars such as Bertone's Carabo, Pininfarina's Cuneo and Italdesign's Navajo, which was presented as late as 1976.

A number of the chassis were occasionally used by private owners in minor races and one car made an appearance in the feature film "Un bellissimo novembre" by Mauro Bolognini.

Tipo 33/2 Daytona

TRIUMPH IN AMERICA CONSECRATES THE TIPO 33. BIRTH OF A LEGEND

Engine

Rear, longitudinal, vertical 90° V8, block and cylinder heads in light alloy, two valves per cylinder, four chain-driven overhead camshafts. Lucas indirect fuel injection, two distributors, two coils, two spark plugs per cylinder, dry sump lubrication

Displacement

1995 cc (78x52.4 mm)

Power and torque

270 hp at 9600 rpm

Transmission

Rear-wheel drive, hydraulically actuated rear-mounted single dry-plate clutch, 6 speeds + reverse

Chassis

Welded tubular elements, fibreglass bodywork

Bodywork

Coupé (Hard-top)

Suspension

Front: independent, wishbones, coil springs, hydraulic dampers, anti-roll bar

Rear: independent, wishbones, coil springs, hydraulic dampers, anti-roll bar

Brakes

Dual circuits, discs all round, rear in-board

Dimensions

Wheelbase: 2550 mm, Length: 3960 mm, Width: 1760 mm, Height: 980 mm

Weight

580 Kg

Maximum speed

298 kph (long tail)

Cars produced

30 (1967-1969)

On the strength of the experience gained with the Giulia TZ and TZ2, Alfa Romeo rediscovered a desire to go sports car racing again. Alfa had abandoned the category in the early Fifties at the time of the 6C 3000 and Disco Volante projects, but sports car races enjoyed enormous popularity in the Sixties, with the two-litre class being contested by the most important builders.

From 1964 onwards, Progettazione Alfa Romeo, under the guidance of Orazio Satta Puliga, started work on a project to build a new car, which was to be developed by Giuseppe Busso in particular.

The chassis, built by Aeronautica Sicula, was composed of three large aluminium tubes, 20 cm in diameter and arranged in an asymmetrical H shape. A subframe made of a single magnesium casting produced by Campagnolo, was attached to the front end. Two "arms" also made of aluminium were located at the rear. The rubber petrol tanks were housed inside the frame tubes. The whole assembly weighed a mere 55 kg, with the car having an overall weight of 580 kg in running order.

The two-litre V8, made of aluminium alloy, had four overhead camshafts, fuel injection fed by a Lucas mechanical pump and dual ignition. The definitive version was producing 270 hp. The top speed was between 260 and 300 kph depending on the aerodynamic configuration.

However, before the engine, already designed and built at Alfa Romeo, could be run for the first time on the test bench, the 33 project (the code number was in fact 105.33) was sold by Giuseppe Luraghi to Autodelta, to the displeasure of the Alfa technicians. That was on the 14TH of January 1966. In the meantime, however, a car that had been finished but was powered by a provisional engine (the 1600 "twin-cam" from the TZ2) had been driven on the track at Balocco in the winter of 1965.

The development of the 33 was long and complex, in particular because of the ground-breaking chassis, so the first official outing was planned for the 7TH of January 1967 at Monza, when the tester and racing driver Teodoro Zeccoli had a terrible accident on a track that was still covered in snow. Redemption came a few months later with victory in the Fléron hillclimb in Belgium. At the wheel of the "periscope car", a nickname deriving from its conspicuous upper air intake, was Zeccoli once again.

Despite a good start, 1967 was not a very successful year and it was not until the following season that things started to look up when a new car with enclosed bodywork had 15 outright and six class wins, including the Daytona 24 hours where it came first and second in its class and Le Mans where it finished first, second and third in its class. It was the win in the American marathon that led to this version of the car being known as the "Daytona" — the example on display was prepared for the museum by Autodelta themselves.

By the end of the season the Tipo 33/2 had won the 2 litre class of the World Championship for Marques, while in the years to follow the baton was taken up by the three-litre version of the car.

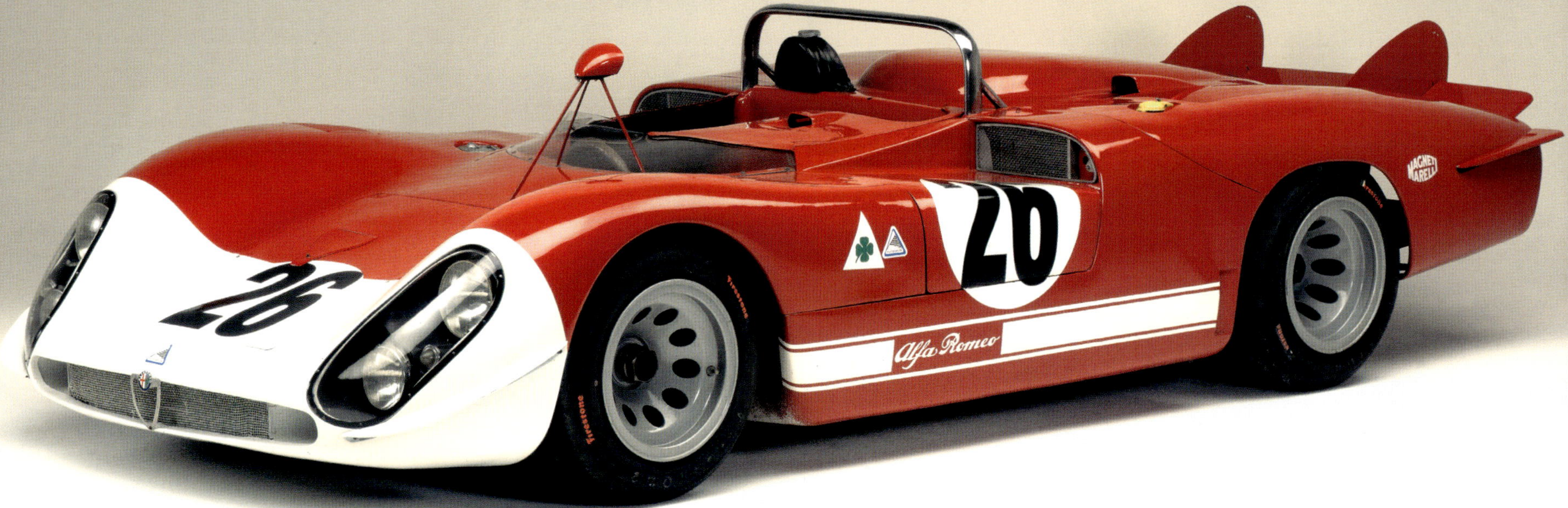
26
20
Alfa Romeo

ROMEO 37
ALFA-ROMEO 35
38
37

YPF

5

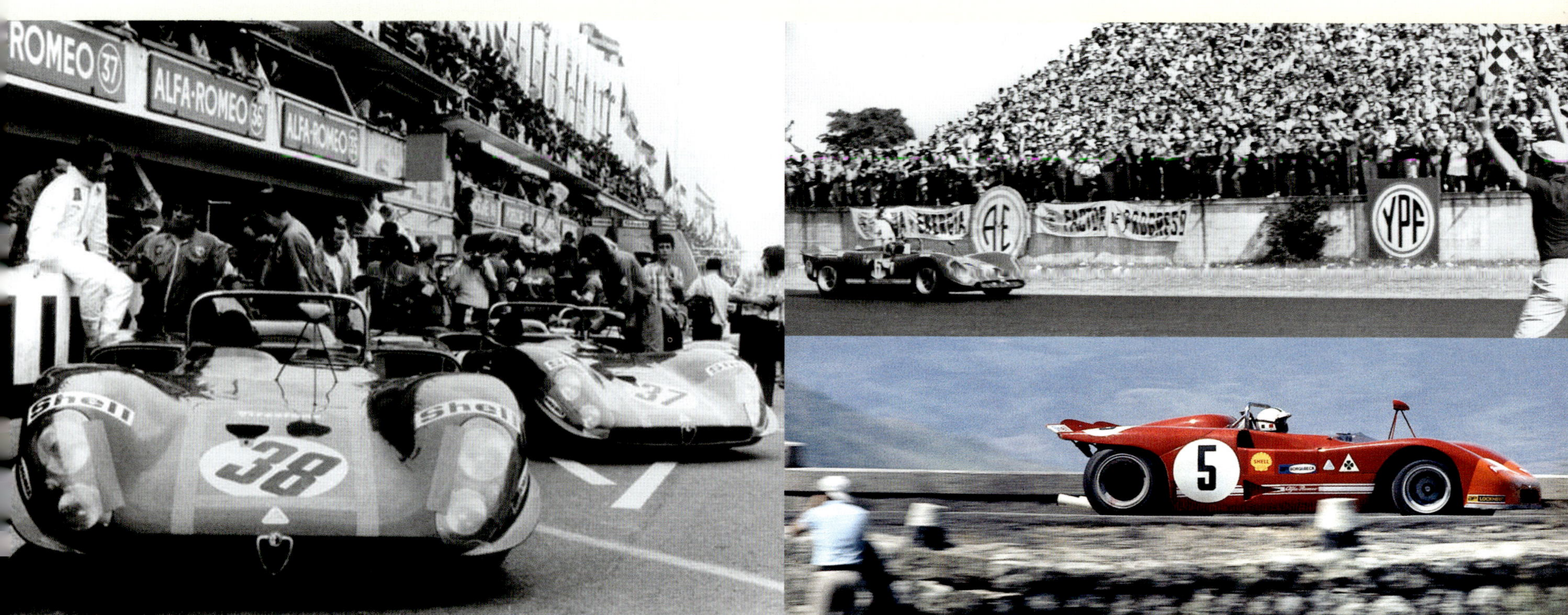

Tipo 33/3

THE "THIRTY-THREE" GROWS TO THREE LITRES
AND BRINGS THE TARGA FLORIO BACK TO ALFA ROMEO

Engine

Rear, longitudinal, vertical 90° V8, block and cylinder heads in light alloy, four valves per cylinder, four chain-driven overhead camshafts. Lucas indirect fuel injection, Dinoplex electronic ignition, dry sump lubrication

Displacement

2998 cc (86x64.4 mm)

Power and torque

400 hp at 9000 rpm

Transmission

Rear-wheel drive, hydraulically actuated rear-mounted dual dry-plate clutch, 5/6 speeds + reverse

Chassis

Load-bearing bodyshell with panels in aluminium and titanium, fibreglass bodywork

Bodywork

Spider

Suspension

Front: independent, wishbones, coil springs, hydraulic dampers, anti-roll bar

Rear: independent, wishbones, trailing arms coil springs, hydraulic dampers, anti-roll bar

Brakes

Dual circuits, discs all round

Dimensions

Wheelbase: 2240 mm, Length: 3700 mm, Width: 1900 mm, Height: 980 mm

Weight

700 Kg

Maximum speed

310 kph

Cars produced

20

Alfa Romeo's return to sports car racing in 1967, with the Tipo 33 project, ushered in a process of evolution that would last for ten years. Following the successful debut of the two-litre car at Fléron, and ahead the great wins of 1968, Autodelta began work on a new version with a three-litre engine that would be able to compete for overall victory.

The light alloy eight-cylinder engine was not completely redesigned but the displacement was increased to 2998 cc and the power output went up to 400 hp. The modification that made the 33/3 a completely new car was the abandoning of the futuristic H shaped tubular frame, which had been criticised by drivers from the beginning for its lack of stiffness, to a box-section structure made of Avional with the gearbox cantilevered beyond the rear axle. With regard to the body, various configurations were tested and often changed according to the track: in most cases the open version was chosen, but there were also several closed cars.

Things looked promising, but on the car's debut in the Sebring 12 Hours in 1969, it was forced to retire because it had not yet been set-up properly. Revenge came that same year however, with wins at Zeltweg and Pergusa. 1970 was a very different year: there were no wins at all, with just a few good results keeping the Alfa Romeo flag flying. This was the stimulus that Autodelta needed to make an updated version of the car.

Although there were no changes to the name, the car prepared for 1971 was thoroughly revised: the engine now produced 420 hp, the gearbox was redesigned with 5 speeds and dog clutches, while front wheels now had 13" rather than the usual 15" rims.

The weight too, which had always been one of the 33's weak points, was reduced to 650 kg: even though the chassis of the 33/2 shared a similar weight to that of competing cars, Autodelta had been unable to keep up with subsequent versions, partly because it was necessary to over-engineer all components for safety reasons. This was even more necessary because this was a state-owned company.

The modified car proved to be competitive out of the box and at the end of the season its palmares was supplemented by victories for Andrea de Adamich and Henri Pescarolo in the Brands Hatch 1000 Kilometres, and de Adamich, this time with Ronnie Peterson, in the Watkins Glen 6 Hours. The high point of the season, however, was another win in the Targa Florio where Nino Vaccarella, the "Flying Headmaster", and Toine Hezemans, drove the Tipo 33/3 to victory.

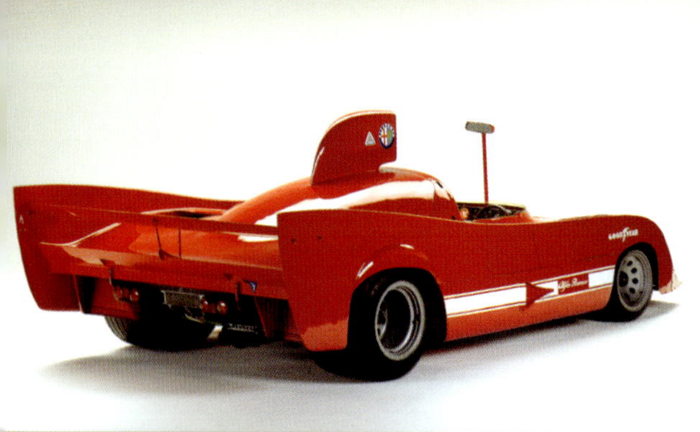

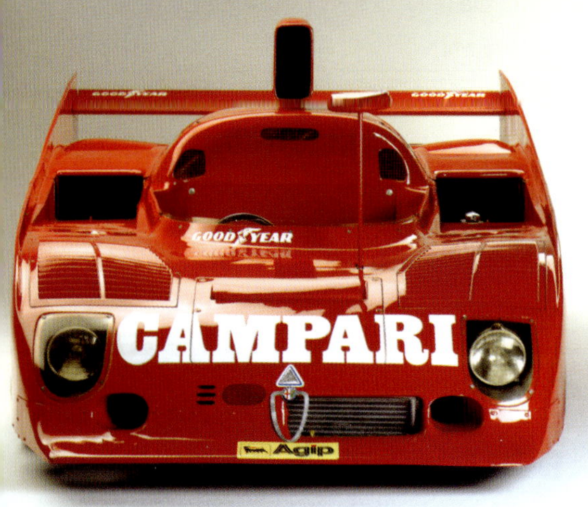

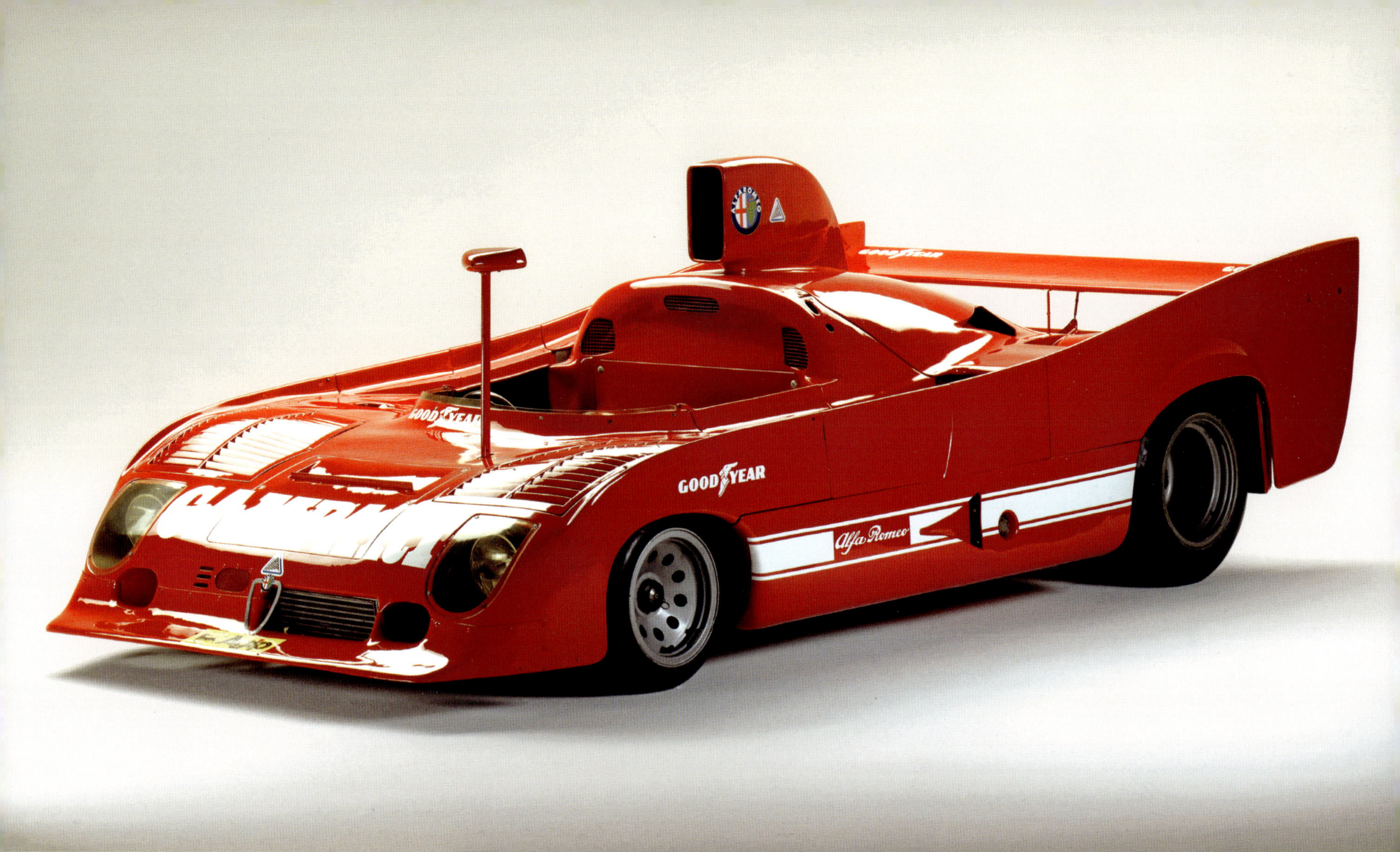
GOOD YEAR
Alfa Romeo

GOOD YEAR
CAMPARI
Agip

Shell
Shel

TEXACO
TEXACO
TEXACO

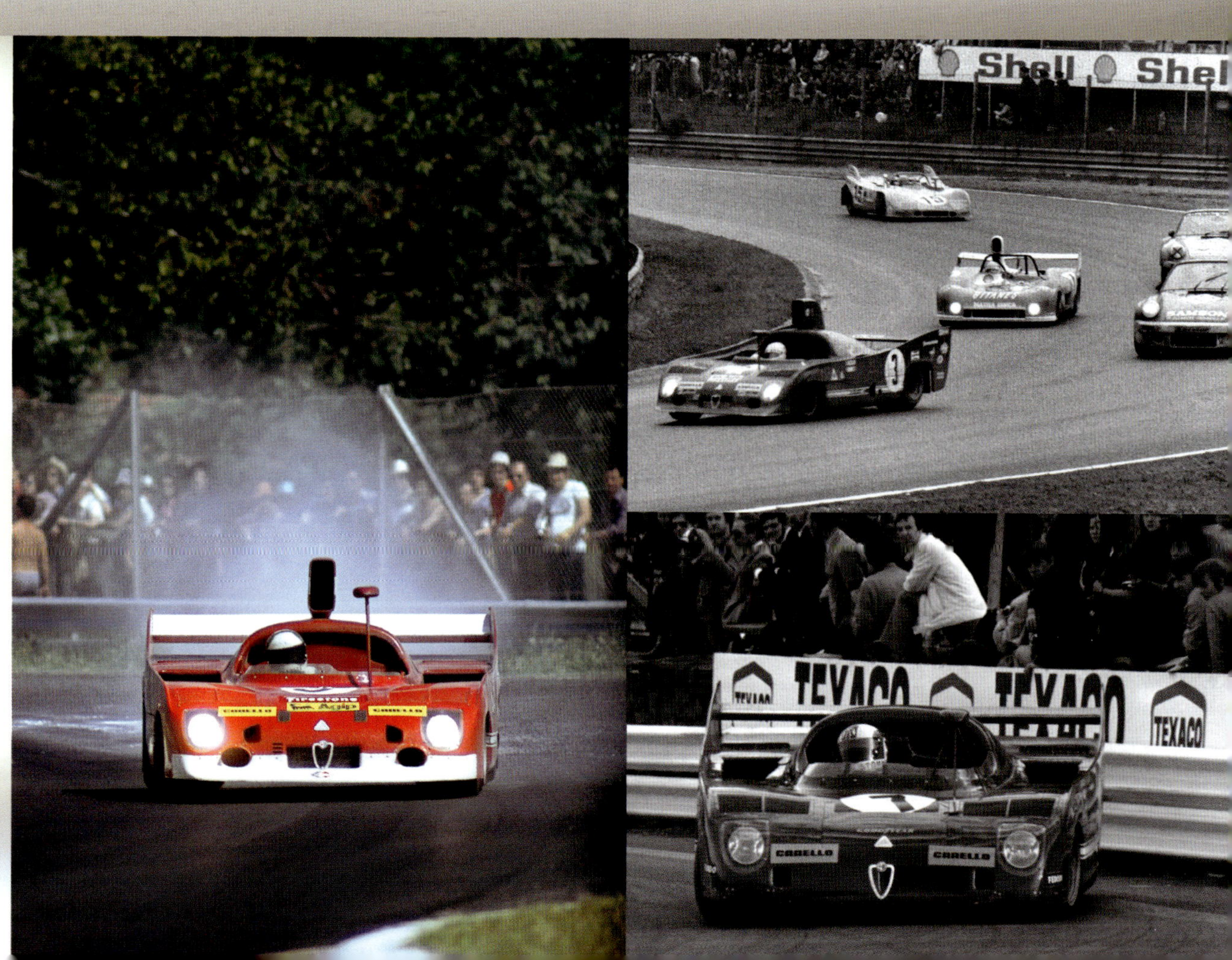

33 TT 12

TUBULAR CHASSIS, 12 CYLINDERS AND SEVEN VICTORIES IN EIGHT RACES.
ANOTHER WORLD CHAMPIONSHIP FOR ALFA ROMEO

Engine

Rear, longitudinal, 12-cylinder boxer, block and cylinder heads in light alloy (aluminium and magnesium), four valves per cylinder, four gear-driven overhead camshafts Lucas indirect fuel injection, Dinoplex electronic ignition, dry sump lubrication

Displacement

2995 cc (77x53.6 mm)

Power and torque

500 hp at 11500 rpm – 35 kgm at 9000 rpm

Transmission

Rear-wheel drive, hydraulically actuated rear-mounted dual dry-plate clutch, 5 speeds + reverse, rear-mounted gearbox

Chassis

Tubular steel with reinforcing panels, bodywork in fibreglass

Bodywork

Spider

Suspension

Front: independent, wishbones, coil springs, hydraulic dampers, anti-roll bar

Rear: independent, wishbones, trailing arms, coil springs, hydraulic dampers, anti-roll bar

Brakes

Dual circuits, discs all round

Dimensions

Wheelbase: 2340 mm, Length: 3800 mm, Width: 2050 mm, Height: 960 mm (excluding the air intake)

Weight

670 Kg

Maximum speed

Over 330 khp

Cars produced

6

A new tubular steel space-frame chassis for the 33 with an advanced driving position and the five-speed gearbox set within the wheelbase was designed during what proved to be a disappointing 1970 season for the Tipo 33/3. This new chassis was designed from the outset with the use of both the "old" V8 engine and a new 12-cylinder boxer that was to make its debut in 1973 in the Tipo 33 TT 12. The new engine, designed entirely in-house at Autodelta by Carlo Chiti, had a monoblock and cylinder heads in light alloy, a displacement of 2995 cc, four valves per cylinder, chain-driven double overhead camshafts and Lucas mechanical fuel injection. The choice of a boxer engine, a configuration much in vogue at the time, allowed the centre of gravity to be lowered and the overall height to be reduced. Early versions produced a maximum power output of 470 hp, but in 1975 the 500 hp barrier was broken giving a maximum speed of over 330 kph and extremely high performance thanks also to a weight of just 670 kg. The other side of the coin was an ever-criticised lack of structural rigidity that put great demands of the driver. The bodywork too was completely new, with an unusual aerodynamic configuration very different to those of its rivals, with a conspicuous air scoop behind the cockpit.

The 33 TT 12 made its race debut at Spa in 1973 with Rolf Stommelen and Andrea de Adamich, but the pair were forced to retire after an accident. The team had to wait until the Monza 1000 Km in 1974 for the car to secure its first victory, when Mario Andretti and Arturo Merzario, after the American had claimed pole position, dominated the race, winning ahead of the sister cars of Ickx and Stommelen and de Adamich and Facetti. Further encouraging results came during the course of the season.

1975 was instead to be a triumphant year for the car and concluded with the long awaited victory in the World Championship for Marques. The cars were again run by Autodelta, but took to the track in the colours of the Willi Kauhsen Racing Team, which brought a great deal of extra sponsorship. Merzario and Jacques Lafitte dominated at Dijon, Monza and the Nürburgring. Henri Pescarolo and Derek Bell won at Spa, Zeltweg and Watkins Glen. It was victory in the 1000 Km in Austria that confirmed Alfa Romeo as World Champion well before the end of the season. Subsequently, Merzario and Jochen Mass also had the opportunity to climb to the top of the podium at Pergusa. Another great victory, this time with an all-red car entered not by WKRT but directly by Autodelta, was obtained in the Targa Florio, with the "Flying President" Nino Vaccarella paired with Arturo Merzario. This was Alfa Romeo's 10th and last win in the Madonie mountains, in a race that in 1923 had consecrated the marque as one of the greats and had seen the debut of the Quadrifoglio or cloverleaf symbol.

Tipo 33 SC 12 Turbo

EIGHT WINS IN EIGHT RACES.
ALFA ROMEO CHALLENGES THE WORLD OF TURBOS

Engine

Rear, longitudinal, 12-cylinder boxer, block and cylinder heads in light alloy (aluminium and magnesium), four valves per cylinder, four gear-driven overhead camshafts. Lucas indirect fuel injection, two KKK turbochargers, electronic ignition, dry sump lubrication

Displacement

2134 cc (77x38.2 mm)

Power and torque

640 hp at 11000 rpm – 48 kgm at 9000 rpm

Transmission

Rear-wheel drive, hydraulically actuated rear-mounted triple dry-plate clutch, 5 speeds + reverse, rear-mounted gearbox

Chassis

Box section aluminium alloy

Bodywork

Spider

Suspension

Front: independent, wishbones, coil springs, gas dampers, anti-roll bar

Rear: independent, wishbones, coil springs, gas dampers, anti-roll bar

Brakes

hydraulically actuated, self-ventilating discs all round

Dimensions

Wheelbase: 2500 mm, Length: 3800 mm, Width: 2000 mm, Height: 960 mm (excluding the air intake)

Weight

770 Kg

Maximum speed

352 kph

Cars produced

2

After the triumphant march of the 33 TT12 cars in the 1975 season, the following year saw a change in FIA rules, which focused on the new Group 5, the group for silhouette cars, while the old Sport category cars, with a few modifications, were moved to Group 6, the World Sports Prototype Championship. Autodelta fielded the new 33 SC12, where the letters SC stood for "scatolato" (box-section) seeing as the new chassis featured an aluminium alloy monocoque. It was longer and narrower than the TT12, about 40 kg lighter and stiffer. The power output of the twelve-cylinder boxer was increased to 520 hp with a top speed of 330 kph. After their debut at the Imola 500 Km, the third race of the season, where Merzario-Brambilla finished second, the 33's took part in the 4 Hours race at Enna and the last event at the Salzburgring, ending with two retirements.

At the beginning of 1976, Autodelta had already announced a new 2140 cc turbo engine, a displacement which according to the rules was the equivalent of a naturally aspirated three-litre. It was announced that the engine was achieving good results on the test bench and was giving an output of about 600 hp. Throughout the season the debut of the 33 turbo was continually postponed and at the beginning of the 1977 season too the announcement of its debut had by now become a contentious issue.

In the meantime, however, 1977 saw revenge for the 33 SC 12 in its new Fernet Tonic livery in a championship that had now reached its swansong. On paper there should have been few and not very competitive rivals, but from the very first race the Osella cars and Rolf Stommelen's Toj gave them a hard time. Nonetheless, Merzario was the dominant driver at the Dijon 500 Kilometres. The Alfas continued march on victoriously at Monza, Vallelunga and the Salzburgring too. Then came the Avus interlude, a race that was valid for the Interserie Championship: Derek Bell won the second race on the German circuit with an extremely fast "experimental" 33 SC12, which the driver claimed to have taken to 345 kph. Arturo Merzario won at Enna and the Paul Ricard circuit, while at the Estoril, Carlo Chiti, despite fears the race would be cancelled for a lack of competitors, decided to enter three cars: it was to be the last time they would take the first three places, allowing Alfa Romeo to win the title, with eight victories in eight races.

Despite the succession of announcements it was only in the last race that the turbo engine made its debut. The 12-cylinder 2134 cc boxer was boosted via two KKK turbochargers and gave a maximum power output of 640 hp. The top speed, recorded by Teodoro Zeccoli at Balocco, was 352 kph. The car suffered from noticeable turbo-lag and had a chassis and brakes that were undersized with respect to the enormous power available. Merzario only managed to finish in second place, due by a lengthy pit stop caused by problems in restarting the overheating. Merzario's revenge at the wheel of the 33 SC12 Turbo, now on display in the museum, came a few weeks later at Hockenheim, one of the races in the Interserie championship. But by now the lights had been dimmed...

Racing **in the Blood**

Cars, drivers, challenges.
Every era has its victories

6C 3000 CM

THE LAST FIFTIES SPORTS CAR: NO MILLE MIGLIA BUT REVENGE AT MERANO

Engine

Front, longitudinal, vertical straight-six, block in cast iron, removable cylinder head in light alloy, two valves per cylinder, two duplex chain-driven overhead camshafts. Six single-choke carburettors, magneto ignition, dry sump lubrication

Displacement

3495 cc (87x98 mm)

Power and torque

275 hp at 6500 rpm

Transmission

Rear-wheel drive, front-mounted multiple dry-plate clutch, five speeds + reverse

Chassis

Tubular with central girder

Bodywork

Barchetta

Suspension

Front: independent, wishbones, coil springs, hydraulic dampers, anti-roll bar

Rear: De Dion axle, coil springs, hydraulic dampers

Brakes

Hydraulically actuated drums all round, in-board at the rear

Dimensions

Wheelbase: 2250 mm, length: 2834 mm, Width: 1616 mm, Height: 1140

Weight

930 kg

Maximum speed

250 kph

Cars produced

6 (2 spiders + 4 coupés)

At the end of the 1940s, Alfa Romeo's standard bearer in the Sport class was still the 6C 2500 Competizione, which was closely related to the production car and therefore based on a design dating back to well before the Second World War. A new three-litre engine was installed for the 1950 Mille Miglia that had been designed in 1948 by Giuseppe Busso for the prototype of the 6C 3000. The performance figures were promising but it took some time for it to achieve the desired results.

A completely new car for the Sport class was, however, prepared in 1952. The CM initials added to the well-known name 6C 3000 stood for "Competizione Maggiorata". The engine capacity was increased to 3495 cc, with a maximum power output that very quickly rose from the original 246 hp to 275 hp. The top speed was more than 250 kph.

The new Sport model retained very little of the old 6C 3000 — the redesigned chassis was tubular with a central main beam, the front suspension was independent with wishbones, coil springs and an anti-roll bar while a de Dion rear axle was fitted — a configuration that Giuseppe Busso had championed for some time. Drum brakes with helical finning were fitted, the rear ones located in-board.

The car's race debut came in the 1953 Mille Miglia. After the start the race was led by Sanesi as far as Pescara, where he retired with a broken chassis. The lead passed to an identical car driven by Kling with right behind him another driven by Juan Manuel Fangio.

In Rome, Kling's chassis gave way too and on the Futa Pass the front end of Fangio's car also started to "flutter" indicating that the infamous defect had not spared his car either. The Argentinian hung on for a long time but after Florence he had to slow down, conceding victory to the Ferrari driven by Gianni Marzotto. The next day the tester Bonini revealed the seriousness of the damage — while driving the car back to Milan all he had to do was turn the steering wheel while stationary as he manoeuvred around the cars in the *parc fermé* for the chassis of Fangio's car to break with a soft 'crack'.

Subsequently the three 6C 3000 CM cars were entrusted to the same drivers for the Le Mans 24 hour race, and here too they were forced to retire as a result of hurried preparation of the cars at a time when the company was concentrating hard on the new Giulietta project. For the same reason it was decided to send only one car to the Spa 24 Hours and the Nürburgring 1000 Km. At Spa, the car driven by Sanesi-Fangio skidded off the road in the rain, while in Germany Kling did irreparable damage to his car during practice when he ran off the road after a hare hit the windscreen.

As well as the four coupé's with Colli bodywork, two spiders were also assembled. And it was the latter that finally scored a win when Fangio dominated the first Supercortemaggiore Grand Prix in Merano. In 1955, this car was developed further and fitted with disk brakes before being retired and later put on display in the Alfa museum.

Giulia TZ 2

EVOLUTION. LIGHTER, FASTER AND EVEN MORE SEDUCTIVE

Engine

Front, longitudinal, vertical straight-four, block and cylinder head in light alloy, two valves per cylinder, two duplex chain-driven overhead camshafts. Two twin-choke carburettors, distributor ignition, Two spark plugs per cylinder, wet sump lubrication

Displacement

1570 cc (78x82 mm)

Power and torque

170 hp at 7500 rpm

Transmission

Rear-wheel drive, hydraulically actuated rear-mounted single dry-plate clutch, five speeds + reverse

Chassis

Welded tubular spaceframe

Bodywork

Coupé in fibreglass

Suspension

Front: independent, wishbones, trailing arms, coil springs, hydraulic dampers, anti-roll bar

Rear: independent, wishbones, trailing arms, coil springs, hydraulic dampers, anti-roll bar

Brakes

Hydraulically actuated and assisted discs all round, inboard at the rear

Dimensions

Wheelbase: 2200 mm, Length: 3680 mm, Width: 1540 mm, Height: 1050 mm

Weight

620 kg

Maximum speed

245 kph

Cars produced

12

While the TZ was bringing the company considerable satisfaction during the 1964 season, on the Carrozzeria Zagato stand at that year's Turin Motor Show, the logical evolution of that car appeared, the Giulia TZ 2 (even though TZ remained the official name), a car which, even today, deserves a place of honour among the Alfa Romeo's that have made racing history.

The tubular spaceframe chassis, the TZ's jewel in the crown, was substantially unvaried, but it now carried lightweight fiberglass bodywork designed by Ercole Spada with parts of the chassis immersed in the body's resin with the aim of making the whole structure more rigid. At first glance the TZ 2, even though it retained the overall shape of the TZ, with its prominent front overhang and the upper body which followed a continuous line as far as the abruptly truncated tail and boasted an expansive wraparound rear window, was in fact lower, more shapely and more "muscular", lending it an even more dynamic appearance.

Styling apart, the main changes were to the suspension, with shock absorbers which now operated vertically (a modification that had also been made to the TZ) and which made room for the new 13" wheels in place of the previous 15" ones.

The by now timeless four-cylinder twin-cam 1570 cc engine, with a bore and stroke of 78x82 mm and dry sump lubrication managed to develop a maximum power output of 170 hp at 7500 rpm thanks to double ignition (not fitted to the very early examples) and a new dynamic air intake. The 100 litre fuel tank, disk brakes on all four wheels and a 5-speed plus reverse gearbox which, depending on the gear ratios, allowed the car to reach a speed approaching 250 kph, were some of the other main features which made up the technical specification of the TZ 2.

Apart from the aforementioned extremely lightweight bodywork, another "weight-loss programme" for the interior of the car meant that it was about 40 kg lighter than the TZ.

From its first race on the 25TH of April 1965 in the Monza 1000 Kilometres, the TZ 2 proved to be a winner with Roberto Bussinello and Andrea De Adamich finishing seventh overall and first in class (GT up to 1600 cc). However, some of the most significant triumphs of this extraordinary car came in the 1965 season with class wins for Rolland-Consten in the Sebring 12 Hours, Bianchi-Rolland in the Targa Florio, De Adamich-"Geki" in the Nürburgring 1000 Kilometres and also in the Melbourne 6 Hours, in the Giro d'Italia and in the Criterium des Cevennes. More class wins came in 1966 at Monza (De Adamich-Zeccoli), Sebring (Andrey-"Geki"), the Targa Florio (Pinto-Todaro) and the Nürburgring (Bianchi-Schultze).

GTA 1300 Junior

"SMALL", BUT ONLY ON PAPER. FURTHER VICTORIES FOR THE "ALLEGERITA"

Engine

Front, longitudinal, vertical straight-four, block and cylinder head in light alloy, two valves per cylinder, two duplex chain-driven overhead camshafts, with Kugel-Fischer mechanical fuel injection, twin spark distributor ignition, wet sump lubrication

Displacement

1290 cc (78x67.5 mm)

Power and torque

165 hp at 8400 rpm

Transmission

Rear-wheel drive, hydraulically actuated single dry-plate clutch, five speeds + reverse

Chassis

Pressed steel unitary construction, light alloy panels

Bodywork

Lightened coupé

Suspension

Front: independent, wishbones, coil springs, hydraulic dampers

Rear: live axle, triangular central element, trailing arms, coil springs, hydraulic dampers

Brakes

Hydraulically actuated and assisted discs all round

Dimensions

Wheelbase: 2350 mm, Length: 4080 mm, Width: 1580 mm, Height: 1315

Weight

760 kg (dry)

Maximum speed

210 kph

Cars produced

447

With the idea of attracting a younger clientele with a sparkling model capable of guaranteeing performance and driving pleasure with reasonable purchase and running costs, in 1966 Alfa Romeo introduced the GT 1300 Junior, an aggressive yet elegant coupé bodied by Bertone and powered by the 1290 cc twin-cam engine from the Giulietta. This latest successful model formed the basis for the development a year later of the GTA 1300 Junior, in a process identical to that which had led to the launch of the Giulia Sprint GTA (1965) based on the Giulia Sprint GT (1963).

Although the GTA 1300 Junior retained the same 1290 cc displacement as the base model, the bore and stroke dimensions were completely different at 78x67.5 mm against the 74x75 mm of the Bertone coupé; the fuel system featured two twin-choke carburettors, twin spark ignition with a distributor and specific timing that brought the power putput up to 96 hp at 6000 rpm, with a maximum toque value of 11.6 kgm at 5600 rpm.

That the new GTA 1300 Junior was a car conceived for racing was clear at first sight. Externally the coachwork boasted supplementary air intakes at the front and conspicuous stripes on the flanks along with the cloverleaf symbol. A large Alfa serpent instead embellished the bonnet while the boot carried the "GTA 1300 Junior" script. These elements were either white on red coachwork or green on a white ground.

As had been the case with the GTA, race tuning of the Junior was entrusted to Autodelta which, over time, coaxed the 1300 twin-cam into producing power outputs in the order of 160 hp at 7800 rpm, with maximum speeds of around 210 kph. In 1971, the "testa stretta" or narrow head version with valves inclined at 45° (rather than the normal 80°) and Spica (occasionally Lucas) mechanical fuel injection was to achieve 165 hp at 8400 rpm, while in 1974 a new head with four valves per cylinder was homologated that was to permit power outputs of up to 180 hp at 9300 rpm.

"Junior 1.3/1.6, the Giulia that wins" ran a celebrated advert published by the company in those years. Never was a slogan more appropriate for a car that between 1968 and 1972 won two European Championships (1971 and '72). Two Spa-Francorchamps 24 Hours, the Jarama 4 and 4 Hours (1969 and '70), the Nürburgring 500 Km and 6 Hours (1969, '70 and '72) and other important races at Monza, Zandvoort, the Paul Ricard circuit and Silverstone. In total, 447 examples were constructed.

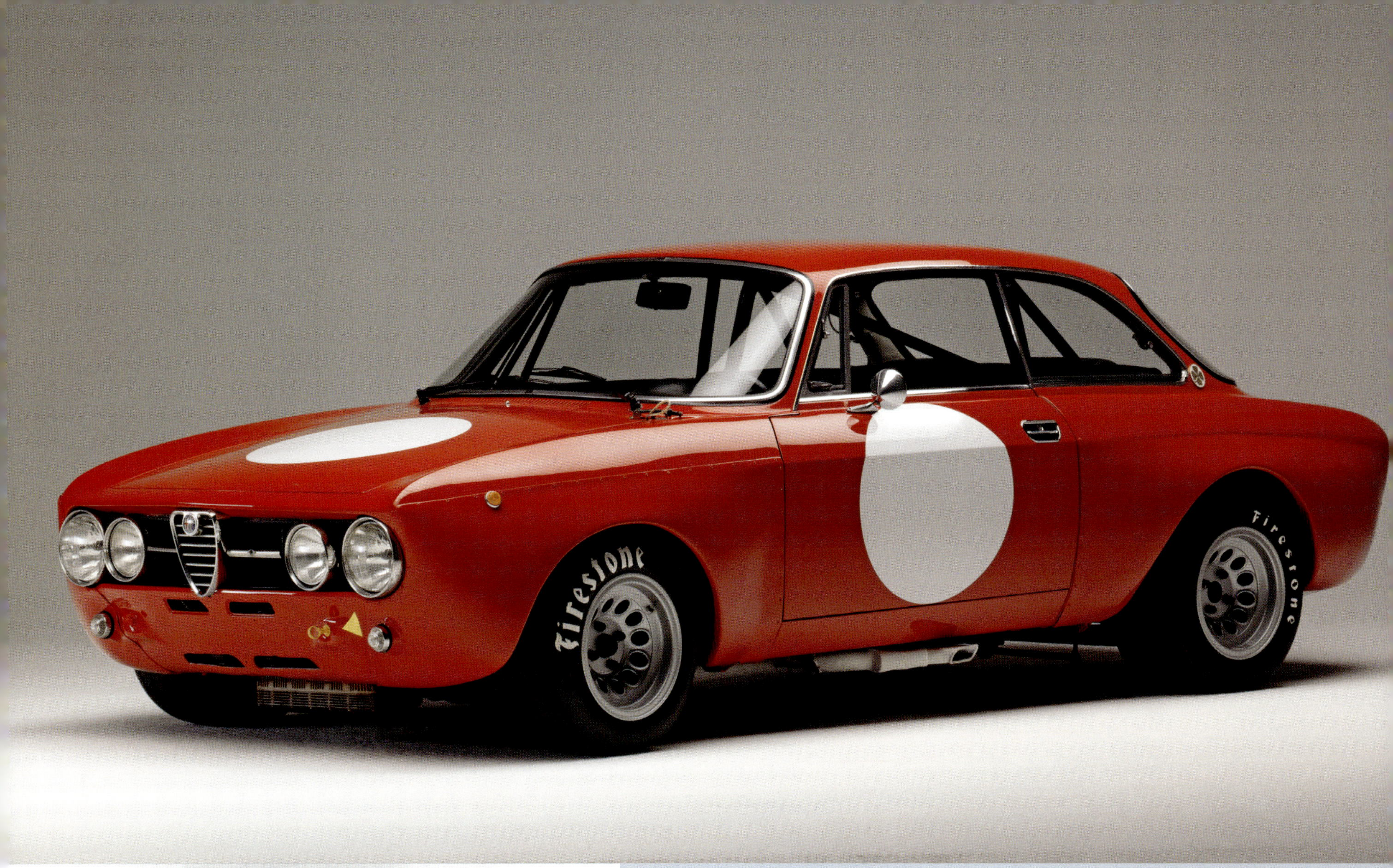
Firestone

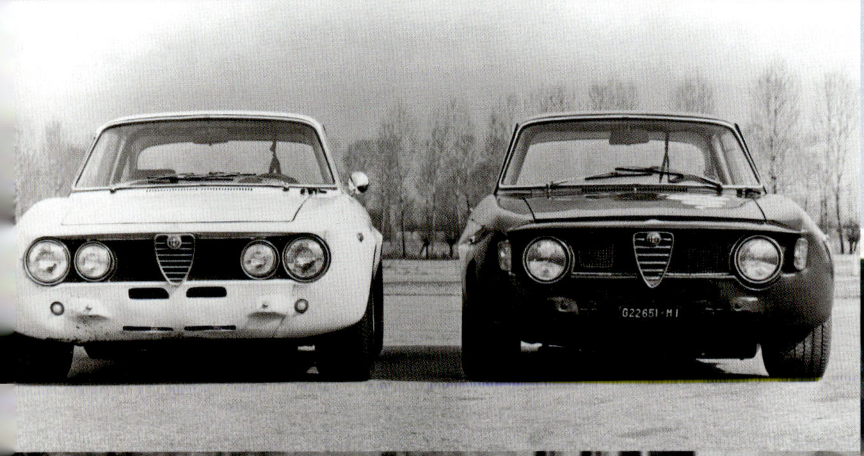
022651-MI

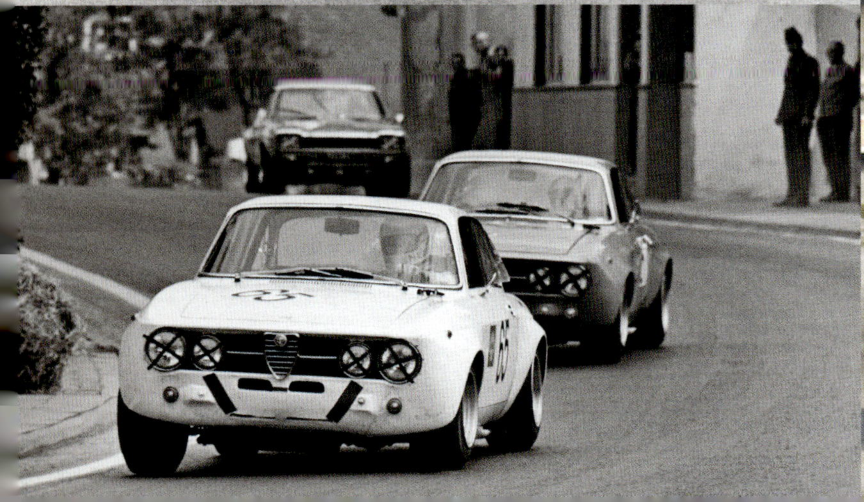

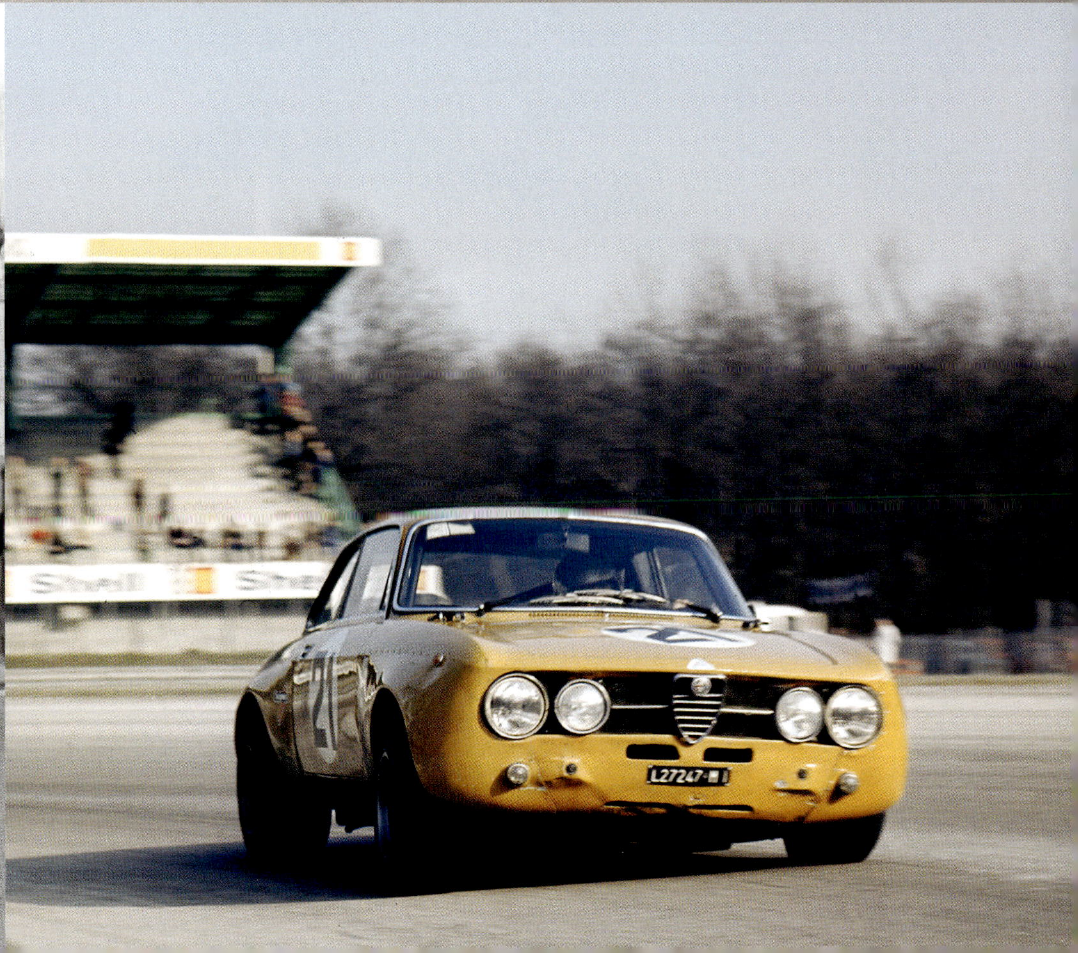
L27247-MI

1750 GTAm

DERIVED FROM THE "AMERICA" VERSION: PEERLESS IN EUROPE

Engine

Front, longitudinal, vertical straight-four, block and cylinder head in light alloy, two valves per cylinder, two duplex chain-driven overhead camshafts. Spica indirect fuel injection, twin spark distributor ignition, wet sump lubrication

Displacement

1985 cc (84.5x88.5 mm)

Power and torque

210 hp at 7500 rpm

Transmission

Rear-wheel drive, hydraulically actuated single dry-plate clutch, five speeds + reverse

Chassis

Autodelta modified unitary construction steel bodyshell

Bodywork

Coupé

Suspension

Front: independent, wishbones, coil springs, hydraulic dampers, anti-roll bar

Rear: live axle, triangular central element, trailing arms, coil springs, hydraulic dampers, anti-roll bar

Brakes

Dual circuits with servo, discs all round

Dimensions

Wheelbase: 2350 mm, Length: 4080 mm, Width: 1668 mm, Height: 1320

Weight

940 kg

Maximum speed

230 kph

Cars produced

40

A displacement of between 1300 and 2000 cc with a minimum of 1000 cars produced. Such were the requirements for homologating Group 2 cars from the beginning of 1970. Alfa Romeo was not caught napping and on the 1ST of October, the 1750 GTAm derived from the American version (as that "Am" in the name indicates) joined the category. This was a car that was different to the one sold in Europe in that it had Spica indirect mechanical fuel injection (which was necessary to satisfy the severe anti-pollution norms already in place in the USA at the time) and which also made it all the more suitable for competition. Autodelta, which once again had the task of preparing the GTAm cars for racing, decided to use this set-up although the more traditional Lucas system was also used on occasion.

The main differences in the bodywork, compared to the Giulia Sprint GTA from which the GTAm was derived, were first of all the use of steel instead of aluminium (which was subsequently used for the doors only) and the use of fibreglass extensions riveted on to the wheel arches housing 13" front and rear tyres which gave the car an even more aggressive and race-bred appearance.

Just as important were the modifications to the engine where the bore was increased by 4 mm while the stroke was left unchanged (thus 84.5x88.5 instead of 80.5x88.5 mm), with the overall displacement increasing to 1985 cc. This increased bore created rather too many problems in terms of the reliability of the block and for this reason it was decided to insert a monosleeve rather than four individual liners, which became a distinguishing feature of the GTAm.

Compared to the 1750 GTV the compression ratio was increased to 11:1, the cylinder head had valves with an angle of 45° and twin spark ignition with a distributer while the engine produced maximum power output of between 195 and 220 hp at 7200 rpm. The dry weight of the GTAm was around 940 kg and its declared maximum speed was over 230 kph.

The GTAm was soon enjoying success in the European Touring Championship with Toine Hezemans winning at Monza, Budapest and Jarama and taking the title at the end of the season. Adamich-Picchi also won at the Nürburgring with this last also winning at Zandvoort.

The European title was added to the collection in 1971 too with the latest version of the 2000 GTAm. The car had the same displacement, but the power output rose to 240 hp at 7500 rpm, giving a top speed of more than 230 kph. Another modification compared to the 1750 GTAm version was the homologation weight that was 20 kg greater.

The Dutch driver Toine Hezemans took the championship title again with the GTAm, winning a Monza, Brno, Zandvoort, the Nürburgring and the Paul Ricard Circuit together with van Lennep and at Spa-Francorchamps with Facetti.

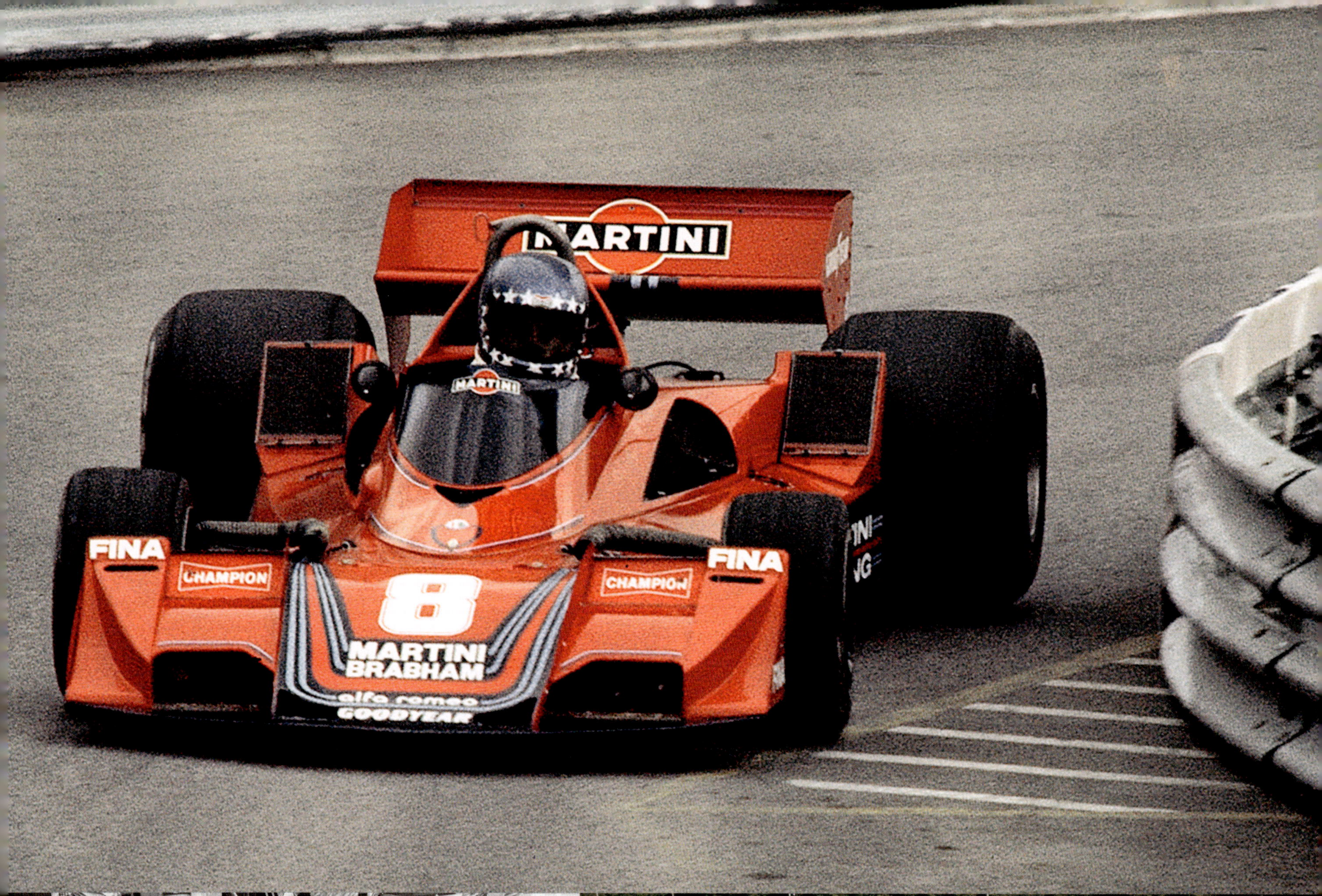
MARTINI
MARTINI
FINA
CHAMPION
8
FINA
CHAMPION
MARTINI
BRABHAM
alfa romeo
GOODYEAR

MARTINI
FINA
CHAMPION
8
FINA
CHAMPION
MARTINI
BRABHAM
Alfa Romeo
GOODYEAR

MARTINI
RACING
Alfa Romeo
7
FINA
FINA
CHAMPION

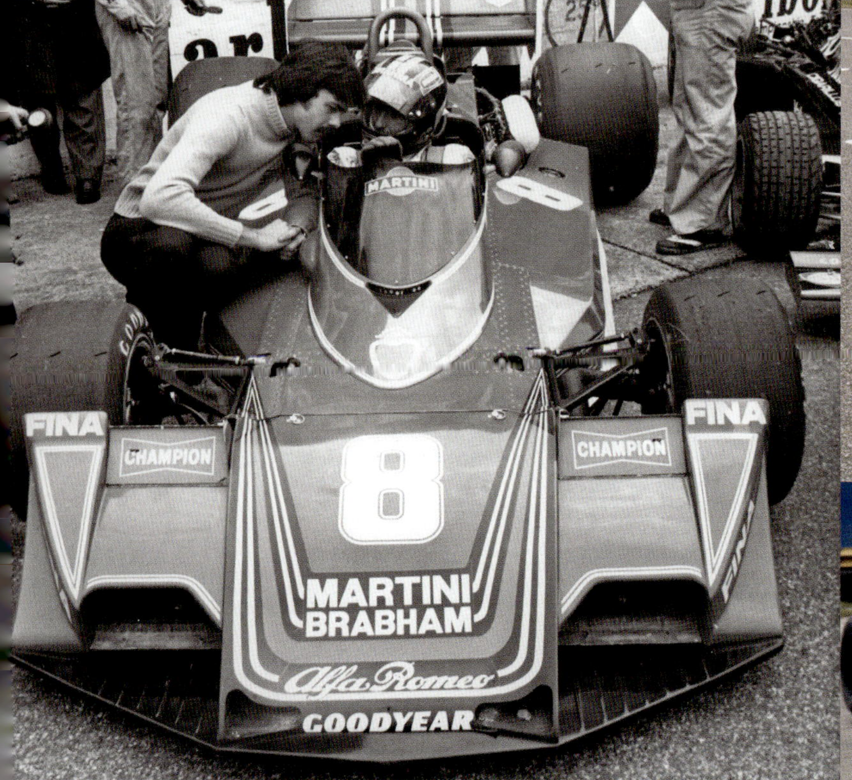

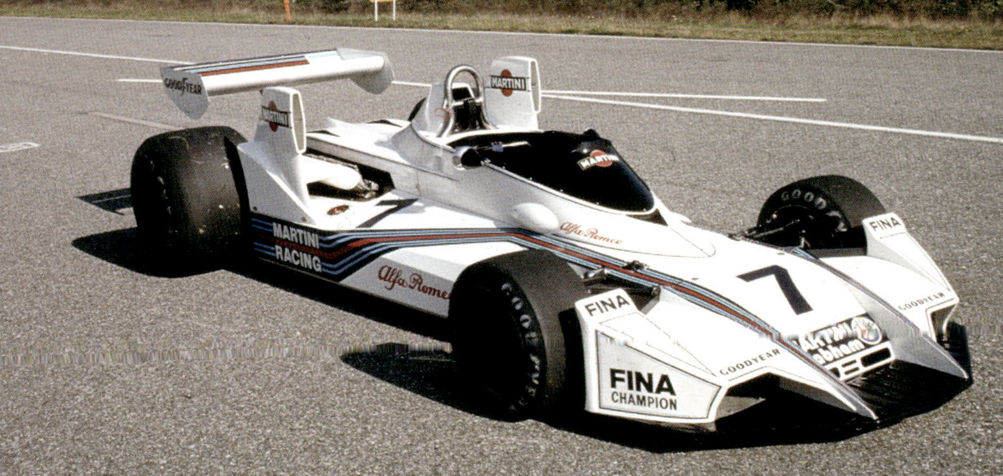

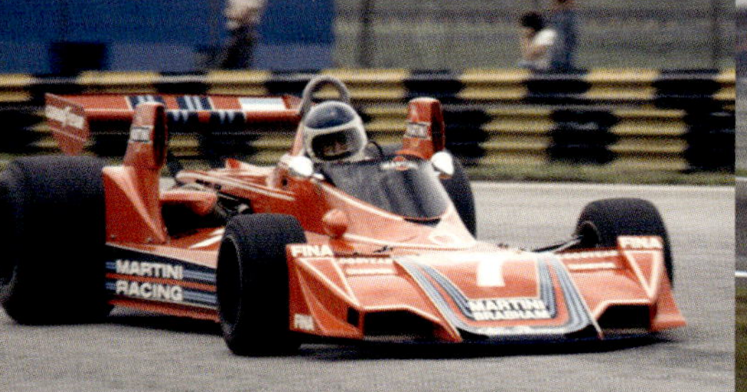

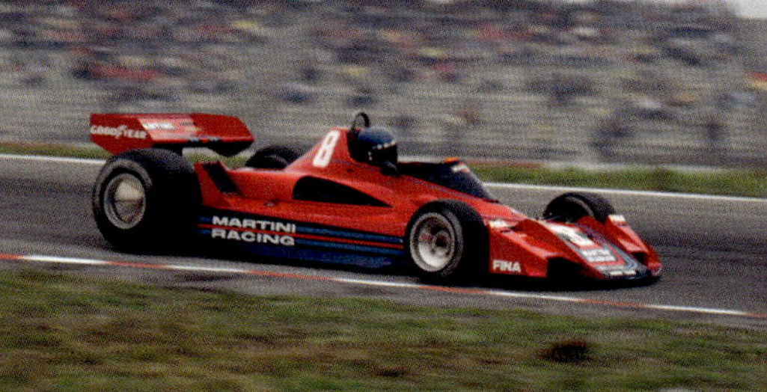

Brabham BT-45B

THE ENGINE FROM THE 33 "MONDIALE" FOR ALFA ROMEO'S RETURN TO FORMULA 1

Engine

Rear, longitudinal, horizontal flat-12, block and cylinder heads in light alloy (aluminium and magnesium), four valves per cylinder, four gear-driven overhead camshafts. Spica indirect fuel injection, Dinoplex electronic ignition, dry sump lubrication

Displacement

2995 cc (77x53.6 mm)

Power and torque

500 hp at 11500 rpm – 33 kgm at 9000 rpm

Transmission

Rear-wheel drive, hydraulically actuated dual dry-plate rear clutch, 5 speeds + reverse, rear-mounted gearbox

Chassis

Light alloy Brabham monocoque

Bodywork

F1

Suspension

Front: independent, wishbones, trailing arms, coil springs, hydraulic dampers, anti-roll bar

Rear: independent, wishbones, trailing arms, coil springs, hydraulic dampers, anti-roll bar

Brakes

Dual circuits, self-ventilating discs all round

Dimensions

Wheelbase: 2464 mm

Weight

585 kg

Alfa Romeo's official participation in Formula 1 had ceased at the end of the 1951 season after the two World Championships won by Nino Farina and Juan Manuel Fangio in the Alfetta 158 and 159. Years later there were to be a few occasional experiments with the V8 engine from the Tipo 33 installed in the McLaren M14D chassis in 1970 and in the March 711 the following year, with Andrea de Adamich above all taking them out onto the track. In neither case was the outcome sufficiently successful as to suggest that there would be a follow-up.

The chance to make a comeback to Formula 1 in style arose again in 1975, the season in which Autodelta finally managed to take the World Championship for Marques with the Tipo 33 TT12, winning seven races out of eight and demonstrating the undoubted qualities of power and reliability of their 12-cylinder boxer. An agreement was thus reached with the brilliant Brabham Martini Racing Team, one of the most high-profile outfits of the moment, then run by Bernie Ecclestone and sponsored by the well-known drinks manufacturer, which was still firmly in the hands of the aristocratic Rossi di Montelera family. Alfa Romeo agreed to supply 12-cylinder engines from the 33, which made some modifications necessary as the engine was load-bearing in the monocoque BT 45. The car designed by the talented Gordon Murray was presented in a beautiful white livery with blue and red stripes and during the event favourable comparisons were made with Ricart's Tipo 512, the only Grand Prix Alfa Romeo to have had a centrally-mounted engine. Marketing strategies later dictated a change to red and blue colours. Problems soon arose: the engine was powerful and reliable but still too heavy for Formula 1. Over the years the team took on a number of top-class drivers including Carlos Pace, John Watson and the World Champion Niki Lauda who won two races in 1978. The first was in Sweden, where the car was disqualified because it had been fitted with a rather eccentric large fan designed to suck air from underneath the car to increase downforce and the second was at the Dino Ferrari Grand Prix at Imola, a non-championship race. The car on display is a BT 45B used as a reserve car during the 1977 season. In 1979, the BT48 was given a new 60° V12 engine that permitted an improved ground effects configuration because it was smaller. However, results were not forthcoming and while a completely new Alfa Romeo single-seater had already made an appearance on the track, the contract was terminated even before the season ended.

Tipo 179F "test car"

THE ALFA ROMEO FORMULA 1 WAS AMBITIOUS AND HAD GREAT POTENTIAL. THEN EVERYTHING CHANGED

Engine

Rear, longitudinal, 60° V12, block and cylinder heads in light alloy, four valves per cylinder, two gear-driven overhead camshafts per bank. Lucas mechanical fuel injection with electronic adjustment, electronic ignition, dry sump lubrication

Displacement

2991 cc (78.5x51.5 mm)

Power and torque

Over 525 hp at 12300 rpm
34 kgm at 9500 rpm

Transmission

Rear-wheel drive, dual dry-plate clutch, six speeds + reverse

Chassis

Light alloy monocoque

Bodywork

F1

Suspension

Front: independent, wishbones, trailing arms, coil springs, hydraulic dampers, anti-roll bar

Rear: independent, wishbones, trailing arms, coil springs, hydraulic dampers, anti-roll bar

Brakes

Hydraulic self-ventilating discs all round, floating at the rear inboard

Dimensions

Wheelbase: 2740 mm, Length: 4670 mm, Width: 2150, Height: 1030

Weight

585 kg

At the end of the Seventies, development of the Tipo 177, the Alfa-Alfa Formula 1 car was long and tortuous. Subsequently, the widespread use of single-seaters with ground effects soon made conventional cars obsolete, which led Autodelta to work on the new Tipo 179.

The chassis was an aluminium alloy monocoque boasting a wide use of composite materials and a load-bearing engine. Composite materials were employed in the bodywork too, a crucial element in a "wing car": carbon fibre, Kevlar and above all aluminium honeycomb. The need to create Venturi ducts on the underside of the car, obviously sealed off by sliding sideskirts, made the 12-cylinder boxer that had been improved for the Brabham unusable in the new car because it was too wide. For this reason, in just a few months a new 60° V12 was designed that had a lot in common with the old boxer, starting with the 2995 cc displacement. The power output was over 520 hp.

Development of the 179 proceeded in parallel with the 177's debut and on the 9TH of September 1979, when both cars took to the track at Monza for the Italian Grand Prix, the new car was entrusted to Bruno Giacomelli, who did not however finish the race. The 1979 season was drawing to a close and for 1980 Alfa Romeo chose the promising Patrick Depailler as Giacomelli's teammate but tragically he was killed in a controversial accident at Hockenheim on the 1ST of August. For the remaining races the second single-seater was entrusted to Vittorio Brambilla and the young Andrea De Cesaris. In the meantime, the Tipo 179 was improving quickly, to the extent that Giacomelli was able to take pole position at Watkins Glen: he opened up an enormous lead in the race until he was betrayed by a melting coil that robbed him of a certain victory. With a build-up like this 1981 had to be the turning point: at last the 179 was competitive and the great Mario Andretti was signed as the main driver. Although the displacement and configuration were the same, the engine was a new V12 with a different bore and stroke and an increased power output of 525 hp.

Then came a dramatic turn of events that was worse than a cold shower for the team: in order to limit ground effects, sliding sideskirts were banned, making the promising 179 uncompetitive from one moment to the next. Its best result was Giacomelli's third place at Las Vegas, while Mario Andretti did not even finish the season. This was the beginning of a crisis for Autodelta that led to it closing down shortly afterwards. In the meantime, the designer Gérard Ducarouge started working for Autodelta and in view of the Tipo 182, starting experimenting on the old 179 with various ideas including a carbonfibre chassis. The car on display was one of these experimental cars used for testing at the end of the season: it was later rebuilt and handed over to the museum.

Larini
Philips Car Systems
ALFA CORSE
MICHELIN
RECARO
DEKRA
8
SELENIA
MAGNETI MARELLI
BÄUMLER
men's fashion
ERG
speedline
TRW Sabelt
sparco
soteco
schön
Eibach
CECOMP
brembo
BILSTEIN

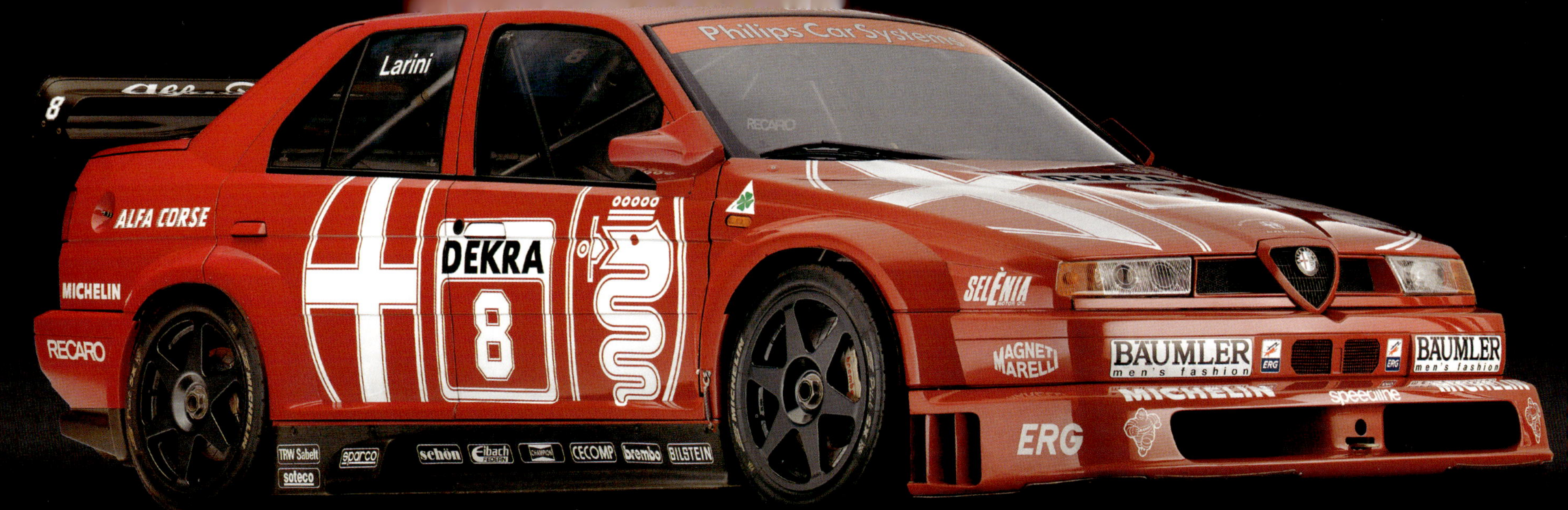

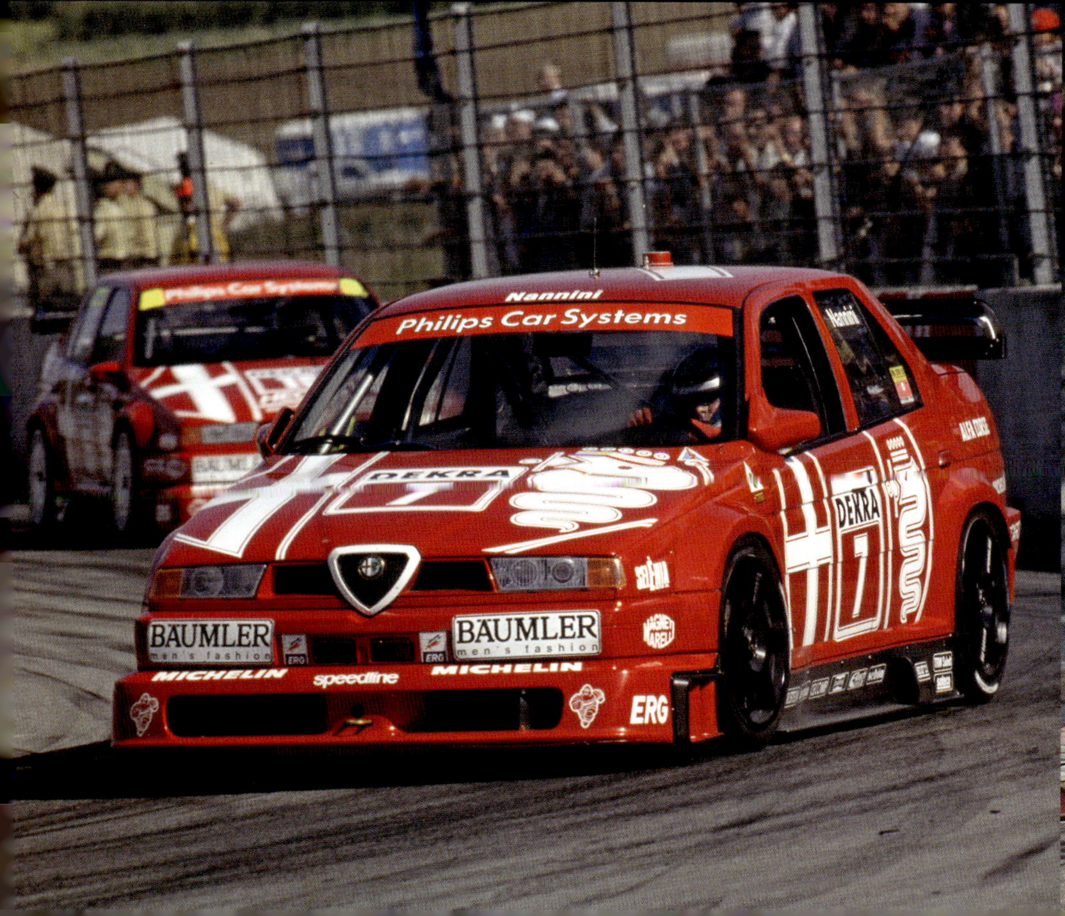
Nannini
Philips Car Systems
DEKRA
7
BÄUMLER
men's fashion
MICHELIN
speedline
ERG

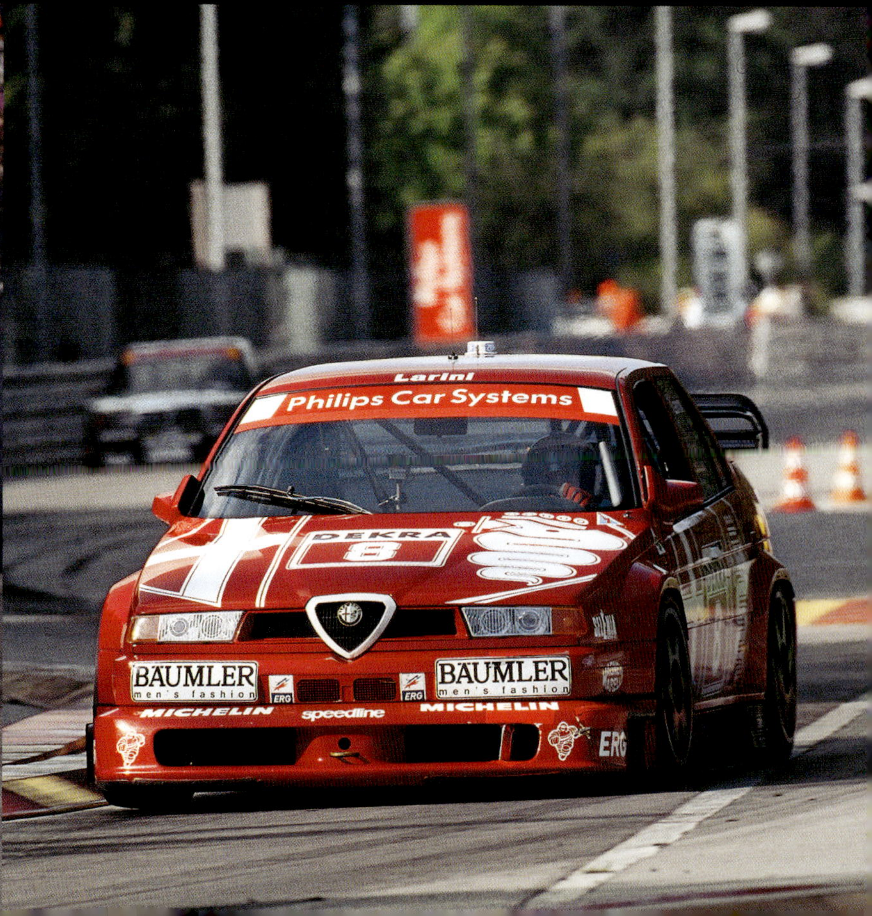
Larini
Philips Car Systems
DEKRA
8
BÄUMLER
men's fashion
MICHELIN
speedline
ERG

155 V6 TI

ALL RECORDS BROKEN AND COMPETITORS ANNIHILATED IN THEIR OWN BACKYARD

Engine

Front, longitudinal, 60° V6, block and cylinder heads in light alloy, four valves per cylinder, four gear-driven overhead camshafts. Weber-Marelli electronic fuel injection, electronic ignition with one coil per cylinder, dry sump lubrication

Displacement

2498 cc (93x61.30 mm)

Power and torque

420 hp at 11800 rpm – 30 kgm at 9000 rpm

Transmission

Permanent four-wheel drive, multiple dry-plate clutch, six speeds + reverse (sequential)

Chassis

Steel unitary construction bodyshell, front subframe, bodywork with carbonfibre panels

Bodywork

Saloon

Suspension

Front: independent, wishbones, McPherson struts, coil springs, hydraulic dampers, anti-roll bar

Rear: independent, wishbones, McPherson struts, coil springs, hydraulic dampers, anti-roll bar

Brakes

Hydraulically actuated and assisted self-ventilating discs all round

Dimensions

Wheelbase: 2540 mm, Length: 1576 mm, Width: 1750, Height: 1410

Weight

1100 kg (dry)

After the excellent racing season of 1992, when the 155 turbocharged four-wheel drive GTA dominated the Italian Superturismo Championship, Alfa Corse decided to increase their range of activity by working on several racing versions of the 155. Alongside the birth of the D2 version, which was suitable for most European championships, the most ambitious objective was the DTM (Deutsche Tourenwagen Meisterschaft), the German touring championship, an extremely competitive environment with a vast following, to the extent that there was an average of 62,800 spectators at every race.

The 155 made full use of the tuning opportunities permitted by the generous rules of the D1 class and was drastically revised, going well beyond the usual extent of modifications. The standard 60° V6 engine in light alloy was transformed whilst still observing the two main limitations imposed: both the distance between the cylinders and the material used for the engine block had to be the same as on the production versions. For everything else a wide range of fundamental modifications were allowed: it had dry-sump lubrication, four valves per cylinder, with inlet valves made of titanium, a displacement of 2498 cc, with a power output of 420 hp at 11800 rpm and a maximum torque value of 30 kgm at 9000 rpm. The engine, which weighed only 110 kg, was fitted length-wise in the 155, ahead of the front axle and mounted on a subframe.

The six-speed gearbox was connected to the engine by means of a magnesium casting which also contained the oil reservoir and the front differential, as the transmission was four-wheel drive with a epicyclic unit, a viscous coupling, and limited-slip front and rear differentials.

Thanks to these modifications, the car's 1040 kg weight was now equally distributed between the two axles: the bodywork was made of carbon fibre and the chassis was reinforced with a roll cage. While retaining the standard McPherson layout, the suspension had special geometry and components. From the second season onwards 18" in place of 19" wheels were fitted, while during the course of the season the fuel injection system was improved and a new sequential gearbox was adopted.

The Alfa Corse team, under the guidance of Giorgio Pianta, prepared two 155 V6 TI cars which were to be driven by Nicola Larini and Alessandro Nannini. Two sister cars belonging to the Schubel team were driven by Christian Danner and Giorgio Francia, the driver and road-tester who followed the development of these cars and all the other Alfa Romeos from the Seventies.

The car's victorious debut at Zolder was just the first stage of Nicola Larini's journey to winning the championship, defeating the reigning champion Klaus Ludwig, standard bearer of the powerful Mercedes team. Larini won the most races in the history of the DTM, no less than 10 out of 20, with Nannini also contributing with two wins and the non-championship Donington race.

Appendix

In addition to the cars on display in the museum, the collection of the Museo Storico Alfa Romeo has been enriched in continuation and continues to be expanded. Over the years, production cars through to the latest models and styling or mechanical prototypes have been added. Cars from the Press Workshop, demonstration chassis and a number of donations. The collection also features engines, scale models, trophies and mechanical components of various kinds.

A selection of cars is represented here.

1908

Darracq 8/10 HP

1914

40/60 HP Corsa

1919

Trattrice Romeo

1920

20/30 HP ES Sport

1924

RL Targa Florio

1924

RM Sport

1926

RL Super Sport

1927

RL Super Sport "Mille Miglia"

1928

6C 1500 Sport

1929

6C 1750 Super Sport

1930

6C 1750 Gran Turismo

1933

6C 1900 Gran Turismo

1934

6C 2300 Gran Turismo

1934

6C 2300 Gran Turismo

1934

GP Tipo B "Aerodinamica"

1939

6C 2500 SS Corsa

1947

6C 2500 Super Sport

1949

Ambrosini S1001 "Angelo dei Bimbi"

1951

1900M – AR 51

1951

GP Tipo 159

1952

1900 C52 Disco Volante

1954

1900 Sport Spider (2000 Sportiva)

1955

750 Competizione

1956

1900 Super Sprint

1958

2000 Berlina

1958

2000 Sprint

1960

Tipo 103

1962

1300 Sprint

1962

2600 Berlina

1962

2600 Spider

1962

Giulia Sprint

1963

Giulia Sprint Speciale

1963

Giulia TZ

1965

2600 De Luxe

1965

2600 SZ Prototipo

1965

Giulia Super

1966

Scarabeo

1966

Giulia "Torpedo"

1967

1750

1967

Montreal Expo

1971

Caimano

1971

Cuneo

1972

Alfetta Coupé

1973

GT Junior 1.3

1973

Scarabeo II

1975

Eagle

1975

Tipo 33 TT12

1976

Navajo

1976

NY Taxi

1979

Tipo 177

1982

Sprint 6C

1983

GTV6

1983

Zeta 6

1987

Alfa Boxer

1988

164 ProCar

1988

75 IMSA

1989

March 89CE

1989

SZ

1989

SE 048 SP

1991

Lola T9000

1991

Protéo

1993

164 Q4

1996

155 V6 TIF3

1998

156 D2

2001

Kamal

Print by

D'AURIA PRINTING SPA - ASCOLI PICENO

JUNE 2015